Mosaic of Thought

Mosaic of Thought

The Power of
Comprehension Strategy Instruction

SECOND EDITION

Ellin Oliver Keene
Susan Zimmermann

HEINEMANN
Portsmouth, NH

Heinemann

A division of Reed Elsevier Inc.

361 Hanover Street

Portsmouth, NH 03801–3912

www.heinemann.com

Offices and agents throughout the world

© 2007 by Ellin Oliver Keene and Susan Zimmermann

The authors and publisher wish to thank those who have generously given permission to reprint borrowed material:

"Books" from *The Apple That Astonished Paris* by Billy Collins. Copyright © 1988 by Billy Collins. Reprinted with the permission of the University of Arkansas Press, www.uapress.com.

(continues on p. xvi)

Library of Congress Cataloging-in-Publication Data

Keene, Ellin Oliver.

   Mosaic of thought : the power of comprehension strategy instruction / Ellin Oliver Keene, Susan Zimmermann. —2nd ed.

     p. cm.

   Includes bibliographical references and index.

   ISBN-13: 978-0-325-01035-9

   ISBN-10: 0-325-01035-8

   1. Reading comprehension.   2. Literature—Study and teaching.

I. Zimmermann, Susan. II. Title.

LB1050.45.K435 2007

372.47—dc22   2007005803

Editor: Thomas Newkirk

Production management: Abigail M. Heim

Production: Sarah V. Weaver

Typesetter: Gina Poirier Graphic Design

Cover and interior design: Joyce Weston Design

Cover photograph: Fotosearch

Manufacturing: Louise Richardson

Printed in the United States of America on acid-free paper

11   10   09   08   07   ML   2   3   4   5

To our children
and to the teachers
whose innovative practices
inspired the second edition of this book

Contents

Foreword

In Nick Hornsby's bestselling novel *High Fidelity*, the main character, Rob, reflects on his surprising success with women, particularly given the fact that he is not particularly good-looking and that he is definitely downwardly mobile financially. He concludes that women like him because he "asks questions"—a tactic, by the way, that a lot of men have not managed to figure out.

My involvement with this amazing book came from a question (though perhaps not the kind Rob is referring to). I had just finished a workshop in Denver for the Public Education & Business Coalition (PEBC), and Ellin Keene was about to drive me to the airport. At that time, about 1995, the PEBC was a dynamic and innovative staff development organization in the Denver area—but not well known outside that area. As we began to head north to the airport, I asked Ellin whether she was working on any project.

As a matter of fact she was—and it had to do with comprehension. She explained to me that there was a body of research on comprehension that pointed to the extraordinary power of a small number of strategies. Ellin and a group of staff developers had been explicitly teaching these strategies to children, and had results to show their effectiveness. I was familiar with some of this research; in fact, my colleague Jane Hansen had worked with David Pearson on schema theory and comprehension. I had read some of the reports from federally funded national centers for reading, but this research hadn't made its way into the classroom, so far as I could tell. Except for tacking "comprehension questions" onto reading passages, no one seemed much interested in the topic.

Since the Denver airport is about halfway to Canada, we had time to talk, and by the time its unmistakable teepee-like silhouette came on the horizon, I had invited her to propose the book to Heinemann. Ellin teamed up with the incomparably gifted Susan Zimmermann (cofounder of the PEBC), and soon a proposal and chapters started coming my way. The book was accepted, published, and not only became one of the all-time best sellers for Heinemann, but also helped open the door for Cris Tovani, Debbie Miller, Stephanie Harvey, and other Denver-based teacher educators who became national figures in their own right.

It would be nice to claim Heinemann somehow saw all this coming. But I don't think anyone did. The cover design was garish (mercifully replaced in this new edition); there was no big send-off, no publicity push. If ever a book sold itself, this one did. Yet in retrospect, the topic and timing—and of course the writing itself—couldn't have been better.

At that time, the whole language and reading/writing process approaches to literacy instruction were under attack for their lack of direct explicit instruction. Sometimes this attack came from the educational right wing that wanted extensive phonics instruction, but it also came from thoughtful educators like George Hillocks and Lisa Delpit, who argued for more deliberate teaching of reading and writing processes, particularly for students who had not "naturally" internalized them in home-based literacy experiences. Clearly many children flourish in literature-rich environments, where they can, in Frank Smith's words, learn to read "through the act of reading itself" (1983, 23). They can experience a positive cycle of reinforcement: Success in reading leads to more reading and more success in reading, with minimal instruction from the teacher.

But for some students this cycle was a negative one. Difficulty with reading led to avoidance, unproductive strategies, and negative self-attitudes, all of which made reading even more difficult—and more likely to be avoided. For these students, the incidental, "intuitive" approach to instruction that Smith and others promoted was simply not adequate.

Even successful readers need metacognitive strategies that can help them deal with difficulty, when normal habitual reading processes are not fully adequate to the task. Marvin Minsky, a leading cognitive scientist, makes clear the importance of these monitoring strategies:

> Thinking is a process, and if your thinking does something you don't want it to, you should be able to say something microscopic and analytic about it, and not something enveloping and evaluating about yourself as a learner . . . it may be all right to deal with other people in a vague global way—by having "attitudes" toward them, but it is devastating if this is the way you deal with yourself. (quoted in Bernstein 1981, 122)

Humans, after all, have a capacity no other animals have—we can think about our thinking. We can stand back and reflect upon our own thought processes, and if necessary alter them. We are not prisoners of reflex and habit. *Mosaic of Thought* provides a language and set of strategies to do this thinking.

When the chapters for the first edition of *Mosaic* made their way from Denver to Durham, I was struck by the way they opened. Susan and Ellin picked evocative, rich pieces of literature and showed how they would use comprehension strategies in responding to them. I remember one reviewer of the manuscript suggested these all be cut because teachers would want to get immediately to the "practical" procedures for the classroom. To our credit, we immediately recognized that as a bad idea.

In reading this new edition, I see even more clearly how crucial these openings are. Not only do they model the strategies, but they universalize them; they show that comprehension is for grown-ups too, and that some of our deepest pleasure as readers comes from slowing our thought processes so that we can contemplate them. All of these openings have been rewritten in this new edition, with new excerpts, yet they retain the wonderful attractiveness that made the first edition so welcoming to readers.

There are other significant changes. The authors draw on a decade of teacher innovation in the use of comprehension strategies. Ellin spent a good part of that decade helping teachers in some of the poorest school districts in the country, and she reports on what she did and what she saw. There are examples of reading conferences that focus on comprehension strategies, and a new model for the reader's workshop. And there are new illustrations of how "think-alouds" can push students to comprehend deeply—and how students rise to the challenge.

Susan and Ellin also respond to some unintended applications of their ideas. To my knowledge, neither author is heavily invested in companies that market sticky notes, and they never intended that fluent readers should have their pleasure drained by constantly stopping to affix them. Strategy instruction was never intended to be a complete reading program; it was part of a curriculum in which there should be extensive independent reading and regular opportunities to hear great literature read aloud—for the sheer pleasure of it. And they never—ever—saw using strategies as an end in itself. Strategies are a *means* to deepen the reading experience and to give students a language to talk about their processes. In this edition, the authors clarify some of these teaching issues by clearly describing the place of strategy instruction in the wider reading curriculum and by answering questions about the sequencing of instruction.

So it is with great pleasure that Heinemann offers to you this edition, what will surely become the definitive edition, of this classic text. I am honored to be associated with it, and count it a special privilege to have worked with these two extraordinary women.

I'm so glad I asked that question.

Thomas Newkirk
University of New Hampshire

Acknowledgments

Someone once said, "Working together works." It has been a pleasure for us, once again, to collaborate on work that we each view as our most important. Rewriting and expanding this book has caused us to read differently, to slow down, to go deeper, to think about what really matters in teaching children to read (and to love it!), to do every day what we ask teachers and students to do (think about our thinking). Our own children, who interrupted us mercilessly during the writing of the first version of *Mosaic*, are now grown or largely so. We have to admit that we desperately missed their interruptions, and this revision process (while much smoother and more efficient) reminded us of how much they brought to the original *Mosaic*. They kept us focused on the importance of relationships and the joy of reading together. Our thanks and love to Elizabeth, Katherine, Helen, Alice, and Mark. You, along with the wonderful children in the classrooms where we have worked, were the true inspiration for *Mosaic of Thought*.

Susan's husband Paul served as the informal editor-in-chief of this *Mosaic*. With the precision of a samurai, he approached each chapter, editing sword (red pen) in hand. Without his thoughtful review, feedback, and patience, this would be a lesser book. Thank you, Paul, for taking this on with skill and enthusiasm and always, always letting us know how much you believed in the importance of literacy for all children.

David Keene continues to make it all possible for Ellin. He is the master of both keeping the laundry going and providing moral support; throwing away the junk mail and putting everything into perspective; ensuring the dogs and Elizabeth don't starve and listening to all those travel stories; sending the overnight packages filled with transparencies Ellin forgot for a workshop; and reminding Ellin that it is all worth it. Support doesn't begin to describe what David has contributed—no words can.

Looking back, we didn't realize what a brain trust we had sitting around the PEBC conference table as we wrestled with the overarching question of how we could teach children to understand what they read. Those were stimulating, fast-paced days and we are forever grateful to Laura Benson, Anne Goudvis, Steph Harvey, Chryse Hutchins, Debbie Miller, Liz Stedem, Cris Tovani, and Marjory Ulm for rolling up their sleeves, working tirelessly in classrooms, and opening our eyes and minds to new ideas and possibilities for children. It was through those early discussions that the model for reading described in *Mosaic of Thought* was invented. It is difficult to imagine a more rewarding collaboration. Our thanks go to all for their contributions to the thinking described here and, more importantly, for their early work in literally hundreds of classrooms where the concepts were developed and refined.

We had the good fortune of tracking Don Graves down in his office at the University of New Hampshire in 1985, picking his brain, and persuading him to come to Denver to help us set up some writing workshops. Don, the grandfather of writer's workshop, wrote our first foreword and hugely influenced our work in reading, as did Richard Allington, Isabel Beck, Kylene Beers, Lucy Calkins, Smokey Daniels, Janice Dole, Nell Duke, Ralph Fletcher, Mary Ellen Giacobbe, Shelley Harwayne, Georgia Heard, Peter Johnston, Don Murray, Tom Newkirk, P. David Pearson, Michael Pressley, Joanne Hindley Salch, and Keith Stanovich.

Tom Newkirk has been and continues to be believer-in-chief of this project. It was Tom who suggested we write *Mosaic* in the first place, who pitched the idea of a second edition, and who persevered through our initial reluctance. Tom's editorial insights are potent, to be sure, but it has been his steadfast belief in the power of comprehension strategy instruction that has sustained us. Tom field-tested our ideas in conversations with his brilliant network of New Hampshire teaching colleagues, including Louise Wrobleski, Tomasen Carey, and his wife, Beth, a superb first-grade teacher. Together, they helped us refine and clarify our message so the book would be practical for teachers.

Huge thanks go also to the team at Heinemann—Leigh Peake, Sarah Weaver, Abby Heim, Stephanie Colado, Eric Chalek—who with grace and good humor took care of myriad details to make this book happen.

Ellin thanks her new friends and colleagues at the Cornerstone Initiative at the University of Pennsylvania, especially Kevan Collins, Rahshene Davis, Suzanne Fraley, Kelly Hunter, Lu Lewis, Becky McKay, Steve Prigohzy, Martha Roberts, Sara Schwabacher, Brian Summa, Edna Varner, and Mary Jean Whitelaw, for helping her to reshape ideas into more coherent frameworks for teachers' learning. She especially thanks principals and teachers in Cornerstone schools for allowing her to teach alongside them and learn from their ever-present belief in the ability of children, including those in high-poverty schools, to learn at the highest levels every day.

The most profound thanks we can offer goes to teachers throughout this country who have led the charge for more effective, thoughtful, inquiry-based classrooms where children and adults learn together. We have been touched by and learned from hundreds of teachers and can't here do justice to all of them. From our original guides to great teaching at the PEBC—Patrick Allen, Leslie Blauman, Colleen Buddy, Lori Conrad, Mimi DeRose, Anne Henderson, Sue Kempton, Leslie Leyden, Missy Matthews, Debbie Miller, Bruce Morgan, Mary Urtz, Kristin Venable, and Cheryl Zimmerman—to those we have worked with most recently and whose work is added to the mosaic in this edition, we thank you for deciding to dedicate your lives to making children's lives better. There is no more important work.

Mosaic of Thought

CHAPTER 1

Creating a New Mosaic

Books

From the heart of this dark, evacuated campus
I can hear the library humming in the night,
a choir of authors murmuring inside their books
along the unlit, alphabetical shelves,
Giovanni Pontano next to Pope, Dumas next to his son,
each one stitched into his own private coat,
together forming a low, gigantic chord of language.

I picture a figure in the act of reading,
shoes on a desk, head tilted into the wind of a book,
a man in two worlds, holding the rope of his tie
as the suicide of lovers saturates a page,
or lighting a cigarette in the middle of a theorem.
He moves from paragraph to paragraph
as if touring a house of endless, paneled rooms.

I hear the voice of my mother reading to me
from a chair facing the bed, books about horses and dogs,
and inside her voice lie other distant sounds,
the horrors of a stable ablaze in the night,
a bark that is moving toward the brink of speech.

I watch myself building bookshelves in college,
walls within walls, as rain soaks New England,
or standing in a bookstore in a trench coat.

I see all of us reading ourselves away from ourselves,
straining in circles of light to find more light
until the line of words becomes a trail of crumbs
that we follow across a page of fresh snow;

when evening is shadowing the forest
and small birds flutter down to consume the crumbs,
we have to listen hard to hear the voices
of the boy and his sister receding into the woods.

— Billy Collins, *The Apple That Astonished Paris*

First Reader

I can see them standing politely on the wide pages
that I was still learning to turn,
Jane in a blue jumper, Dick with his crayon-brown hair,
playing with a ball or exploring the cosmos
of the backyard, unaware they are the first characters,
the boy and girl who begin fiction.

Beyond the simple illustration of their neighborhood
the other protagonists were waiting in a huddle:
frightening Healthcliff, frightened Pip, Nick Adams
carrying a fishing rod. Emma Bovary riding into Rouen.

But I would read about the perfect boy and his sister
even before I would read about Adam and Eve, garden and gate,
and before I heard the name Gutenberg, the type
of their simple talk was moving into my focusing eyes.

It was always Saturday and he and she
were always pointing at something and shouting, "Look!"
pointing at the dog, the bicycle, or at their father
as he pushed a hand mower over the lawn,
waving at aproned mother framed in the kitchen doorway,
pointing toward the sky, pointing at each other.

They wanted us to look but we had looked already
and seen the shaded lawn, the wagon, the postman.
We had seen the dog, walked, watered and fed the animal,
and now it was time to discover the infinite, clicking
permutations of the alphabet's small and capital letters.
Alphabetical ourselves in the rows of classroom desks,
we were forgetting how to look, learning how to read.

— Billy Collins, *Questions About Angels*

Ellin's Reflections

I stumble across Billy Collins' poem "Books" as I prepare for a workshop at the University of New Hampshire in July 2006. I will work there with dear friends and colleagues Tom Newkirk, Louise Wrobleski, and Tomasen Carey in Hamilton Smith Hall, where Donald Graves and Donald Murray launched the writing process movement in the early 1980s.

It is somehow fitting that we return to Collins' poetry here, having begun the first edition of *Mosaic of Thought* with his poem "First Reader." Former poet laureate of the United States, Collins creates poems that appeal to a broad cross-section of readers, bringing poetry to thousands who previously thought it was too difficult for them to understand.

In both "First Reader" and "Books," Billy Collins asks us to think differently about books and readers. That is what we tried to do in the original *Mosaic of Thought.* In this edition, we offer a deeper look at the ideas we presented ten years ago. These two poems speak of a deepening process as well. To me, "First Reader" makes a more direct statement than "Books," which offers a more complex view of the world of the reader and the role of books.

In "First Reader," Collins challenges the conventional wisdom that has long defined learning to read as the process of using texts with severely limited vocabulary to master a sequence of little skills that accumulate until one day, almost magically, kids figure out the mysterious code and "learn to read." Collins exposes the flaw in that assumption: In learning to read through little books where perfectly dressed, well-behaved, white, middle-class characters say, "Look!" he warns, "we were forgetting how to look, learning how to read."

"First Reader" prompts me to flash through a brisk chronology of my own learning-to-read days. Miss Gregg looks down fondly from her desk. My six-year-old fingers prop my book at an angle on the desk, just like all the other children in the classroom who hold the same reader, in the same position. I see Dick and Jane standing politely on those wide pages. I must have liked Dick and Jane. They no doubt affirmed my small place in the world. My family looked a lot like theirs: mom, dad, one brother. Dick and Jane preserved the status quo. They didn't encourage me to look beyond the pages into their lives. They didn't stimulate me to think.

Who were the first characters for me after Dick and Jane? Why is it so difficult to remember them? Mrs. Schoonmaker was my fourth-grade teacher. She played bridge with my grandmother on Wednesday nights and was always a little grumpy on Thursday morning. She introduced me to *Black Beauty* and *National Velvet*, but she also put me in the middle math group with Miss Schakelford. I knew what that meant.

My next years as a reader were characterized by learning that words on the page constituted a literal, finite truth that wasn't to be challenged by the reader. We learned to identify main ideas and write short book reports. We answered comprehension questions at the end of abridged stories in basal readers. Looking at layers of meaning in text was never even considered. Examining text was abandoned in favor of three reading groups a day and free reading on Friday afternoons. There were no questions about why Cathy wouldn't marry Heathcliff, or what drove Emma Bovary to suicide. Rereading, understanding symbolic meanings, or talking with others about books—the activities that define my reading as an adult—were not part of my life as a reader back then.

It wasn't until Honors English my senior year of high school that things changed. Jan Call was the teacher. She suggested, for the first time in my life, that I look beyond the text, consider multiple meanings, propose an interpretation different from that posed by the rest of the class, or ponder symbolism. Willy Loman, the protagonist in *Death of a Salesman*, became the subject of several weeks of discussion. It would never have occurred to me that his name could symbolize his plight. Jan Call suggested we embrace many ways of knowing a book and that we—how radical!—reread it in its entirety or in small pieces. I felt utterly ill prepared for this type of discussion. And, given that school hadn't included this kind of discussion before the twelfth grade, I *was* unprepared. Everyone joked that the notoriously talkative Ellin Oliver was mysteriously quiet in Honors English. I was one of those students who in "learning how to read" had forgotten "how to look."

The poem "Books" provides a different perspective. Collins writes of a "man in two worlds" whose real-world presence ebbs as he pours his conscious energy into books in which the "suicide of lovers saturates a page." I see a professorial-looking man in the 1960s. He is in black and white—like an old movie—though his surroundings, in my mind, are in muted colors. He wears a suit, attire more formal than his slouched posture in a forgotten corner of the library would lead one to expect. He has been in that spot—a hard wooden chair, worn but substantial—for hours. The New England winter light has drained from the hillside outside the library windows, but the color changes are minimal: from gray tinged with yellow, to gray tinged with pink, to the steel gray of the moment.

The man runs a hand through his thinning hair and, for those short hours, he escapes the anxiety of his tenure battle and the gnawing truth that he hasn't heard from his son in months. For now, he inhabits a world of characters who mostly allow him to forget. He is "reading [himself] away from [himself], straining in circles of light to find more light," to move beyond his own life, to discover in those pages something deeper, more universal.

I reread the poem but don't hear the murmur and hum of authors Collins describes. To me it is a cacophony and it startles me as I read: all those characters straining to be heard from the pages of the books that surround this solitary man. Their voices and actions are unpredictable, savage, and loud. I wonder that he isn't distracted by them. Strangely, through the din, I can hear his heart beat, slow, steady, loud in its own right.

As I listen, my professor (*my* professor!?) leans back in his chair, takes a long look at his watch, steals a resigned look outside, and gathers his coat to move back into the night of his world.

Such liberties I have taken with "First Reader" and "Books." I do so without apology. I am the reader. It is my will I impose on Collins' poetry. I cherish my right and ability to do so. I know also that if I read these poems again next week or next year or ten years from now, they will speak to me differently. I know that if I have a conversation with my husband David or daughter Elizabeth about them, more tiles will be added to the mosaic of my understanding. How can I help but long for children to have the same rights? How can we rest until all our children have immersed themselves in a literary world that encourages and teaches them to read, reread, invent, explore, question, and imagine?

Into the Classroom

It was 1989. The fifth graders stared at me like I was crazy when I got them to sit on the floor in Claudia Keeley's classroom at South Street Elementary. "C'mon, why do we have to be on the floor like first graders?" one boy groaned. When I pulled out Roberto Innocenti's *Rose Blanche*, a story about a young girl during World War II, another asked, "Mrs. Keene, why are you going to use a book for little kids with us?"

"It's okay," I replied. "You're going to find this book startling. There are ideas in it that are really more appropriate for older kids."

Still they squirmed; complained they were uncomfortable; whined they were missing snack time. Claudia looked embarrassed. I shot her a don't-worry-let's-stick-to-the-plan look.

"I'm not going to read this book from beginning to end the way you're used to hearing stories read aloud," I told them. "I'm going to share my thinking with you as I read. I want you to hear the questions that form in my mind when I read *Rose Blanche*. Usually you don't know what questions people ask as they read. Today I'm going to share mine, and I want you to think about your questions as well. Great readers ask questions as they read."

The kids exchanged uncomfortable glances. I overheard a girl whisper, "What's the point of that?" I was beginning to wonder myself.

"When I read certain kinds of books, my mind is filled with questions. I can answer some of them, but some are more interesting to leave unanswered. I'm going to stop reading when one of those questions pops into my mind, and I'm going to share it with you."

I paused—too early, I now realize—at the end of the second page and wondered aloud why the soldiers would wink at the children. Twenty hands shot up, each kid eager to answer.

"Wait, I'm not sure I want to answer that right now." At least I had the sense to ask them to wait and let me think about my own question; I realized quickly that it wasn't a very searching question.

I paused again several pages later and wondered aloud why a little boy would jump out of a truck and try to run away. And I wondered why the mayor grabbed the child and gave him back to the soldiers. This time, as I looked at the kids' faces, I could see they were thinking about the answer. All except a couple hand-raisers had already learned to let me linger with the question, rather than try to answer it for me. After a few pages, something had changed in that classroom. As I kept reading, the students started asking their own questions. "Why are the kids in prison?" "What could they have done wrong?" "Why did they wear yellow stars on their clothes?" "Why don't they give them food?" No more grumbling about being treated like little kids or missing snacks. They were *listening*.

This think-aloud in Claudia's classroom was a maiden voyage for me. It was practice, pure and simple. I wasn't totally sure what I was doing. I had read some research, had conversations with graduate school professors, and, honestly, it just made sense to share my thinking out loud about the comprehension strategies—in this case questioning—with those fifth graders. How else could I *show* them what could be going on in their minds when they read? They needed to know that reading is an action sport, and that the action takes place in their minds. They also needed to know that *their* questions would be—and should be—different from *my* questions.

After Claudia's kids headed off to lunch, we sat in her quiet classroom and debriefed the lesson. After a shaky start, the kids had definitely become engaged—they wanted to answer the questions I posed; they were eager to find out what happened in the text; they started asking their own questions. We talked about their questions. They were primarily clarifying questions—answerable questions that readers use to ensure they understand before they read on—but at least they had taken the baton when I handed it off. They weren't only going for the answers to my questions. They saw a role for themselves in generating the questions.

"Okay, what's next?" Claudia asked. "What should I do with them tomorrow?"

"I have no idea," I told her. We laughed, but I didn't.

What We've Learned

I've learned a lot since that late-1980s foray. I know when reading picture books, it's often more effective to wait several pages before thinking aloud. I know that to think aloud about an easily answered question is less effective than tackling tougher, more provocative questions. With *Rose Blanche,* a book conducive to reflection, I should have discouraged the students' early answers in favor of speculating about the more complex issues the questions brought to mind. I should have previewed *Rose Blanche* more carefully so that when questions arose, I would have known which focused on the most important aspects of the book.

I know better now. But what I remember eighteen years later is how intoxicating that session in Claudia's classroom was. I remember the change that came over the students as they lost themselves in thought about *Rose Blanche* and began to share their questions and search for answers, even though my teaching and their responses weren't very refined. I remember how challenging it was to try to read aloud in an engaging way, simultaneously considering questions and deciding when to think aloud about them. I remember the energy and the engagement I saw in the kids' faces. In Claudia's and other classrooms where we were testing our ideas about explicitly teaching comprehension, a new world of teaching opened to me, far more engaging, stimulating, and *fun* than following any teacher's manual.

Now I know that to help kids peer into the mind of a proficient reader—and thereby develop an understanding of what they must do as they read—many think-alouds over a long period of time are necessary. Since those early trial-and-error days, my thinking about comprehension strategy instruction has evolved in myriad ways—but its essence is unchanged. If I were to work with Claudia's students today, I would still teach questioning as an essential comprehension strategy that proficient readers use to deepen understanding. I would still use thinking aloud as the instructional bread and butter of reader's workshop; still ask kids to generate questions as they read independently; still choose the best in children's literature for my lesson, using fiction or nonfiction that I personally found provocative and multifaceted; still gather the kids, no matter what their ages, around me on the floor so I had eye contact and a sense of intimacy in the classroom.

But there are differences—some I've taught myself, some I've gleaned from reading the research, some I've learned from watching hundreds of extraordinary teachers around the country as they teach comprehension strategies. I remember frustration when, early in a strategy study, children didn't do much more than imitate my responses. As, over time, they built confidence in their own thinking, their responses became progressively stronger, deeper, and more articulate. Working with colleagues, we found that comprehension strategy study needs to be built on a gradual release of responsibility from teacher to student. The teacher first demonstrates the use of the strategy in numerous types of books and then creates a safe and stimulating environment for students to practice the strategies in their own reading. Most effective is fluid instruction that encourages the sharing of responses in heterogeneous large groups and then reinforces that thinking in small groups and through individual conferences.

Most important, I realized that I could raise my expectations far higher than I had imagined. When immersed in compelling text and equipped with comprehension strategies, children will reach further, probe deeper, and understand complex material from the earliest ages.

Humble Beginnings

Nine of us sat around a table in a 1920s-era office building—converted apartments—located across the street from the Colorado State Capitol. The room had fallen from its glory days, but crown molding, wainscoting, and a handsome tile fireplace remained. The windows opened to a courtyard with summer flower beds. The sound of cars passing on the busy one-way street mixed with the splashing of the fountain. Elizabeth Keene, two months old at the time, slept in her car seat after having been passed around for all to admire.

We came together monthly—staff developers and Public Education & Business Coalition (PEBC) staff—to share what we'd experienced in the schools and classrooms where we were working. From the small kitchen across the hall, we helped ourselves to tea. There was always the unmistakable smell of popcorn "fresh" from the microwave. A bell rang whenever the front door opened, announcing a new arrival.

The chairs were wobbly and squeaked as we shifted positions. Talk began in earnest well before those meetings officially began.

Several years before, the PEBC had launched its Literacy League pilot school project in five schools—two in inner-city Denver, three in outlying suburban districts—initially with a focus on improving students' writing skills. Ellin and Liz Stedem, an elementary teacher with broad experience in reading and writing, began by cautiously stepping into a few classrooms. They wanted to serve as coaches, not experts, to learn alongside teachers. They were eager to help analyze the teachers' strengths and weaknesses, but also to examine their classrooms in light of the groundbreaking writing process work of teachers and researchers in New Hampshire, New York, and around the country. Language Arts classes were being converted into writing workshops in which children wrote every day from their own experiences, learned to revise their own work, and shared their writing with classmates. Children were being taught to replicate the *process* used by real writers, and the result was more compelling, detailed writing and greater student engagement.

We sat around that table in 1989 with Laura Benson, Anne Goudvis, Steph Harvey, Chryse Hutchins, Debbie Miller, Marjory Ulm, Liz Stedem, and Cris Tovani. The energy was palpable. By then more schools and more staff developers were involved in the Literacy League. The work was going well. Kids were writing more. Teachers were writing with their students. Students were overcoming their discomfort with writing and even looked forward to writing time. Much of their writing was infused with their unique voices. They were writing (as writers do) about topics of their choice to explain ideas that mattered to them. But there were rumblings.

"Kids aren't reading enough," Steph Harvey blurted. "They're writing stories about their dogs, their grandparents, their passions. They're having fun, but they're just not reading enough. Even worse, I'm seeing kids who seem to read fluently, but when I try to have a conversation with them about what they read, they don't have a clue. Their decoding is excellent, but they aren't getting it."

We had noticed a dichotomy: The tone and feeling of engagement the students had during writing disappeared when they shifted to reading, took out their basals, and, too often, checked out intellectually. We knew there was a problem. Their teachers knew there was a problem. Teachers were working to build their classroom libraries so kids had more choice in the books they read. They were creating writing/reading blocks where students could shift from writing to reading, all in a workshop setting. Nonetheless, something was lacking.

Steph told of a conversation she had with Leslie Blauman, an upper-grade teacher at Meadow Point Elementary School. "Even Leslie, who is a *gifted* teacher, just doesn't feel like she's teaching reading. She says things like, 'My kids are fluent readers, but it's not enough just to put more books in their hands and check in once in a while.' Leslie wants her instruction to be more focused, but she doesn't know *what* to teach. She wants the kids to have the same engaged experience with reading as they're having with writing. She just doesn't know how to make that happen."

"I have an idea," Ellin said.

Ellin was in Jan Dole's graduate reading methods class at the University of Denver in the early 1980s and had kept in close contact with her. Important research was under way about reading comprehension. Ellin, always the research junkie, was intrigued about a body of research Jan had shared with her called the proficient-reader research. It identified seven principal comprehension strategies that good readers use when they read (see Figure 1.1).

"I think Jan and her colleagues are tossing around the notion that these strategies could form the core of a very effective comprehension curriculum. If we give explicit, long-term instruction using the strategies, they think we can actually *improve* comprehension. We've always thought of comprehension as something 'caught not taught,' but this is fascinating stuff and it makes sense."

Figure 1.1

Metacognitive Strategies
(listening to the voice in your mind that speaks while you read)

- **Monitoring for meaning**—knowing when you know, knowing when you don't know

- **Using and creating schema**—making connections between the new and the known, building and activating background knowledge

- **Asking questions**—generating questions before, during, and after reading that lead you deeper into the text

- **Determining importance**—deciding what matters most, what is worth remembering

- **Inferring**—combining background knowledge with information from the text to predict, conclude, make judgments, interpret

- **Using sensory and emotional images**—creating mental images to deepen and stretch meaning

- **Synthesizing**—creating an evolution of meaning by combining understanding with knowledge from other texts/sources

"That's really interesting, Ellin," Susan said, "Can we pursue it? We've grappled with *what* to teach for a long time. It's logical that good readers use certain thought processes. If we know what great readers do when they read, that's what we should teach, right?"

A sense of urgency arose. We began an exploration that led to some important early answers. The teachers and PEBC staff developers started with conversations about their own reading. When Liz Stedem read Wallace Stegner's *Crossing to Safety*, she told us to put down anything else we might be reading and read it immediately. We read Nadine Gordimer's *My Son's Story* and Lawrence Thornton's *Imagining Argentina* and talked about parts we loved, sections that surprised us, events we didn't fully understand, and mutual friends who might enjoy them. We started a PEBC book club. By the time we talked about *Love in the Time of Cholera* by Gabriel Garcia Marquez and *Beloved* by Toni Morrison, a year later, our lives as readers had changed permanently.

"The only time I recall anyone teaching me directly how to improve my reading was a speed reading course my mother forced me to take the summer before I went to college," said Chryse Hutchins, one of the PEBC staff developers. "This new way of looking at reading is incredible. I mean, I read and I'm thinking at two different levels now. I'm taking in the content, the events in the story, the editorial, the gardening hints, whatever, but I'm also posing and answering questions, pondering, really living in my visual images as I read. I'm thinking about experiences I've had and books I've read that relate to this text and I'm making decisions about what I think is most important. I'm driving myself a little crazy. I'm talking about metacognition at cocktail parties," she moaned. After telling her to "get a life," the others had to admit they did the same.

Ellin said, "We need to think about what this means for kids and for our work with teachers. If proficient readers use these strategies to make meaning when they read, could it be possible to help kids become more aware of their own reading processes and then teach them to improve their comprehension? Could we help kids learn to comprehend in the first place, and deepen their comprehension once they're reading fairly independently? Is that too simplistic?" Ellin paused. "My mother always told me that elegance and strength are found in simplicity." Smiles spread around the table.

We focused more on the proficient-reader research that Ellin had introduced. This body of work examined the cognitive processes (strategies) used most commonly by proficient readers, whether adults glued to a gripping novel or advanced placement seniors making their way through a physics text.

In our adult reading groups and at the PEBC staff developers' meetings, we tested the strategies on our own reading. We became more conscious of our own thinking processes as readers. We realized we could concentrate simultaneously on the text and our ways of thinking about it. What seemed most extraordinary, however, was that by thinking about our own thinking—that is, by being *metacognitive*—we could actually deepen and enhance our comprehension of the text.

The Problem: How to Teach Comprehension

In the 1980s teachers around the country began to abandon basal-driven reading instruction for several reasons. Primarily, like the students we observed, their students were disengaged. As teachers, they were uncomfortable with the instructional model based on rote learning, which left little room for serious analysis and exploration. But, most alarming, they were moving away from this type of instruction because too many of their students were not learning how to comprehend what they read.

For six years Ellin directed the Chapter One (now Title I) program in the Douglas County, Colorado, School District. She and the Chapter One teachers spent many hours observing and scrutinizing the work of elementary students identified for these services. The profiles of many of the children troubled them. These were children who successfully read words from word lists on comprehension inventories. They were able to decode words accurately with acceptable pronunciation. Some even read passages fluently. Yet after they read, many were unable to tell what the passages meant. These children didn't know when they were comprehending and when they weren't. Many didn't know what they were supposed to comprehend when they read. Others didn't seem to know that text is supposed to mean something.

Often when the Chapter One children listened to stories read aloud, it was clear they weren't aware that they should be thinking about the story or that they should be prepared to talk about it afterward. They paid little attention to the illustrations and showed only slight interest as their classes undertook activities related to the content of the books. Increasingly, Ellin became aware of a growing group of students who could decode words, but couldn't really understand what they read.

The problem wasn't limited to upper-grade students like those Steph Harvey talked about in Leslie Blauman's fifth-grade class. Debbie Miller, a superb first-grade teacher then at Denver's Knapp Elementary (and later author of *Reading with Meaning*), bemoaned the fact that she spent so much instruction time focused on word learning. She didn't feel she was teaching comprehension either. She wondered if it was possible to teach young children to use the comprehension strategies.

Ellin's teaching colleagues in the Douglas County Chapter One program as well as thousands of teachers around the country lost confidence in traditional reading instruction because their students weren't engaged and too many of them didn't comprehend what they read. They knew there had to be a better way. They knew that teaching reading implies more than hoping that all the worksheets and comprehension questions somehow add up to the real thing.

Nonetheless, when teachers made significant changes in their reading classrooms, they continued to raise a collective voice: "We have moved on. We have left controlled, teacher-proof reading programs that instruct 'Say this' in bold print. We have created reader's workshops instead of reading classes, and they are inviting places where children can learn to love to read. We have filled our shelves with wonderful children's literature. We read to our students for hours every week. Children in our classrooms love books and spend time with them every day. As teachers we are happier and more creative than before, but if we don't want to return to programmed reading instruction, we're going to have to know what to teach instead."

It became clear that many of these important questions focused on the content to be taught for comprehension. Teachers felt increasingly confident about how the classroom environment and management should be handled. They were absorbed and enthused about the process of transforming their classrooms into reader's and writer's workshops, and they felt an enhanced sense of engagement from their students, as well as for themselves. Teachers were beginning to understand the need to articulate and focus instruction on the mental processes that underlie reading.

The teachers at the cutting edge in literacy instruction who asked tough questions and discussed important issues with us believed the set of skills lifted from the basal scope and sequence was irrelevant and uninteresting in terms of teaching children how to comprehend. But they didn't yet know what to replace the scope and sequence with.

Experimenting with Comprehension Strategies

The brilliance of the proficient-reader research is that it gave us new insight into what to teach: the comprehension strategies. We tested them in our own reading and in classrooms like Claudia Keeley's and Leslie Blauman's. We read differently having used them ourselves. When confronted with a challenging article in the *Economist* or the *New Yorker*, we found that we used the strategies consciously and successfully. In general, as we read, we were simply more aware of our thinking. We paid more attention to the thought processes that we used as we read, and as a result became more aware readers. If we could do that as adults, we reasoned, think what it might mean for children.

A search began. Through journals and visits to reading projects in school districts around the country, we looked for settings in which children studied in workshop environments surrounded by high-quality fiction and nonfiction; *and* where they were given ample opportunity to read every day as well as to talk and write about their interpretations of books; *and* where the teacher explicitly taught the comprehension strategies identified in the proficient-reader research. We wanted to see if teachers anywhere in the country were implementing the proficient-reader research by using the strategies and helping children practice them in a workshop setting.

We found classrooms where teachers had created reader's workshops that focused primarily on selecting books and on sharing in book clubs. Minilessons centered on ways children, working alone or in groups, could create vivid written and artistic responses to what they read. We found classrooms where children developed elaborate projects around concepts from books they read. In many classrooms, teachers taught children to use graphic organizers such as webbing and mapping processes to help them remember details about characters, setting, and plot. The tools were primarily enrichment activities. Teachers used them to assess what children remembered from their reading, but the activities did little to actually improve children's comprehension while they were reading. We also found many classrooms where a great deal of direct instruction focused on a string of isolated and unrelated skills.

Something was missing. It was, we came to believe, the study of literature in a workshop setting combined with deep, focused comprehension instruction—instruction that targeted the thinking that occurs during reading, thinking that determines how deeply the text is understood.

As we designed the Reading Project, we turned to teachers like Leslie Blauman, Debbie Miller, Anne Henderson, Patrick Allen, Mimi DeRose, Colleen Buddy, and Mary Urtz. We observed early demonstrations like the one Ellin conducted in Claudia Keeley's fifth-grade classroom and watched the children closely to take our direction from them. When Claudia asked Ellin, "What's next?" we knew we were forging new territory. We saw that thinking aloud was a potent instructional tactic. It permitted us to let children in on one of the best-kept secrets of human cognition—what we think about as we read. We noticed that when we modeled and thought aloud about a strategy, children could begin to apply that strategy on their own, first in pairs and trios, later in their independent reading.

Anne Henderson's kindergartners at Meadow Point and Summit Elementary schools taught us that the youngest children could become deeply engaged and excited about being metacognitive (able to think about their thinking). Mary Urtz' fifth graders taught us that the comprehension strategies worked just as well in nonfiction as in fiction. Leslie Blauman's third, fourth, and fifth graders taught us how far children can delve in their book club discussions. Colleen Buddy helped us develop a working language to define and describe each strategy. Debbie Miller taught us how to include comprehension strategy instruction in a reader's/writer's workshop that honored children's choices and interests and cultivated thinking in an environment of respect and high expectations. Patrick Allen explored the outer limits of long-term strategy instruction, finding that the longer we focused on a strategy, the more students were able to use the strategy to plumb the depths of meaning. Mimi DeRose worked with us to understand how strategies can be applied across content areas.

Talking around that conference table, applying the comprehension strategies in our own reading, and learning from these teachers and their students enabled us to piece together the initial mosaic of thinking about comprehension instruction.

We were figuring things out as we went, discovering the power the comprehension strategies unleashed in classrooms. We were astonished at the quality of thinking kids shared when they took the strategies for a test drive themselves. Lessons like the one Ellin taught at South Street School were not driven by orthodoxy. The hope was that we were aligned closely enough with the proficient-reader research to begin answering some questions that had been troubling us at the PEBC.

We never imagined that *Mosaic of Thought* and the other books written by PEBC colleagues on comprehension strategy instruction and professional learning[1] would touch a chord in teachers around the country. We didn't realize then that we were not alone. Teachers throughout America were struggling with the same issues we faced in classrooms in the Denver area. We wanted to challenge the conventional wisdom about the way teachers approached comprehension instruction and to invite young readers into a world where they could read as real readers do, with depth and insight. We wanted to make comprehension teaching and learning more accessible to teachers and, through them, to students who had never experienced a book so deeply that it could become an anchor for the development of their emotions, beliefs, and values. We were just beginning to hear from teachers about their frustration in working with children who were fluent readers but who struggled to understand. We knew we had to be as honest as possible about what worked and what didn't, and that we had to keep going until we had answers.

This edition of *Mosaic of Thought* is about what remains true—and what is different—since those early days at the PEBC. It's about the evolution of our thinking about comprehension strategy instruction as we've traversed the country working with extraordinary teachers in all fifty states and throughout Canada. It's about listening and talking with others whose thinking we admire. People like Don Murray, Don Graves, Tom Newkirk, Lucy Calkins, Shelley Harwayne, Mary Ellen

---

1. *Nonfiction Matters*, Stephanie Harvey; *Strategies That Work*, Stephanie Harvey and Anne Goudvis; *Reading with Meaning*, Debbie Miller; *I Read It, But I Don't Get It*, Cris Tovani; *Do I Really Have to Teach Reading?* Cris Tovani; *7 Keys to Comprehension*, Susan Zimmermann and Chryse Hutchins; *Learning Along the Way*, Diane Sweeney; *Pathways*, Marjorie Larner; *Writing Through the Tween Years*, Bruce Morgan; *To Understand*, Ellin Oliver Keene.

Giacobbe, Joanne Hindley Salch, Ralph Fletcher, and Georgia Heard provided the foundation and inspiration for our early work and caused us not only to teach differently, but also to think differently about children's capacity to think at high levels. This book is about listening to and watching great teachers at work.

In the prologue to the first edition of *Mosaic of Thought*, we wrote, "Children need to learn letters, sounds, words, sentences, books, and they need to learn to comprehend literally and inferentially." We would now add the word simultaneously. Children need to learn letters, sounds, words, sentences, and how to comprehend what they read—*simultaneously*. Children do not learn to read in a lock-step, linear fashion. Small children are building the foundation for later reading when they listen to and respond to stories being read to them. When a child falls in love with a story, a huge step has been taken. That child knows the power of words and understands that words on a page contain important meaning. Of course, children need to learn letters, sounds, and words, but simultaneously they must be learning about the *meaning* held in those symbols on the page. They must be able to become as immersed and enchanted by the written word as the "professor" was in Billy Collins' "Books."

In that prologue we also said, "Our hope is that this book gives teachers new ways to think about their own reading, and effective ways to inspire children to read deeply and carefully. Ultimately, we will be most gratified if teachers move beyond this book—expanding and deepening the concepts, sharing their insights with other teachers and parents, working through obstacles together, creating new mosaics of thought." This has happened beyond our wildest dreams. Everywhere we go, teachers regale us with stories from their classrooms, ways they have embraced and elaborated upon the concepts outlined in *Mosaic of Thought*. There is no doubt who the true experts are: those teachers who have a thorough understanding of the reading process and the determination to understand and respond to each child's needs as a reader. When they call upon the comprehension strategies to help their students gain understanding, magic happens. We applaud their work and thank them for having the courage, moxie, and good sense to create an even more beautiful and effective mosaic.

CHAPTER 2

Changing Times

A scream torn from midair,
the sound of twisted metal clamors
out of blurry televised images.
The t.v. silent,
but the images screamed in my head.
People will say:
it was a morning like any other,
and that is what it was.
The sun still rose,
not anticipating the horrors
it would illuminate.
People rose,
innocent of the terror they would witness
and the strength.
Which is what I will remember.
The miracle cries united
so many courageous voices
drowning out the sound of
buildings falling silently,
the giant damaged blossoms of humanity
crushed against the perfect sky.

      —Elizabeth Keene, written in 2001; revised, 2006

Ellin's Reflections

My daughter, Elizabeth, now a high school senior, was in seventh grade in September 2001. I recall muting the television before we left for school that morning—a meaningless act, I now realize. Part of me wanted to protect her from the emerging news, part of me couldn't turn it off, and muting the sound was a sort of numb compromise. I took her to school, listening to the radio, and as we drove down a busy city boulevard, she pointed out that everyone in the cars around us had a hand on their face and fear in their eyes. I glanced at dozens of fellow drivers and passengers; their eyes met mine, and it was true, most had a hand on a cheek or over their mouth. They seemed to say, "Someone has made a terrible mistake and the reporting is in error. This can't be true." We were silently bound in that hope but knew it was in vain. I recall especially the worn eyes of an elderly man that seemed to suggest he wished he had not lived long enough to endure this pain.

I was hesitant to leave Elizabeth at school and called the principal from the car on my way to work. What precautions was he taking? He said, "I honestly don't know what to do, Ellin." That was not what I wanted to hear.

Elizabeth wrote about the events in a journal in 2001. Five years later, she reworked the words into a poem. I'm struck that her recollected images are of sound—perhaps intensified by the silent TV. I'm horrified that she lives in a world where, at age twelve, she had to experience that day, but glad that she used her journal to try to think through such complexity. She was resolute, then and now, to remember the "miracle cries united"—to focus on the courage and unity that grew out of the tragedy. It is to "that perfect sky" in New York City she will go when she attends Barnard College—the women's college at

Columbia University—in the fall of 2007. The strength and courage she chooses to remember from that day in 2001 will, I hope, sustain her in the city she and I find the most beautiful—and complex—in the world.

I write these words on the fifth anniversary of 9/11 and find it difficult to fathom the change we have all experienced. From coping with security lines in airports to wincing each time we read of another fallen soldier in Afghanistan or Iraq, to realizing the scope of civilian casualties in those countries, to arguing with friends, colleagues, and family about the right path for America to follow, we live with new weight on our shoulders.

If we could fast-forward a hundred years to gain the perspective of history, perhaps we would find some insight. Perhaps these troubled years will lead to some strength we can't yet envision. But we are here now, trying to do our best in a changed world. As teachers we are searching with more urgency than ever for the right answers, the way to reach the children of the post-9/11 era. We know that education that leads to understanding, tolerance, wise decisions—and the ability to function in a complex, global society—has never been more critical to our sense of well-being and our democracy.

What We Know

Today there is wide body of research supporting the effectiveness of explicit comprehension strategy instruction and the need for students to become metacognitive, to think about their own thinking as they read. Numerous articles and books provide detailed information about and overviews of the comprehension research. These include *Best Practices in Literacy Instruction* (Gambrell, Morrow, Neuman, and Pressley 1999*), Improving Comprehension Instruction: Rethinking Research, Theory, and Classroom Practice* (Block, Gambrell, and Pressley 2002), *Comprehension Instruction: Research-Based Best Practices* (Block and Pressley 2002), *Progress in Understanding Reading* (Stanovich 2000), *Reading for Under-*

standing: Towards an R&D program in Reading Comprehension (RAND Reading Study Group 2001), *Reading Instruction That Works,* Second Edition (Pressley 2002), *When Kids Can't Read, What Teachers Can Do* (Beers 2003), *Promising Practices for Urban Reading Instruction* (Mason and Schumm 2004), and *What Really Matters for Struggling Readers: Designing Research-Based Programs,* Second Edition (Allington 2006). There is near unanimity in the field of literacy education that strategic readers are more active readers and that active readers both retain more and are more likely to reapply what they remember in new contexts. (See Block and Pressley 2002.)

Traditional practices in which comprehension *instruction* was really comprehension *assessment*—asking students an endless string of comprehension questions or asking them to retell what they read instead of to share their thinking—often failed to teach children how to better understand what they read. Teaching reading meant dealing with the visible and audible manifestations of reading, rather than the cognitive aspects. If children completed drill sheets and workbook pages and sat in their ability groups to read aloud, it was taken on faith that students would somehow come to comprehend complex text.

In fact, many children did not. Many students read words well, but had little sense of the meaning of what they read, especially meaning that went beyond the literal. These children could decode well, but they weren't becoming proficient, independent, critical readers. Because teachers and children lacked a clear language to describe the thinking used by proficient readers, thinking wasn't addressed. Before comprehension strategy instruction, there was little consideration of what children thought about while they were reading.

The research is now clear that instruction that actively engages students in asking questions, summarizing and synthesizing text, and identifying important ideas improves comprehension, and that proficient reading involves using more than one strategy at a time: "It involves a constant ongoing adaptation of many cognitive processes" (Sweet and

Snow in Block, Gambrell, and Pressley 2002, 39). Using background knowledge, inferring, creating mental images, and monitoring comprehension also contribute to active and engaged reading. The goal, of course, is to have children use all of these strategies at once, shifting effortlessly from one to another as needed to understand what they read.

Comprehension strategy instruction is an important step in the right direction, but it is not a panacea and by itself is not enough to develop avid, proficient readers. It is also critical to provide explicit instruction in decoding, fluency, word analysis, text structures, and vocabulary for children learning to read. Students need to spend abundant time every day reading increasingly difficult text, and they benefit from having a purpose and focus for their reading, as well as the common language that the strategies provide to articulate their thinking. *Nothing* should stand in the way of time to read independently.

In those early PEBC conversations, we knew reading instruction needed to be different if we were going to produce students who were truly literate. We were committed to finding better ways, but we were better at asking the tough questions than answering them. We knew teachers were the best people to make adaptations and adjustments as they implemented strategy instruction. Only they know their students' needs and can make judgments accordingly. Armed with an understanding of the research and firsthand knowledge of their students, teachers can generate the most effective plans for literacy instruction. Therefore, the questions and ideas we raised were meant to challenge the status quo and help teachers consider alternatives, not provide "the" answer.

Today's Literacy Landscape

Federal and state legislation has increased public demand for accountability, largely demonstrated by "high-stakes" testing. These tests take a large amount of class time and often work against students learning to think at higher levels.

Some packaged programs purport to lay out a research-based set of practices for teaching literacy. Inevitably, they limit teachers' decision making about their students. In an effort to raise test scores, schools and districts have turned to "silver-bullet" programs in the hope that rigid adherence to a scripted, one-size-fits-all program will lead to better performance and higher achievement in the guise of improved test scores.

But what do better performance and higher achievement really mean? Do higher standardized test scores necessarily equate to either? Are we comfortable with classrooms where students follow directions, complete assignments, and sit at literacy centers doing activities but aren't asked to read broadly and think deeply? Do we believe that the skills that matter most in a complicated, interdependent world are those that can be tested in a multiple-choice format? Are we providing students with materials that are readable, interesting, multifaceted, and challenging? And are we certain that students are actually doing the one thing that makes the biggest difference in their reading performance—spending extensive periods of time every day actually reading?

Judith Langer from the State University of New York, Albany, has studied "thoughtful classrooms" in which students score well on high-stakes assessments, though their daily classroom work is interactive and conceptual, not packaged and scripted. After evaluating eighty-eight classes in Florida, New York, California, and Texas over a period of two years each, her research team concluded that students who achieve a higher-than-expected level of literacy benefit significantly from their teachers' skills in classroom instruction. "Increased performance," Langer notes, regardless of the school's characteristics or demographics, "is measured by students' engagement in thoughtful reading, writing and discussion and by their use of knowledge and skills in new situations" (Langer 2002).

Research like Langer's confirms what we have observed in classrooms throughout the country: Kids who think well test well. Skill-and-drill, one-size-fits-all programs, which are increasingly prevalent, are an illusory solution. Evaluating programs over the past forty years shows that "packaged reforms simply do not seem to reliably improve student achievement" (Allington 2006, 14). Valuable resources that could be used to improve school and classroom libraries, decrease class size, redesign the school day for productive academic work and real reading, and provide effective staff development to teachers are being squandered on tests and costly materials that too often don't make a difference for children.

The Joy of Reading

As we travel the country, we see multifaceted, engaging classrooms and committed teachers. We see people who want the best for their students. And we see children who live in drug-infested neighborhoods, who switch schools with each eviction notice, and who attend schools where discipline is maintained with a bullhorn. Deep anxiety about reading permeates classrooms. That anxiety is exacerbated by high-stakes testing that can carry punitive consequences.

Everywhere we go teachers feel under the gun to get their students to read and understand. Of course, we all want children to read and read well. Too frequently, however, something critically important is lost somewhere along the line: the joy of reading. What we fear—and what the research indicates—is that we are producing "school readers": students who seldom crack a book once they've left the classroom.

In *Reading at Risk: A Survey of Literary Reading in America*, the National Endowment for the Arts surveyed literary reading habits of more than 17,000 adults over a twenty-year period from 1982 to 2002. Its principal finding was that "literary reading in America is not only declining rapidly among all groups, but the rate of decline has accelerated, especially among the young" (NEA 2004, vii). The NEA found that the number of Americans who say they've even opened a single book of fiction, let alone a poem or a play, over the course of a year declined from an already low 56.9 percent in 1982 to 46.7 percent in 2002. Perhaps most disturbing is that the age group with the steepest decline in literary reading was young adults aged eighteen to twenty-four. In 1982, 59.8 percent in that age group read literature. In 2002, the number had dropped to 42.8 percent (NEA 2004, xi).

Electronic media, including the Internet, video games, and portable digital devices, have increasingly drawn Americans away from reading books. Nonreaders watch more television than readers. It's not that electronic media are intrinsically bad. The Internet gives access to an extraordinary range of information, and some video games require real focus. The problem is that often these pursuits take less concentration, less active engagement, and less attention than reading. As a rule, they require less mental engagement from the participant. They tend to foster shorter attention spans. Used to excess and to the exclusion of reading, they become a factor in the decline of reading. The NEA study also found that readers tend to play a more active and involved role in their communities: "The decline in reading, therefore, parallels a larger retreat from participation in civic and cultural life. The long-term implications of this study not only affect literature but all the arts—as well as social activities such as volunteerism, philanthropy, and even political engagement" (vii).

Current political fashion cannot kill common sense. We must have the goal of educating children to become real readers, not simply students who answer test questions correctly but leave school with no interest in picking up a book ever again. If we want engaged, active readers and citizens, we must make reading a joyful adventure.

There is no program, no recipe, no prescription that will ever supersede the power of a well-informed and caring teacher. Teachers must stay informed about what works (and what doesn't) and guard the right to make decisions about their own students. They also must be committed to making reading a meaningful and joyful experience, so that when their students leave school, they continue their reading journeys.

Q&A on Comprehension Strategy Instruction

In the last ten years, many teachers have adapted comprehension strategy instruction to meet the needs of their students. Teachers have created Internet listservs to share strategy ideas and learn from one another. Researchers are investigating more applications. Whole conferences are devoted to classroom strategy instruction. Teachers are asking provocative, far-reaching questions about how to best help their students become avid readers.

We want to share some of the questions we hear most often and do our best to answer them.

Q: *Why do we need to teach comprehension strategies?*

Few of us were taught to use comprehension strategies when we were in school, and we learned to read without them. If we became proficient readers, we intuited how to use these strategies, though we didn't label them. We might have learned how to determine importance when we desperately faced reading five hundred pages in one evening; to question when we disagreed with something a professor presented; to create images when we sank into a page-turner; to activate and build background knowledge as we mastered a subject of interest; to infer when we read poetry; to synthesize when we researched and wrote a term paper. Why, then, do we need to teach comprehension strategies explicitly? Isn't it inauthentic to ask kids to monitor their comprehension and call upon the other strategies? Shouldn't they just spend a lot of time reading and discussing what they read?

We explicitly teach the comprehension strategies to ensure children don't simply become expert decoders but also learn to create meaning naturally and subconsciously as they read, far earlier than in the past. Today's students face a wider variety of texts and must contend with a larger volume of reading material. They must be able to think critically and make judgments about the credibility of authors and the intention behind publications more frequently and earlier than pre-Internet generations. They must absorb and apply more information in a wider variety of contexts. Our complex global society calls for all children to be able to think and learn at high levels. Explicit comprehension instruction arms all of them—not just those aiming for a college education—with the tools to do so.

Some suggest that children find using strategies intrusive, that strategies slow them down and make learning to read less enjoyable. We need to listen to the message behind these protestations. If we impose rigid, inauthentic processes on children (e.g., cover your text with sticky notes and write about every connection you make as you read), we are simply taking strategy teaching too far. Children's learning experiences should be authentic and enjoyable. There should be times when teachers read aloud simply to give children the pleasure of listening to beautifully crafted literature, poetry, or nonfiction. There should be times set aside for instruction, thinking aloud, modeling, and demonstrating how proficient readers comprehend more deeply. There should be times when children read independently for the pleasure of reading, and there should be times when they are asked to employ strategies to deepen and amplify their understanding.

For today's students, two factors—the overwhelming amount and variety of text they must learn to manage, and the fact that many kids start school having had few experiences with books—make early and ongoing failure in comprehension a real possibility. Test scores and teachers' observations make clear that is exactly what is happening for too many children. We cannot look the other way, hoping children will figure out how to comprehend on their own. Fortunately, we have a large and growing body of research that wasn't around thirty years ago. The purpose of teaching comprehension strategies is to enable children to read with deeper, longer-lasting understanding. We should never lose sight of that goal.

Q: *Is there an order or chronology for comprehension strategy instruction?*

The research does not indicate a particular order or chronology for teaching comprehension strategies. Teachers should make decisions about the order based on their knowledge of their students, the demands of the text being used in the classroom, and the strategy instruction they may have had in earlier grades.

The teacher or school can decide what order works best for teaching the strategies. That said, through trial and error, we have found that there is an order that makes sense for many teachers. It differs slightly in primary and intermediate classrooms:

- **Primary:** monitoring, using background knowledge, questioning, creating mental images, inferring, determining importance, synthesizing

- **Intermediate:** monitoring, using background knowledge, inferring, determining importance, synthesizing, questioning, creating mental images

This order is not set in stone but reflects the different demands most intermediate teachers face related to high-stakes testing. Many children struggle to infer and determine importance on such assessments. Ideally, they've been exposed to all of the strategies in an earlier grade, so they have some practice using them. We've found that introducing inference, determining importance, and synthesis before the (typically) spring assessments is helpful in preparing them both for tests and for the expository text they will confront in the upper elementary grades, as well as in middle and high school.

Q: *Should children study different strategies based on their reading level?*

It is important to remember that one strategy is not inherently more difficult or more important than another. Rather, it is the difficulty and type of text in which students *apply* the strategies that makes a comprehension task more difficult. We differentiate for students' present proficiency level, not by strategy, but by the *text in which they apply the strategy.* In the same classroom, all children will be studying the same strategy, but applying that strategy in different levels and genres.

Too often, we draw negative conclusions about a child's ability to comprehend or think at high levels when the problem is related to his or her ability to *articulate* that thinking. The vast majority of our students can and do think at high levels—what separates them is often the ability to speak and write eloquently about that thinking. Language about thought can be taught, and strategy instruction allows conversation among a wide range of students—talk that seldom occurs when children are broken into ability groups. Children at different levels are able to discuss text and strategy use with each other. Often we've seen children who typically work with lower-level texts suddenly find themselves "in the game" when participating in conversations about books. In fact, these children frequently provide insightful, unexpected perspectives on books, authors, and topics.

Q: *Should comprehension strategies be taught one at a time or in an integrated fashion?*

This is a much-debated question. Some studies have shown a larger immediate effect from integrated strategy instruction, but we do not yet have data comparing the results from integrated instruction with those from in-depth instruction, which focuses on one strategy at a time and then integrates them cumulatively. We have also observed that children, especially those who have had little strategy instruction, can become confused with the language pertaining to each strategy when they are taught in an integrated manner.

Again, through trial and error, we have found that teaching one strategy at a time, but cumulatively, is most effective. For example, if teachers begin by teaching monitoring for meaning and move to background knowledge, they continue to discuss ways in which readers monitor for meaning during the study on background knowledge, and so on with each new strategy, so that children gain a cumulative knowledge of the strategies.

Ultimately, the goal is to be able to use all the strategies in an integrated manner, but there are times when children should purposefully use one or two strategies, depending on the demands of the text. Sometimes we want kids to be able to either "turn up (or turn down) the volume" on a strategy during reading. By "turn up the volume," we mean that we want children to recognize when they are working in a text that requires them to use one strategy more than others. For example, if they are reading dense, expository text, they may need to "turn up" determining importance and "turn down" inference and images. Or, if they're reading a novel that is fairly easy for them or a text for which they have plenty of background knowledge, they will find that using the strategies in an integrated, seamless manner will work best. They may be unaware that they are even using the strategies. This is fine, and exactly what most adult, proficient readers do.

Q: *What about teaching the comprehension strategies across the curriculum? If you read in science, math, and social studies, don't you use the same thought processes?*

Yes! In many ways comprehension strategies are thinking strategies. We ask questions, use our background knowledge, synthesize information, and so forth throughout the day, at home, at school, and at work. Children certainly use all of the comprehension strategies in all of their coursework, not just in the language arts (see Appendix A). A story from our colleague, Colleen Buddy, brought this home to us. Colleen told us about Kevin, a second grader in her first/second-grade classroom. She was teaching a lesson on predicting, presenting the concept as a type of inference. Kevin raised his hand and asked, "Mrs. Buddy, how come when we're in reading you teach us about predicting, and when we're in math you teach us estimating, and when we're in science, you call it hypothesizing; aren't they all sort of the same thing?"

Bingo! Kevin helped us see that comprehension is about understanding ideas, not just in text, but in the world. Sure, there are subtle differences between predicting, estimating, and hypothesizing, but conceptually they are in the same ballpark. Kevin helped us realize that comprehension strategies are *tools for understanding* across the curriculum.

We particularly like Art Hyde's book *Comprehending Math* (2006), in which he shows how each of the strategies can be applied in mathematics instruction.

Q: What if I don't teach all seven strategies every year? Are some more important than others?

Some schools and districts teach each strategy every year, and individual teachers and/or grade levels determine the order. Other schools choose to teach one strategy through all the grade levels simultaneously, giving the teachers at all grade levels an opportunity to discuss instruction on the same strategy at the same time. Schools that wish to focus on each strategy for a longer period of time (six to nine weeks) assign primary emphasis to three or four strategies each for grades K–1, grades 2–3, and grades 4–5 so that children have had two or three in-depth experiences with each strategy by the time they leave the school. The same configuration can be applied across the three middle school years, with different grade levels assuming primary responsibility for two or three strategies. Of course, the strategies taught earlier can be discussed and woven into instruction on a new strategy.

Q: Don't think-alouds rob children of authentic read-aloud experiences in which a literary piece is read simply for the beauty of the language and the joy of the story?

Comprehension strategy instruction should never, ever cut into the time teachers spend reading aloud to their students, just for the joy of the story.

Reading a fiction, nonfiction, or poetic piece aloud to savor the beauty of the language or learn new facts is vital across all grade levels. Students don't "outgrow" the usefulness of listening to text read aloud. The most important lessons have to do with the pure enjoyment of listening to a story and discussing it later with the teacher and other students. Reading aloud and providing comprehension strategy instruction are both needed.

It is also helpful to provide a natural and "safe" environment—one in which varying opinions are welcomed and honored—so that children feel comfortable discussing and writing about what they read. The comprehension strategies can help "break the ice" by providing children with a focus for their oral, written, and artistic responses.

Some teachers are concerned that thinking aloud interrupts the flow of the story. It is important to be clear about the purpose of a think-aloud—to show how a more proficient reader uses a strategy prior to asking students to apply it in their own reading. These interruptions are essential if teachers are to show students what comprehension actually looks like *during* reading. The heart of comprehension instruction is to focus on the cognitive strategies proficient readers use while they read. This is very different from reading aloud for the pleasure of the story and to increase students' attention spans. Teachers should not be overly concerned about the interruptions as long as they still allow plenty of time for uninterrupted reading aloud.

Q: *Are there factors other than strategy instruction that are particularly important in creating avid, thoughtful readers?*

Two factors are vital: providing time to read and time to talk. Both are critically important in creating effective classrooms, and anything that interferes with them needs to be changed.

TIME TO READ

The greatest casualty when excessive time is spent in test preparation and skill-and-drill learning is time for children to actually read. The adage "the more you read, the better you get; the better you get, the more you read" happens to be true, and is one of the few things that has been proven time and again in the research (*Reading Report Card for the Nation*, NAEP 1999; *What Really Matters for Struggling Readers*, Allington 2006, 36–39). The more children read, the more apt they are to become good readers who attain higher-order literacy proficiencies (Cipielewski and Stanovich 1992).

The simple fact is that good readers read more. That we must give children the chance to read more therefore seems a most common-sense conclusion. Anything that stands in the way of allowing time to practice reading is a serious problem.

Too often children are asked to engage in a range of literacy-related centers, projects, and activities *about* reading, when what they should be doing *is* reading. There is an assumption that students cannot sustain independent reading for long periods of time while the teacher is otherwise occupied (in small-group instruction or in conferring with individuals). Our experience tells us otherwise. If students are taught to gradually extend the amount of time spent in independent reading every day from the beginning of the school year, they will rise to the occasion.

This is how we learn many things: We start with baby steps and graduate, over time and with support, to miles or marathons. When Ellin's toddler Elizabeth learned to swim, at first she doubted she could keep her arms and legs going long enough to swim a short distance to Ellin's outstretched hands. With encouragement and the assurance Ellin wouldn't move, eventually she set out from the side, kicking and paddling like crazy. Though it meant fudging on a promise, Ellin backed up ever so slowly as Elizabeth swam toward her, proving that Elizabeth could go much farther than she thought.

The same is true with young readers. We should begin with shorter blocks of time and gradually "back up," adding more and more time to the daily independent reading period. In our experience, it makes sense to begin the school year with fairly short periods of time for independent reading (as brief as five minutes with very young children, fifteen for older ones), during which the teacher can move among the children conferring, assessing present performance level, and helping children make wise book choices. Gradually, that time can increase up to forty-five minutes for young children and an hour for upper elementary. During this time, the teacher can gather small needs-based groups to address particular skill needs and/or to introduce new skills and genres to children who are excelling.

TIME TO TALK

Oral language development plays a critical role in learning to read and write well. Children's syntax (oral and written grammar, story structures, and use of conventions) and vocabulary (using more precise and purposeful words) develop because they spend time talking at home, to their teachers, and with other children. Too often young children, those who are learning English as their second language, and/or children who struggle seem as if they aren't thinking critically. However, children—particularly those in these three groups—can in fact be thinking at high levels. What they may lack is the language to describe that thinking. Rather than assuming they aren't capable of thinking in more sophisticated ways, we must help them develop the language to define and describe their thinking. Peter Johnston, in his book *Choice Words* (2004), calls our attention to the ways in which teachers' talk in the classroom influences students' learning and how we must take every available opportunity to teach children the language of thought.

When children have abundant opportunities to talk about books, when classroom discussion in small and large groups is encouraged, comprehension improves. Conversations can focus on the content of a book, the comprehension strategies children are using to understand it more deeply, their real-life connections to what they read, their personal stories, or a combination of all of the above. If we want students to be articulate about their thinking, they need daily time to practice talking. To encourage this, we often ask children to "turn and talk" to one another in the middle of a large-group lesson. It gives them a brief, but essential, chance to try out their ideas on one another, quickly solidifying their thinking before moving on. We also encourage teachers to set up book clubs in which students can share ideas and push each other to think at high levels. Providing time to talk, in a purposeful and truly interactive manner, is vital to teaching comprehension.

Q: *What is the best reader's workshop structure?*

We have found that the reader's workshop structure that most effectively supports comprehension learning includes four components (Keene forthcoming). Briefly, these are:

- Large-group meeting time in which the teacher thinks aloud about a comprehension strategy, then encourages children to share their thinking.

- A long period of time for independent reading during which the teacher moves among the children to confer.

- The formation of needs-based groups during independent reading to address specific learning needs.

- A time for children to reflect on their learning with others. This can be in the form of a large-group sharing session, book clubs, written responses, one-on-one sharing between children, or any number of discussion-based forms of sharing.

We provide a fuller description of these components in later chapters.

There has been a resurgence of small-group instruction in the last ten years, a result of the fact that in too many classrooms, children were being taught the same skills from the same text at the same time, even though they had very different needs. The pendulum swing to small-group instruction, while in many ways a positive move, may have swung too far. Now, too often the emphasis seems to be on a continual cycle of small-group meetings with the teacher unavailable to the rest of the class while he or she completes the daily small-group rounds. Frequently, these groups are ability based—a practice that is questionable, especially if the groups stay together indefinitely—and too focused on completing a repetitive process of reading aloud, being corrected, and then having to listen to others read aloud and receive their corrections.

When the small-group meeting structure is too rigid, teachers don't have an opportunity to confer individually with students. Whether the need is for work on decoding or the application of a comprehension strategy, one-on-one conferences provide a potent teachable moment for a child who, for a few moments, has a teacher who is responding directly to his needs.

Q: *What do you do about thoughtful, able readers who complain that comprehension strategies slow them down?*

There are typically four reasons why children complain that strategies slow them down. First, the children may be using texts that are not challenging enough for them. None of us wants to be "slowed down" and forced to use comprehension strategies consciously when it's not necessary. In many schools, children read texts that are appropriate for fluency practice, but lack challenging ideas; they also need more interesting, challenging books.

Second, children in some schools aren't accustomed to reading for deeper meaning, a process that may require them to slow down, pause, think about, write about, and/or discuss ideas with another reader. When they've only been asked to read the words, get to the end of the selection, and answer the prepared questions, it may well take time and additional think-aloud lessons for them to get used to being more thoughtful and critical about their reading. We need to model for children, showing them the joy that comes from understanding and being able to respond to ideas at a deeper level. Frequently, it is the use of the strategies that helps them reach that level.

Third, teachers need to ensure that they aren't "basalizing" comprehension strategy instruction. In our zeal to make sure children are accountable for using the strategies we're teaching, we can force them into techniques that are artificial and boring. When Ellin's daughter Elizabeth was in fifth grade, at the dinner table one night she declared she "hated those strategies!" As Ellin probed a bit, Elizabeth said she "couldn't find five 'determining importances' on each page." A well-intentioned teacher had overdone the application of the strategy by asking the children to mark five things they thought were important on each page of a reading. No wonder Elizabeth said she hated those strategies! No one wants to be forced to use them in a mechanical fashion. We should ask kids to use the strategies purposefully while they're learning them and in an integrated, almost subconscious way later.

Finally, children who are accustomed to reading quickly and responding to questions accurately may be surprised to discover that, with complex text, there are many interpretations and "right answers." They may complain that the strategies slow them down, but in fact may be caught off guard by not having an immediate and "correct" response to a question.

Generally, with children who are avid readers, providing them with more challenging texts is key so that they can experience how consciously using the strategies can help them grasp the material.

~ ~ ~

Remember, the strategies are tools. They are a means to an end—comprehension—not an end in themselves. Our goal is to help children become avid readers who look forward to time alone with a great book in hand. The comprehension strategies combined with a healthy dose of common sense and a commitment to classrooms where children's opinions, passions, and intellects are honored will go a long way toward creating environments in which children will learn to love to read.

CHAPTER 3

Mindful Reading

Monitoring and Revising Comprehension

Girl

Wash the white clothes on Monday and put them on the stone heap; wash the color clothes on Tuesday and put them on the clothesline to dry; don't walk barehead in the hot sun; cook pumpkin fritters in very hot sweet oil; soak your little cloths right after you take them off; when buying cotton to make yourself a nice blouse, be sure that it doesn't have gum on it, because that way it won't hold up well after a wash; soak salt fish overnight before you cook it; is it true that you sing benna in Sunday school?; always eat your food in such a way that it won't turn someone else's stomach; on Sundays try to walk like a lady and not like the slut you are so bent on becoming; don't sing benna in Sunday school; you mustn't speak to wharf-rat boys, not even to give directions; don't eat fruits on the street—flies will follow you; *but I don't sing benna on Sundays at all and never in Sunday school*; this is how to sew on a button; this is how to make a hole for the button you have just sewed on; this is how to hem a dress when you see the hem coming down and so to prevent yourself from looking like the slut I know you are so bent on becoming; this is how you iron your father's khaki shirt so that it doesn't have a crease; this is how you iron your father's khaki pants so that they don't have a crease; this is how you grow okra—far from the house, because okra trees harbor red ants; when you are growing dasheen, make sure it gets plenty of water or else it makes your throat itch when you are eating it; this is how you sweep a corner; this is how you sweep a whole house; this is how you sweep a yard; this is how you smile to someone you don't like too much; this is how you smile to someone you don't like at all; this is how you smile to someone you like completely; this is how you set a table for tea; this is how you set a table for dinner this is how you set a table for dinner with an important guest; this is how you set a table for lunch; this is how you set a table for breakfast; this is how to behave in the presence of men who don't know you very well, and this way they won't recognize immediately the slut I have warned you against becoming; be sure to wash every day, even if it is with your own spit; don't squat down to play marbles you are not a boy, you know; don't pick people's flowers—you might catch something; don't throw stones at blackbirds, because it might not be a blackbird at all; this is how to make a bread pudding; this is how to make doukona; this is how to make pepper pot; this is how to make a good medicine for a cold; this is how to make a good medicine to throw away a child before it even becomes a child; this is how to catch a fish; this is how to throw back a fish you don't like, and that way something bad won't fall on you; this is how to bully a man; this is how a man bullies you; this is how to love a man; and if this doesn't work there are other ways, and if they don't work don't feel too bad about giving up; this is how to spit up in the air if you feel like it, and this is how to move quick so that it doesn't fall on you; this is how to make ends meet; always squeeze bread to make sure it's fresh; *but what if the baker won't let me feel the bread?*; you mean to say that after all you are really going to be the kind of woman who the baker won't let near the bread?

— Jamaica Kincaid, *At the Bottom of the River*

Susan's Reflections

My daughter Helen is teaching a freshman composition class at Brooklyn College. "Mom, I'm using some pretty great essays," she says, and I ask her to send a couple my way.

I read Jamaica Kincaid's "Girl" and am immediately taken by the cadence of the language. There is a beat and a repetition that reminds me of Caribbean music. My first time through, I'm caught up in the language, the stream-of-consciousness nature of the piece, the monumental run-on sentence (this is just one sentence!). After I finish, I need to catch my breath. I realize that—as so often when I listen to songs—I paid more attention to the rhythm and sound of the language than the meaning of the words. I reread it. This time the questions begin: Who is giving the advice? What is her relationship to the girl? What is *benna*? *Doukona*? Wharf-rat boys? Why can't the girl get a word in edgewise?

I'm puzzled and am feeling a cultural disconnect because of the unfamiliar words and the tropical locale. "Wash the white clothes on Monday . . . wash the color clothes on Tuesday . . ." Okay, this is an old woman giving advice to a young woman about all sorts of domestic chores. Is she the girl's mother? Grandmother? Friend?

At first I imagine an older woman generously handing down the household traditions to an adolescent girl. I don't know if this is her home or if she is a servant in someone else's. This could be an older servant teaching a girl who will someday take her place. But then this line: "On Sundays try to walk like a lady and not like the slut you are so bent on becoming." I rushed over that on my first read. Now it stops me in my tracks, not once, but three times. This must be a relative or someone who is close to the girl and cares about her. She is trying to keep the girl out of trouble and she doubts her ability to do so. She sees the girl going downhill fast. Whether the girl is or not is a different issue. The woman's tone changes in my mind from kind to berating. In her laundry list of ways to care for house and yard, what she's really saying is that she wants to keep the girl out of sexual trouble, but maybe she's too late.

Some of the words stump me. I do a quick Internet search, learning that *doukona* is a type of pudding made from starchy foods, sweetened and spiced; *benna* is a folk song about scandalous rumors in a call-and-response form between the leader and the audience; *dasheen* is an edible tropical plant. There is no definition of wharf rats. I guess wharf rats are young men who hang out at the wharf and could entice the girl into indiscretions. Knowing *benna* is bawdy singing helps me understand the woman's accusation and the girl's plaintive response.

The style is confusing: a page-long sentence jammed with advice about mundane housekeeping tasks, interspersed with the most intimate women's counsel: "Soak your little cloths right after you take them off;" "don't squat down to play marbles you are not a boy;" "this is how to make good medicine to throw away a child before it even becomes a child;" "this is how to love a man." I come to see the litany of household "to dos" as a way to mask what the woman is really saying about how females need to behave to be decent and god-fearing. I'm feeling the pressure on this girl to conform to the role that is set out for her: to keep house well and to "be good." I think about that saying, "good girls don't turn into great women." I think about the pressure on women throughout time and across cultures to conform to preconceived and limiting roles. And then this piece becomes a generational clash: The old woman wants to mold the girl so that she doesn't step outside society's boundaries. The girl is too young and unformed to fight back, but I'm hoping someday she will. I'm hoping that her voice, buried under the layers of tradition and convention represented by the woman, will someday be heard.

Surface and Deep Structures

In my mind I review the common stumbling blocks children encounter as they read. I analyze how I surmounted challenges to arrive at my interpretation of "Girl." I wonder, for example, if the comprehension problems I experienced with "Girl" are connected to what reading theorists call *surface structures*, the visible aspects of the text: the letters, words, grammatical structure.

Was mine a problem of deciphering difficult words I was unable to sound out? No, there were unfamiliar words, but I could pronounce all of them with no problem.

Did the text fail to make grammatical sense? The run-on sentence *was* confusing. It contained a lot of information with no pause, no letup in intensity. I deliberately reread it more slowly to take it all in.

But, in the end, my comprehension challenges related more to the *deep structure* of "Girl": the meanings, concepts, and associations underlying the words and phrases; my relevant background knowledge; and my purpose and context for reading. When I first read it, I was captivated by the rhythm and didn't pay enough attention to the meaning. I missed the nuance and subtlety of the piece. There were words I didn't know. Even when I tried to figure them out in context, I wasn't sure and needed to look them up. I had little background knowledge about island living and the constraints on girls. It took some effort for me to connect this girl to women everywhere whose voices are limited by cultural expectations and constraints.

When I first read "Girl," I had to work to understand it—I had to monitor my reading closely, and I needed a number of revision strategies. I read it several times, looked up words I'd never encountered, consciously tackled an unusual text structure, and altered my thinking about the relationship and the motivation of the characters. The more I read and thought about it, the more I realized its simple structure—an old woman giving advice to a girl—was deceptive. Complicated issues of gender and culture are buried in the ordinary words of domestic advice.

Listening to Your Inner Voice

For proficient readers, monitoring for meaning is a natural and often subconscious process. Proficient readers listen to their inner voices as they read, make ongoing corrections and adjustments, and are aware of how meaning evolves. Our goal is to make this process similarly subconscious and natural for *all* students, so that they monitor and revise their thinking in a wide variety of texts long before high school or college—which is where some of us were before we caught on.

In many ways, monitoring is the umbrella under which the other comprehension strategies fall. Each of the strategies is a type of monitoring. When students use them, they automatically revise their thinking as they read. It can be very effective to kick off the school year with a short study, two to four weeks, on monitoring that emphasizes the importance of revising our thinking as we read, being metacognitive, and paying attention so we know when we're understanding and when we're not, and can do something about it. Thinking aloud is key so students have the opportunity to listen in as we reveal how and when our comprehension is thrown off and exactly what we do to get back on track.

When Susan read "Girl," she needed to bring the process of monitoring to a conscious level—to "turn up the volume"—to make sense of the piece. Doing so made it possible to understand the text at a far deeper level than a cursory, "first-draft" type of read would have allowed. The gratification that comes from tackling a challenging piece and coming to a solid understanding of it reinforces the value of monitoring. But the benefit is more than that sense of fulfillment. Monitoring is quite simply vital to comprehension.

Into the Classroom—High School

Cris Tovani is a take-no-hostages, tell-it-like-it-is teacher with an infectious laugh. She is a superb teacher. Before returning to full-time teaching and writing (she's the author of *I Read It But I Don't Get It* and

Do I Really Have to Teach Reading?), she was a member of the Public Education & Business Coalition's staff development team for seven years. Cris now teaches reading and advanced placement English and humanities classes at Smoky Hill High School in the Cherry Creek School District.

Early one school year, Ellin stopped by her sixth-hour class. The summerlike weather had seduced several students not to return to school after lunch. The rest shuffled in. Some flopped into overstuffed chairs bordered by bookshelves while others slid onto stiff chairs behind desks. The way their shoulders slumped and heads hung revealed a body language of defeat from years of painful academic experiences.

Cris had forty-two minutes a day for a semester—for some students, a year—to reverse years of reading frustration and failure. On this particular day she engaged the students in a discussion about how readers monitor and revise their thinking as they read.

"We've been talking about being metacognitive—thinking about your thinking when you read, being aware of when you're understanding and when you're not," she began. "I want to talk to you today about one way readers are metacognitive. We call it monitoring for meaning. When you monitor for meaning, it means that you have to continually attend to your understanding as you read. You need to know what your purpose is as you read. You need to know how to solve problems and change your thinking when meaning breaks down."

"Huh?" a few students queried. The rest seemed to be pretty checked out.

"Okay, we've talked a lot about listening to the voice in your mind that speaks to you when you read. We haven't talked about the specific strategies or forms that voice takes. I want to think aloud for you today to show you how I monitor for meaning and how I change my thinking when I become aware that I'm not getting it. You guys probably think that no matter what adults pick up to read, it's easy for us, but that's not true. I want you to watch what I do so you can start to use the strategies like monitoring that good readers, no matter how old they are, use to make sure they get it."

Cris had an eclectic collection of pieces ready to share. On this day she chose a particularly dense journal article describing a research study. In subsequent lessons, she would use poetry, newspaper editorials, college application instructions, SAT directions, excerpts from Barbara Kingsolver's novel *The Bean Trees*, and a few bureaucratic memos from various school and district administrators—always a great source for incomprehensible material!

"Okay," she began, "I'm going to read this summary of a research study called, 'The processing of lexically stressed syllables in read and spontaneous speech.'"

Loud groans.

"I know, but let's say I have to read it to understand the research behind some of the stuff I'm teaching you guys, okay? Let's say I *have* to understand it. Now listen, because I'm going to think aloud about how I can monitor and revise my thinking or solve some of the problems I have as I read. Ready? 'This research describes four experiments which examined both read and spontaneous speech.' Okay, that's a short summary of the article. I am monitoring my understanding and so far I know there are four experiments. I know a lot about how educators set up research experiments, so I'm okay with that part. I start to have trouble with the part about read and spontaneous speech. What does that mean? I know that one way I can fix up meaning is to keep reading and see if it becomes clearer. That's what I'm going to do, because I haven't read very much yet and I'm going to see if this gets clearer in the next few sentences. If it doesn't, I'll have to go back and try something else. I'm going to read on."

Cris continued. " 'In the first experiment, which focused on read materials . . .' Okay, I read that as *read* with a long *e*, that that doesn't make sense with materials, so I have to go back and change the way I pronounce it to read with a short vowel sound. 'Trisyllabic nouns.'

Whoa! *Trisyllabic* isn't a word I come across very often. Let's see, because that word has a prefix, *tri*, and a root word, *syllabic*, I can take that word apart to see what it means. The prefix *t-r-i* I know means three, like tricounty, three counties, or even triplets, and *syllable* means a word part that makes one sound, so *trisyllabic* must mean three-syllable words. Why don't they just say that?!"

Laughter comes from the students who are now so engaged in watching Cris think aloud that their whole affect has changed.

Cris goes on: " '. . . were presented in three contextually defined conditions.' What in the world is a 'contextually defined condition'? I don't think I have background knowledge for that one! I'm going to skip it and see if I think it's important to come back to it later. If it is important, I can ask my friend Sheila McAuliffe, who is a researcher, or search the Internet to find out what 'contextually defined conditions' means."

Cris then reads, " '. . . to 36 subjects.' Wow, finally something I can understand! My background knowledge tells me that, in research studies, thirty-six subjects, or people on whom the experiment was done, is a pretty small number. I know that the smaller the number of subjects, the tougher it is to conclude that the findings would be true for all kids. I know now that I won't take the findings of this study real seriously because it was so small. I'll keep reading."

" 'Analysis of the responses made by subjects . . .' Okay, this isn't subject like math or science or English. This word *subject* means the people who were in the experiment. There are at least two definitions for the word *subject* and if you emphasize the second syllable, like this— sub-JECT—it means to force someone to do something, which is another meaning. Here I know it means people in the experiment because of its placement in the sentence: 'responses made by the subjects.' I'm going to keep reading: 'hearing only the initial syllable of the stimuli revealed that stressed initial syllables were markedly more intelligible than their unstressed counterparts; but when subjects were presented with the full stimulus, there were no reliable intelligibility differences.' "

Cris says to the students, "Wow, the first thing that happens is that the metacognitive voice in my mind says—TILT—too much information; I want to shut down! But what if I really *have* to understand this stuff? What if I have to report to my graduate school classmates on this article? I know I have to break it down into really small pieces and focus on those chunks until they become more clear. I may need to ask Sheila to read this with me and help me figure out what it means. I may have to reread it several times. I know I'm going to have to slow my reading way down, and it's possible I'll have to read this article in several short periods of time with breaks in between. Those are all ways I can ensure that I'm more likely to get it.

"I'll give it one more sentence. Often when I'm really overwhelmed, I find that if I just read one or two more sentences, things start to become clearer. 'In Experiment Two, a large number of polysyllabic content words, excised'—somehow that just reminded me of having a tooth pulled! I must have heard the word excised being used to describe a tooth being pulled—'from the speech of six speakers, were presented without supporting contexts.'"

Ellin watched from the sidelines in Cris' classroom, impressed with the scope of what she taught. Cris had, for the umpteenth time, shown the students that all readers struggle in some texts. She gave her students a glimpse into the vast array of ways they can repair and revise their comprehension once it has broken down. She also showed them that certain tactics to revise and repair comprehension are more useful in particular situations and that you have to understand your purpose before you know which tactic will be most helpful.

Most important, Cris demonstrated that proficient readers, though they may struggle, are active in solving comprehension problems. Her lesson that day—and on the days that followed—showed students how, as a proficient reader, she solves problems at the word and meaning levels. Gradually, students learned to monitor and revise their thinking using their own texts, most of which came from their content classes, where text is densely packed with concepts and new vocabulary. Throughout, it was clear that the purpose for solving the problems, whatever they might be, was to comprehend.

Cris' work with the high school readers reminded Ellin again that to be proficient, readers must be *flexible, adaptive,* and *independent* in monitoring their understanding. Proficient readers, like surgeons, have a tray of instruments (revision strategies) they can use to operate on comprehension problems. Surgeons use their tools flexibly and interchangeably. They are not limited to a scalpel; they have many tools—lasers, spreaders—to operate on each problem. When Cris told her students she would try reading on to decide whether she needed to understand the phrase "contextually defined conditions," and if so, that she would ask her colleague for help, she revealed the *flexibility* a proficient reader uses, choosing from several revision strategies.

Like surgeons, proficient readers are *adaptive.* They assess a problem and thoughtfully (though quickly) focus on the instrument or problem-solving strategy most likely to work most effectively in that situation. They intentionally use that tool and "shut out" or ignore other tools that would be less useful. When Cris realized she could use her skills in word analysis to arrive at the meaning of *trisyllabic,* she modeled how a proficient reader carefully selects or adapts a problem-solving strategy to match the problem at hand. She was clear when thinking aloud for the students that there really was one revision tool most useful in that situation, and she intended to use it to the exclusion of others.

Similarly, Cris demonstrated throughout that she could and did solve comprehension problems *independently.* Through this lesson, and many other demonstrations, she revealed explicitly and implicitly that monitoring and revision strategies can be used in all reading situations—in class, at home, alone, or with other readers nearby. She talked with the students about the variety of reading tasks they face each day and, specifically, which revision strategies might be used for each if they encounter problems.

Over the three weeks of the monitoring strategy study, Cris' students talked about tackling the density of content in a science book, the technical instructions they had to decipher in computer manuals, and the difficulty of sorting out a lengthy dialogue between several characters in a novel. They spoke openly of the frustration of having a limited repertoire of solutions to the comprehension problems they faced, and they began to build and diversify their arsenal of problem-solving strategies.

A list of reading problems and possible solutions took shape on charts around the room. Together Cris and the students defined problems and discussed ways in which they could actively and purposefully operate on them. They talked about ways questioning, inferring, synthesizing, determining importance, and activating background knowledge could help solve problems that had to do with the meaning of words, passages, and whole text. And they continued to discuss how tools like decoding, word analysis, and using clues from the context could be used when the problem related to recognition, pronunciation, and word definition.

Cris found that when she listened carefully to her students as they described their reading problems, she could respond by modeling a variety of techniques to address a full range of word and meaning-level problems. She watched as her students gradually grew more flexible, adaptive, and independent in their use of the tools.

Unfortunately, in too many classrooms, it is assumed that there are only two kinds of reading problems: failure to decode words and failure to understand word meanings. If we can understand the more subtle features of the reading obstacles themselves, the solutions we teach will be more effective and tailored.

Into the Classroom—Primary

"I don't know what to do about Anne, Ellin. Will you think this through with me?" Kristin Venable, a second-grade teacher in Denver and PEBC staff developer, often posed provocative questions that led to uncharted waters. That simple question began a conversation in which they invented a host of revision strategies to which Ellin has returned many times in other classrooms.

"Anne is a great reader, Ellin. She gobbles up everything in the room and comes to school with loads of library books. My biggest challenge is keeping her challenged! She came in today with a copy of *The Secret Garden* she was given for Christmas, saying she wants to read it during reader's workshop. It's a beautiful edition with those silky pages and color illustrations sprinkled through it. She has seen the movie and is excited about reading a challenging book, but I'm concerned. I looked through the text, and the sentences are lengthy and complex; the language is full of British colloquialisms; and it's a long book. I don't want her to feel frustrated and lose confidence as a reader."

Ellin waited, knowing Kristin would have thought through both sides of the dilemma.

"On the other hand, I've been encouraging all the kids to vary their reading diet. You know, I've said, 'Read in a variety of genres. Read books that are easy or well-loved just for the joy of rereading. Read books that are just right for you and books that are a challenge.' Now Anne wants to do what I've suggested. I'm not sure I can confer with her enough to keep her going through the whole book, but I want to capitalize on her enthusiasm. Do you hear me contradicting myself?" Kristin laughed.

What Ellin heard was nothing like a contradiction. It was a well-thought-out set of questions about a perplexing problem.

"What do you think about asking Anne?" Ellin proposed. "We could tell her exactly what you've told me and ask her to help make a decision about whether she tackles this project." Kristin agreed.

Conferring

They spent a recess with Anne, discussing the pros and cons.

"Well, remember what you tell us all the time, Kristin? We don't have to finish everything we start reading, and I can always finish reading it in third grade if I can't get it done. I really want to try!"

"Okay," Kristin said. "Let's see what happens."

During reader's workshop the next day, Kristin conferred with Anne. "Anne, we've been talking a lot lately about how readers prevent comprehension problems and how they solve those problems if they have them. Let's talk about what you might do to prevent problems before you read."

Anne said, "Well, one of the things good readers do is to think about what they know that's like the book and what they need to know to understand the book."

"Great, we've been calling that activating schema, right? What do you think you know about this book, its author, or the way it is put together—its format?"

Anne replied, "Well, I know what happens because I've seen the movie. Colin walks and his father gets nicer to them all. I don't know anything about the author and I know that it will be the longest chapter book I've ever read!"

"Do you know what country this book is set in?" Kristin asked.

"No, but it's not here and it's a long time ago and it isn't in the city and Mary's parents are both dead."

"That's quite a little spurt of schema, Anne." They both laughed. Kristin quickly went on to build on Anne's knowledge by giving her information about the sentence length, the British figures of speech, and about the relationship between Britain and India in 1911 when the book was published. Kristin read the first two pages aloud so that Anne could begin to hear the cadence of the language and begin to predict more readily in the longer chapter-book format.

"Now, Anne, I want you to read the first few pages—the ones I just read to you—by yourself while I confer with a couple of other readers. Why don't you use these sticky notes to mark places in the text where you are confused by words or ideas? Then I'll come back and we'll talk about ways you can solve problems you might have. Okay?"

When Kristin returned, Anne was intensely engaged in reading and had read most of the first chapter—about five pages. She had marked several places where she had problems. They went to work.

Kristin kept the conference short, five or six minutes, but was able to help Anne solve most of the problems, using a variety of different revision strategies. In a couple of cases, Kristin made an on-the-spot decision not to deal with the problem. She said later that she chose to ignore the mistakes when correct pronunciation or word identification had little to do with whether Anne would understand the story.

Anne began by pointing to the text. "When Mary Lennox was sent to Misselthwaite Manor to live with her uncle, everybody said she was the most disagreeable-looking child ever seen. It was true, too. She had a little thin face and a little thin body, thin light hair and a sour expression. Her hair was yellow and her face was yellow because she was born in India and had always been ill in one way or another."

"I don't know these words," Anne said, her index finger moving from *Misselthwaite* to *disagreeable* to *sour expression*.

"Let's give them a try sounding them out."

"Miss-eel-th-white," Anne said.

Anne didn't get it quite right, but Kristin said, "Go on Anne. It's the name of the house and grounds where they live and it's not really going to be important to say it accurately every time you come to it. You're going to be able to understand the story without saying *Misselthwaite* correctly. Let's move on."

Kristin pointed to the other words that had given Anne trouble: *disagreeable* and *sour expression*. "Give them a try."

"Dis-grace-able. No that's not right. Dis-agree-able." Anne corrected her initial pronunciation of the word.

"Great, Anne, how did you know that was *disagreeable*?"

"Well, I took the word apart in my mind. My mind said *disagree*. Then I saw *agree* in there and I knew that one. When I pulled out *dis*, then I got it."

"So you took the end off that word and saw a smaller word inside?" Kristin asked.

"Yep."

"You already knew the word *agree*?"

"Yep."

"Okay, where's your next sticky note? What kind of a problem did you have here?"

"I don't know what this is." Anne pointed at *sour expression*.

"How could you try to figure it out?"

Anne said what she thought the words were. "Sore expedition, sore expedition," Anne said, visibly frustrated. "I can't say it."

"What if I told you the first word was *sour*?" Kristin asked.

"Sour . . ." Anne looked relieved and reread the sentence.

"Let's see, ex-pid-ition? No! Expression! See? Ex-pres-sion." Anne pointed to each syllable.

"Yes, great Anne. How did you figure that out?"

"Well, it was talking about the way she looked and *expedition* didn't fit that, but light hair and a sour [pause] expression did fit!"

"Great, Anne! You were really monitoring what would make sense in that sentence, and the metacognitive voice in your mind told you that *expedition* didn't fit with the meaning. That's such a smart way to decide what word fits. Go on," Kristin said.

"Her father had held a position under the English Government and had always been busy and ill himself." Anne read *bossy* instead of *busy*. Kristin did not stop Anne as she read this sentence. Anne had not labeled it with a sticky note and the word *bossy* did little to change the overall meaning Anne seemed to be getting. It matched Anne's background knowledge, having seen the movie in which a bossy Mary Lennox changes gradually into a thoughtful child.

Anne kept reading. "She had not wanted a little girl at all, and when Mary was born she handed her over to the care of an Ayah, who was made to understand that if she wanted to please the Mem Sahib she must keep the child out of sight as much as possible."

"I know I didn't read that right." Anne pointed to *Ayah*. "And I don't know what it is, that's why I marked it."

"Actually, Anne, you pronounced it perfectly. How did you decide how it should be pronounced?" Kristin asked.

"Because it had an *a* at the beginning, and I just tried to make the rest of the sound of the word with my mouth."

"Well that was really a smart way to do it. Any guesses about what it might mean?"

"I guess a nanny," Anne said.

"How do you know that?"

"Because it said 'to the care of an Ayah' and that sounded like a nanny, and also I know people who had nannies that lived with them when they were babies. Their nannies were called something weird, too, like a pear."

Kristin laughed.

"*Au pair* is the term the French use for a nanny who lives with a family and takes care of their kids. You're right, though, I think an Ayah is like a nanny or an au pair. Anne, you did exactly what great readers do when they have problems pronouncing a word and knowing what it means. You figured out how to say the word by sounding it out and you figured out what it meant by looking at the sentence it was in, thinking about your background knowledge, and then guessing at the meaning. That's exactly what great readers do to solve problems."

They moved on to *Mem Sahib*.

"I just can't say it, this isn't anything," Anne said, shaking her head. "Mim shahaba . . . Meem shabib." Anne tried the word twice, stopped, and spent time rereading before turning to Kristin.

"I don't get it."

"Do you need help with pronouncing the words or with understanding what they mean?" asked Kristin.

"Both," Anne said.

Kristin took a quick glance at the text. Later she told Ellin that she concluded the context would reveal little about the words in question and that, at first, even she was a little unsure about the exact meaning of the words *Mem Sahib*. From a glance at earlier paragraphs, she drew a conclusion.

"Let me help you with that one," Kristen said to Anne. "That's the name they gave to Mary's mother. I think it means mistress of the house or something like that. Let me tell you how I decided that. I read up here that her mother 'had been a great beauty who cared only to go to parties and amuse herself with gay people.' And then I read that nannies called Ayahs took care of Mary, so when I read that the Ayah has to keep the child out of sight as much as possible, I decided that Mem Sahib must be the mother."

Kristin covered a lot of territory in five or six minutes. Through her responses to problems Anne identified, she armed Anne with problem-solving strategies that addressed phonics, word identification, word and text meaning, background knowledge, and purpose for reading. Kristin helped Anne to identify problem-solving strategies that were immediately relevant in a text Anne desperately wanted to read. Anne's motivation was a key factor in her application of the strategies Kristin taught her that day. She needed to know how to solve problems flexibly, adaptively, and independently if she was to finish the book.

In subsequent conferences, Kristin and Anne talked about getting a reading mentor for her as she read *The Secret Garden*. They were able to identify a fifth grader who had read the book and was willing to meet with Anne twice a week to coach her through it. This relieved Kristin of the need to confer with Anne daily and led to the development of a strong relationship with a reader whose proficiency exceeded Anne's. The fifth grader was taught to converse with Anne and pose questions rather than telling her how to interpret the events she read.

Kristin told Ellin that Anne struggled through the entire book, exactly as she had told us emphatically she would. Did she recognize the subtleties of meaning an older reader might have? Perhaps not. Will she reread the book in fifth or eighth grade or as a parent? Probably, and if she does, the layers of meaning she uncovers will no doubt surprise her. The monumental effort she expended as a second grader to make her way through this book will have an equally lasting impact. She learned that she can set her mind to something and do it. She can move through and beyond the hurdles.

~ ~ ~

Remembering Cris and Kristin's work with their students (who are now headed to college or even raising their own children), we realized how much of their teaching remains exemplary. Both responded using their extensive knowledge of the essential elements that come together to make successful readers. They suggested approaches based on solid, research-based understandings of what proficient readers do to address problems at the word and meaning levels. Both have spent countless hours studying professional literature and discussing it with colleagues. Both still belong to the *same* study group—a group that includes teachers and staff developers representing the K–12 span—in which they discuss each other's writing and professional texts. Both realize that to teach well and to support other teachers, they must keep up with the research and be avid readers and writers themselves.

No program or prescription, no set of materials or student activities can ever substitute for the deep knowledge and caring that Cris and Kristin bring to their teaching and which enables them to respond in such individualized ways to the range of students in their classrooms.

We wonder, for example, what might have happened to Anne if she hadn't landed in Kristin's class. Would she have received the thoughtful and supportive instruction she needed to tackle a book as challenging as *The Secret Garden*, or would she have been told that it simply wasn't "on her level"?

For better or worse, we all learn the most from adversity, not just as readers, but in the wider circles of our lives. Taking on challenges like reading *The Secret Garden* in second grade or figuring out how to make sense of research jargon in high school teaches independent problem-solving skills and steels us for the personal challenges and confusions that life will no doubt throw our way. Learning to monitor for meaning and make ongoing revisions as we're confronted with new information is not only a reading skill, but a life skill, and the feeling of accomplishment when we break through to understanding is hard to beat. The satisfaction in emerging on the other side of these hurdles is deeply personal and memorable. If we can learn to see adversity as opportunity in our lives and in our classrooms, perhaps we will come to view challenges, comprehension problems, and other obstacles as fascinating intellectual opportunities to face together.

Key Ideas for Comprehension Strategy Study

Monitoring Meaning

- Proficient readers monitor their comprehension during reading—they know when the text they are reading or listening to makes sense, when it does not, what does not make sense, and whether the unclear portions are critical to overall understanding of the piece.

- Proficient readers can identify when text is comprehensible and the degree to which they understand it. They can identify ways in which a text becomes gradually more understandable by reading past an unclear portion and/or by rereading part or all of the text.

- Proficient readers know what they need to comprehend from a text—they are aware of their purpose for reading and what will be required of them with respect to reporting on their reading.

- Proficient readers are aware of the purpose for their reading and direct special attention to the parts of the text they most need to comprehend for that purpose.

- Proficient readers are able to assume different "stances" toward a text. For example, a child can read a book from the point of view of different characters, of a book reviewer, or of a writer seeking new techniques for his/her work.

- Proficient readers identify difficulties they have in comprehending at the word, sentence, and whole-text levels. They are flexible in their use of tactics to revise their thinking and solve different types of comprehension problems.

  - Proficient readers solve word- and sentence-level problems with surface structure strategies such as decoding strategies and/or word analysis.

  - Proficient readers solve text-level problems by monitoring, evaluating, and making revisions to their evolving interpretation of the text while reading. They then compare the emerging meaning to their background knowledge and make adjustments to incorporate new information into existing memory stores.

- Proficient readers can "think aloud" about their reading process. They are aware of and can articulate the surface and deep structure strategies they use to identify words, read fluently, and create solutions to reading problems.

- Proficient readers can identify confusing ideas, themes, and/or surface elements (words, sentence or text structures, graphs, tables, etc.) and suggest a variety of means to solve the problems they encounter.

■ Proficient readers are independent, flexible, and adaptive:

- They show independence by using surface and deep structure strategies to solve reading problems and enhance understanding on their own.

- They demonstrate flexibility by using a particular strategy (such as determining importance) to a greater or lesser degree depending on the demands of the text.

- They are adaptive in their ability to "turn up (or turn down) the volume" on a particular strategy or use all comprehension strategies in concert.

■ Proficient readers use text management strategies. They pause, reread, skim, scan, consider the meaning of the text, and reflect on their understanding with other readers.

CHAPTER 4

The Presence of the Past

Using Schema to Understand and Remember

The dress I wore was lavender taffeta, and each time I breathed it rustled, and now that I was sucking in air to breathe out shame it sounded like crepe paper on the back of hearses.

As I'd watched Momma put ruffles on the hem and cute little tucks around the waist, I knew that once I put it on I'd look like a movie star. (It was silk and that made up for the awful color.) I was going to look like one of the sweet little white girls who were everybody's dream of what was right with the world. Hanging softly over the black Singer sewing machine, it looked like magic, and when people saw me wearing it they were going to run up to me and say, "Marguerite [sometimes it was 'dear Marguerite'], forgive us, please, we didn't know who you were," and I would answer generously, "no, you couldn't have known. Of course I forgive you."

Just thinking about it made me go around with angel's dust sprinkled over my face for days. But Easter's early morning sun had shown the dress to be a plain ugly cut-down from a white woman's once-was-purple throwaway. It was old-lady-long too, but it didn't hide my skinny legs, which had been greased with Blue Seal Vaseline and powdered with the Arkansas red clay. The age-faded color made my skin look dirty like mud, and everyone in church was looking at my skinny legs.

—Maya Angelou, *I Know Why the Caged Bird Sings*

Our Reflections

Ellin and I sit at my kitchen table, laptops out, papers strewn. Springtime in the Rockies. Pale green aspen leaves flutter in the breeze. Recent rain has left a life-giving freshness in the air, welcome after a too-dry winter. The Continental Divide rises snowcapped in the distance.

"I've found some good pieces." I hand her a sheet of paper with several excerpts from Maya Angelou's *I Know Why the Caged Bird Sings.*

"This one I love." She points to the piece that opens this chapter. "Why don't you start working on it?"

I reread it and begin jotting down my thoughts.

~ ~ ~

This reminds me of the dress my mother got for me in seventh grade, gray wool with a white collar and red bow at the neck. My first grown-up dress. As a little girl, I wore mainly handmade dresses. Between my mother and my Aunt Biggie, I had a supply of carefully smocked, exquisitely crafted dresses to wear. As store-bought dresses became the norm, I came to view my dresses, labored over with love, as second-rate, inferior to the poorly made, store-bought dresses that you'd get to try on. I complained. Little by little I outgrew the handmade dresses and they were replaced by bland, store-bought models. The gray dress was different, though. It, I knew, made me look elegant and sophisticated. Things I certainly wasn't at age twelve.

Then this piece takes me to the dresses Rita (my mother-in-law) bought for my daughter Katherine: taffeta, organdy, frilly with lace and bows, layers of skirts; elegant, gaudy dresses for a skinny, brain-injured child. Dresses that from a distance might fool people for a little while, until they saw

Katherine's clenched hands and distant look. Momentarily, those dresses were armor for Katherine, hiding her reality, protection from a thoughtless world, proof she was adored.

It also reminds me of the fancy green dress my daughter Helen and I found several weeks ago when she was in town visiting from her small apartment in Brooklyn. Fitted bodice, V-neck, twirling skirt, scalloped hem. "Chiffon," said Helen. "My first chiffon dress." My twenty-four-year-old Helen tried it on in the dressing room at the mall and started spinning around, like she had when she was a little girl in dress-ups. "It's perfect," I said. "Looks like it was made for you. You'll never find anything better." "I'll wear it to my rehearsal dinner," she said, though no wedding is planned. In the dressing room, she removes her scarf. Her bald head looks like alabaster—smooth, sculptural. "A walking-work-of-art" goes through my head. Helen in her green dress swirling with her head exposed.

The dresses lead me to dreams: the dream to create an image of who we want to be, not who we are. A dress to hide Katherine's Rett syndrome; a dress so beautiful it will not mask but will set off Helen's alopecia areata. But this is something different for Maya Angelou. This is the bleak reality in America, even today. It is a black child's yearning for beauty, elegance, for being different from what she is, for being not-black, for being movie-star white. Angelou knew that in that time, in her world, white was better, white was "right with the world."

Her black Singer sewing machine reminds me of the machine my Aunt Biggie had—one with pedals you pushed like an organ—and of the hand-me-down dresses we'd give to Saphrona, my grandmother's black maid in Asheville, North Carolina, in the 1950s, who made biscuits and fried chicken and ironed my grandmother's clothes on an ironing board set up in the dining room. Saphrona, whose own children we never met, though Saphrona was there helping Grandmother day after day. That reminds me of the book *Dear Willie Rudd,* by Libba

Moore Gray, in which Miss Elizabeth writes a letter thanking her caring, hard-working, and now long-dead black maid, Willie Rudd, for all that she did for her as a child. Fifty years too late, she tells Willie Rudd how much she loved her.

I reread the piece and see a young Maya and I am back at a school I visited in Zimbabwe several years ago, a school with broken-out windows, no desks, no books, a worn-out blackboard, an outhouse with a hole in the ground, and hundreds of black children with bright eyes and strong, white teeth, smiling at us, singing for us. Hungry children with such unlimited potential and such limited futures in a country run by the tyrant Robert Mugabe, a country where starvation is a reality and opportunities almost nonexistent.

I feel shame for our country and the segregation of the South (and North); shame for our world where potential is squashed and squandered; shame that we made little Maya feel "dirty like mud" as her innocence is subjected to the unfairness of racism. She wants to look beautiful, to transcend for once the limits the outside world puts upon her, to ride the tucks and frills and elegance of a lavender dress to a place where color doesn't matter, where her perceived physical flaws aren't apparent, where everything that is ugly or unsightly is covered by silk. What Maya sees as wonderful one day is changed the next to an ugly hand-me-down from an unknown white woman. These paragraphs hold the terrible weight of racism and make that racism personal as magic collides with reality and the dreams of a little black girl are shattered in harsh sunlight, leaving me with the image of a skinny, awkward child in a faded, too-big dress.

"Ellin, can you read this and let me know what comes into your mind." Ellin stops typing, rereads the paragraphs from *I Know Why the Caged Bird Sings*, and begins with a sigh.

"This deflates me, right from the beginning. Those words 'sucking in air to breathe out shame.' It's still true today in so many parts of this country. I can see the faces of the children in classrooms where I've worked. They are quiet, well-behaved, compliant. They have a polite deference, especially to white people. Even to this day, they've been born into a society that calls upon them to be subservient. I have this awful sense that nothing we could ever say about how smart, able, full of potential they are could offset societal—and their own—expectations. Sometimes, I sense anger, and I can deal with that more effectively. But I read this and had this overwhelming feeling that too little has changed, and most people in this country are unaware of that. In classroom after classroom that I've been in, I've seen it."

"Amazing, Ellin. That's so different from what I thought about. I had the sadness, but my mind immediately took me to dresses and I started seeing dresses that have been important to me and to Katherine and Helen. I felt that sense of exhilaration and pride that Maya Angelou felt about the lavender dress at first, before it was completely shattered."

"Not to me. I was back in those classrooms. And I thought that as a privileged white person, it was hard to imagine what I could do to help cut through those low expectations. I saw these words"—Ellin points to the piece—"'Marguerite [sometimes it was 'dear Marguerite'], forgive us, please, we didn't know who you were,' as meaning that they didn't recognize her because she was dressed well, and that was such a surprise to them. And then it was like she faded into the anonymity of any other child in poverty. She was wearing a hand-me-down dress. It wasn't really hers. It was someone else's. And then this line, 'the age-faded color made my skin look dirty like mud.' What a denigration, like she was being slapped back down, that she would be kept down.

It was all the vestiges of slavery to me, those deep-rooted perceptions that even generations later, over a century later, remain. How shameful that even with all the opportunities, the Civil Rights Act, the strides that have been made, so much remains the same. That's what I was thinking."

I am struck by the different responses Ellin and I have to the same few paragraphs. We arrived at similar conclusions about the sad sense of loss and the intractability of racism that come from the piece, but our background knowledge gave us very different connections to it. Ellin's mind took her to classrooms throughout the South where she has worked; mine to important dresses, memories of my grandmother's maid, of *Dear Willie Rudd,* and a visit to an African school. I thought of a quote attributed to John Steinbeck: "A man who tells secrets or stories must think of who is hearing or reading them, for a story has as many versions as it has readers. Everyone takes what he wants or can from it and thus changes it to his measure . . . A story must have some points of contact with the reader to make him feel at home in it. Only then can he accept its wonders." I realize once again how important our personal connections are to what we read and how powerful our background knowledge is in affecting how we respond and understand.

Capitalizing on the Known—Schema

In the last twenty-five years, reading research has provided valuable insight into the thinking processes of proficient readers, revealing remarkable consistency in the strategies they use to comprehend text. One of the most significant areas of research has been in schema theory, which "tries to explain how we store our knowledge, how we learn and how we remember what we have learned" (see Maria 1990 for a synthesis), not just in reading, but in all areas of learning.

When applied to reading, understanding schema sheds light on the ways children connect the new to the known, recall relevant information, and enhance their comprehension with insights only they can bring. It has been known for some time that one of the most effective ways to improve comprehension is to "activate mental files" before, during, and after reading. We know that children are far more likely to retain and reapply information if they think about what they already know related to the new information. Through discussions, reading simpler texts on a topic, or having new, relevant experiences, readers can activate existing or create new background knowledge.

For decades, publishers of basal readers have included background information teachers were instructed to share with children prior to reading a story, supposedly to enhance the students' comprehension. Now, in classrooms around the country, it has become common practice to help children recall information from their long-term memory banks (schema) relevant to what will be read, whether that reading is from a textbook, a novel, or an article from *National Geographic.*

As a first-year teacher, Ellin felt satisfied that she was activating children's background knowledge if she shared the information provided in the teacher's manual before they began to read. She probably was activating some background knowledge some of the time for some of the kids. But she was merely saying what a publisher thought might build relevant background knowledge. The students themselves were rarely involved—it was a matter of telling them what they should think about and know before reading the selection. If there was a mismatch between the way she described the background information and a student's mental file on that topic, the publisher's carefully written exposition may not have done a thing to support the complex process of assimilating and storing new information during reading.

Ellin created three reading groups in her fifth-grade classroom, in much the same way she remembers reading groups from her own elementary experience. She was given three different teacher's manuals. Each came with three different sets of ditto sheets to run. Twenty-one years old and three days on the job, she went into the teachers' work-room, carefully slid a purple master for the next day's lesson into the metal teeth, started to operate the machine (ditto machines, or "spirit duplicators," were common before photocopiers became ubiquitous), and noticed midcrank that the master was crooked. With her left hand still cranking, she laid her right on the master to straighten it, dislocated her pinky, and concluded it was a sign that dittos weren't doing her, or anyone in her classroom, any good.

She decided—perhaps not for the right reasons—to abandon the dittos, choose selections from the basal she found interesting, enjoy the pieces with the children, and supplement the basal with trade books.

One evening Ellin reviewed the material provided in the teacher's manual for a story on Indians of the Southwest. It suggested that no one knew why the Anasazi had abruptly disappeared from that region in the fourteenth or fifteenth centuries. She read more, convinced this would give her all the background knowledge she'd need to lead a good lesson on the story. Little did she know.

Bryce was placed in her class by a fourth-grade team that would never have sent him to a colleague they actually knew and liked. They must have believed that, being new, she wouldn't have been exposed to Bryce's reputation prior to his arrival in fifth grade and would therefore be more objective. They must have had good intentions. She was sure that was it.

As she introduced the lesson on the Anasazi with her sketchy facts, Bryce interrupted. "No way! The Anasazi migrated because of drought. They had very sophisticated agriculture and were growing several different kinds of crops, so when the droughts came, they migrated. Trust me. I've been to Mesa Verde."

Ellin had done her job, she thought, in preparing for the story, but she had been naïve and presumptuous in thinking a little bit of reading would make her the expert. Bryce's schema ran circles around hers, and he shared it smugly with his classmates. What he lacked in style, he more than made up for in direct experiences he could apply to thoroughly understand the piece.

How different that experience might have been had Ellin asked the children to identify their background knowledge prior to reading, and then, together, filled in the gaps. How rich the students' understanding might have been if they'd had an opportunity to express themselves verbally, artistically, in writing, or dramatically (certainly Bryce's choice) before, during, and after they read. How different her students' reading experiences might have been had she known that the process of recalling or activating background knowledge should be taught explicitly, in a variety of texts, over a long period of time. How different their reading classes would have been had she regarded activating schema as one of a mosaic of cognitive strategies readers use to ensure they comprehend.

Several years ago, Ellin visited a fifth-grade classroom on South Dakota's Pine Ridge reservation. The teacher was introducing a unit on the Civil War and wanted to start by activating existing background knowledge. She told the children she would be their secretary for the day and record their responses on chart paper. Enthusiastically, she asked the kids to share everything they already knew about the Civil War. Her marker was poised above the chart.

Silence. No child raised a hand.

"Think about it for a second, guys. I really want to know what you already know about the Civil War."

Stone silence.

"What do you already know about the Civil *War*?" She drew out the last word as a bead of sweat dripped down her face. A lone child finally raised his hand. "Yeah, well, my uncle flew fighter missions in it."

She looked to the teachers observing from the back of the room with a look of desperation on her face, but necessity is the mother of invention and this teacher knew she needed to regroup. She drew a deep breath.

"Ladies and gentlemen, I'm sorry. I made a mistake. I should have asked that question in a different way. What I should have said is this: Do you have background knowledge about times when things were unfair for a whole group of people? Can any of you think about times when terrible conflicts existed between groups of people in this country and their government?"

Now the children's hands shot up. They filled the chart with background knowledge about how Native Americans had been treated and how the government had violated their rights. Though no one said, "1861 to 1865, Abraham Lincoln, slavery, the Emancipation Proclamation," or any of the other facts we had all been anticipating, we realized that the children had background knowledge at a conceptual level that would permit them to understand the content in their Civil War study in the far more relevant context of their own experience.

Teaching for the Long Haul: Two Snapshots

Debbie Miller, author of *Reading with Meaning* (2002), long set the standard for comprehension instruction in the Denver area. Kathy Powell, a second-grade teacher at Lansdowne Elementary in Baltimore County, Maryland, has adapted many of Debbie's original teaching tactics while incorporating her own. Both Debbie and Kathy use a Gradual Release of Responsibility Model (Pearson and Gallagher 1983) to plan their comprehension strategy studies. This model can be applied to studies lasting from three to nine weeks and is most effectively used when teachers are focused on one strategy at a time, cumulatively adding strategies that have been taught before. In the later stages of the Gradual Release of Responsibility Model, it will be clear how teachers can integrate strategies taught earlier in the school year.

Let's look at two schema strategy studies. Debbie's and Kathy's studies involve four phases—planning, early, middle, and late—on the Gradual Release Planning Template (Figure 4.1). The studies are quite

Figure 4.1

Gradual Release Planning Template:
Teaching Comprehension Strategies for the Long Haul

PLANNING PHASE

- Teachers identify the strategy to be taught.

- Teachers explore their own use of the strategy in adult text in several genres and discuss the various elements the strategy comprises. They compile lists of various ways they use the strategy in reading and in other learning situations.

- Teachers collect texts representing a wide range of genres and levels they think are particularly conducive for modeling the strategy.

- Parents are notified that an in-depth strategy study is beginning and given information about how they might discuss the strategy with their children.

- Teachers prepare the classroom by creating comfortable, intimate areas in which children can meet to discuss their thinking and the books they are reading. They collect materials necessary to record thinking—for example, chart paper, thinking logs, strategy notebooks, advanced organizer forms, sketching paper.

- Teachers administer portions of *Assessing Comprehension Thinking Strategies* to assess present performance level for the strategy to be studied.

EARLY PHASE

Instructional focus (teachers focus on what the strategy is and why proficient readers need it):

- Teachers think aloud about how a proficient reader uses the strategy (in short text).

- Teachers discuss how they use the strategy when they are reading and how the strategy is useful in other areas of learning.

- Teachers focus continually on how the strategy helps readers understand more.

- Teachers begin to model ways in which proficient readers use the strategy differently in different text genres and levels.

- Reading conferences focus on students' early attempts to articulate their thinking and use of the strategy.

Student focus:

- Students begin to experiment with the strategy in their own work, in groups of four or two, and/or individually.
- Students keep track of their individual application of the strategy using sticky notes, sketches, logs, and/or conversations.
- Students begin to share their use of the strategy in text at their level and in their interest areas.

MIDDLE PHASE

Instructional focus (teachers typically work in large and small groups with increasing time devoted to conferences):

- Teachers continue to think aloud frequently, but may use longer texts.
- Teachers focus on how the strategy is used differently in different genres.
- Teachers model and think aloud to reveal how use of the strategy actually helps them understand more deeply and permanently.
- Teachers show how readers reveal their thinking through the use of oral, written, artistic, and dramatic means.
- Teachers begin to discuss ways in which the strategy relates to strategies previously studied.
- Teachers convene invitational groups (small, needs-based groups) to meet particular needs—for example, students who aren't yet applying the strategy in text at their level, students who aren't yet articulating their thinking about the strategy, students who aren't selecting challenging text in which to apply the strategy.
- Conferences focus on diversifying the text in which students are independently using the strategy.
- Parents are kept up to date about students' progress in using the new strategy. They may be invited into the classroom to review the "thinking made public" students have recorded on charts and in strategy notebooks, and so on.

Continues on next page

Student focus:

- Students begin to diversify the genre in which they apply the strategy.
- Students diversify the oral, written, artistic, and dramatic means they use to share their thinking.
- Students' book clubs focus on strategy use and ways in which strategy use enhances comprehension.
- Students use the strategy in progressively more difficult text.
- Students show evidence of using the strategy independently.
- Students are increasingly able to articulate not only how they use the strategy, but why it helps them comprehend more deeply and permanently.
- Students begin to share experiences in using the strategy to comprehend more deeply with other students and their teacher.

LATE PHASE

Instructional focus (instead of conducting think-alouds and large-group lessons, teachers spend much more time conferring and meeting with small groups):

- Teachers model/think aloud using the strategy in very challenging text in small, needs-based groups.
- Teachers use text they haven't read (cold reads) to authentically reveal through thinking aloud how they use the strategy the first time through a text or passage.

different, but both are very effective and give a sense of the range of successful approaches.

Phase 1/Planning—Debbie's Classroom

Debbie began each strategy study by taking the time to understand the strategy she was about to teach. She read the research, talked to other teachers, and reviewed the description of the strategy to get a

- Teachers reveal the ways in which the strategy integrates with strategies previously studied.
- Teachers administer the same portion of *Assessing Comprehension Thinking Strategies* in different text and discuss growth with students and parents.
- Teachers begin the planning phase for the next strategy.

Student focus:

- Students assume responsibility for articulating their use of the strategy clearly and concisely in conferences and to other students.
- Students teach some of the crafting sessions, thinking aloud about how using the strategy helps them comprehend more deeply and permanently.
- Students use the strategy and can articulate their thinking about the strategy in several genres.
- Students share ways in which they use the strategy independently (without teacher prompting and outside class reading time).
- Students show eagerness to use the strategy in increasingly difficult text.
- Students use the strategy flexibly (they use it when needed but can "turn down the volume" when the strategy is less appropriate).
- Students use more than one of the strategies adaptively (they may use different strategies for different types of text).

---

sense of the range of crafting lessons she needed to plan. To ensure she had a firm grasp of how she used it herself, Debbie deliberately applied the strategy in her own reading—professional books, novels, magazines, newspapers. Prior to starting the study, she told the parents about it, reminding them that they would not be seeing a blizzard of completed worksheets with smiley faces and stars. Instead, she invited parents to talk to their children about the books they read at home and specifically to talk about the children's personal connections to the stories.

Phase 1/Planning—Kathy's Classroom

During the planning phase, usually the last week of the previous strategy study, Kathy collects a dozen or so different types of books that she can use for her early think-alouds. She chooses books that are meaningful to her, will be engaging for the children, and will be conducive to modeling different aspects of schema (see Figure 4.2). She may not end up using all of them, but likes having a cluster of books she has previewed close at hand so she can be prepared but spontaneous in addressing needs as they arise. Some of the selections come from the district's basal, others from her extensive classroom library, and others from the school library.

Kathy read the books at home in relative peace and quiet and thought about where she might stop for think-alouds. Because she wanted the think-alouds to be authentic, however, she didn't consider herself bound to these predetermined possible stopping places.

Prior to launching her study, Kathy assessed her second graders' understanding of background knowledge using the Major Point Interview for Readers (MPIR) from *Assessing Comprehension Thinking Strategies* (Keene 2006). She selected only questions related to schema and conferred with each child, focusing the questions on the child's schema in a book he was reading independently. She then scored each child's responses and tucked them away. This quick procedure gave Kathy a great baseline. At the end of the study she repeated the process to gauge her students' improvement.

Phase 2/Early—Debbie's Classroom

The second graders gathered at Debbie's feet in her classroom's "gathering place"—the area where Debbie sat in a rocking chair and the children congregated cross-legged around her—as she launched a

Figure 4.2

How to Choose a Good Think-Aloud Text

When selecting material for think-alouds, teachers should look for these types of texts:

- a short selection or excerpt from a book that provides several natural stopping points for the teacher to pause during a think-aloud, share her thinking about the strategy, and explain how the strategy helps her better understand the text

- an interesting, perhaps provocative text in which children are likely to be engaged in the topic because it is relevant, compelling, or intriguing

- a text that is more challenging than one that all of the children would be able to read independently

- a selection that is (or may become) a familiar, well-loved text for a particular group of children

- a selection from a student's own writing that is conducive to thinking aloud about a particular strategy

- for later stages in the strategy study, a variety of genres in which the teacher and/or students can think aloud about how to apply the strategy differently

---

comprehension study on schema. She began with a description of people known as researchers who study the way people think and read.

"These researchers were like scientists with a hypothesis. You know, a good guess," she told them. "They wanted to know what really great readers thought about while they read. And you know what? They really did find out! Do you want to know what one of the most important things is?"

Several "yeahs" filled Debbie's pause.

"The researchers found out that readers think about things they already know, things that have happened to them that are like the things that happen in a book. That means that great readers—like you guys are getting to be—whether they're reading by themselves or listening to someone reading, understand the story better if they think about their own experiences while they read."

"Yeah, that's what I always do," piped Jack. "I think about my family or my pets. I have four—"

"Let me show you how it works," Debbie gently interrupted, "because all of you probably do what Jack does already, but you might not have thought about it." Debbie pulled *The Two of Them* by Aliki from the shelf. "First, I'm going to share my thinking as I read, and later, you'll have a chance to share what you thought as I read to you."

Debbie made it look as if she'd pulled a book randomly off the shelf. In fact, she'd done her homework. Prior to reading the book to the students, she had identified where she might pause and think aloud. She selected *The Two of Them*, a book about a young child and her grandfather and how their roles reverse as he ages and eventually dies. A central concept for the book, and therefore the focus of her think-alouds, was the connections she could make to the idea of oral narrative as a way to preserve a family's history. Debbie is careful to ensure that her schematic connections are tied to the essential themes and concepts in any book. In *The Two of Them*, not only could she make connections to her life, but the children (who had heard the book several times before) could as well. For some strategies, teachers like Debbie prefer to begin with books the children know well so they can focus on the strategy rather than working to grasp a brand-new story line. (Many teachers prefer to use unfamiliar text when introducing inferring and questioning, however.)

Debbie began. "Okay, you guys, this is how it's going to work. When I'm reading, you'll see me looking at the book and showing you the pictures like I always do. I'm going to read the book all the way through one time. Then, I'll go back, and as I reread, you'll see me stop and think aloud about things I know or have experienced that are like the book in some way. I'll probably look up at the ceiling, so you'll know I'm telling you what I was just thinking as I read the book."

Debbie read six pages before stopping to look up. "When I read this part about the grandfather singing songs and telling his granddaughter stories of long ago," Debbie said, "I remember my own grandfather. He used to gather all the grandchildren around him and tell us the stories that were true for our family, just like the grandpa in this book. It was like he wanted us to know those stories before he died, and he was afraid if he didn't tell them, they might be forgotten forever. When I read those words, I could see all of us sitting around him. There were too many grandchildren to sit in his lap like the little girl in this book, but he told us stories about my mom and my aunts and uncles. And you know what? When I had children, I told them those same stories so they would remember all the different people in my family." Debbie closed the book on her lap for a moment to show she was shifting gears.

"When a book makes me think of my own life," Debbie said, "I'm making text-to-self connections—you know, connections from the text or book to myself."

She stopped to write *text-to-self* on the far left side of a six-foot length of chart paper (an anchor chart) labeled "Making Schema Connections" that hung horizontally on the wall nearby. She wrote the title of the book under the "text-to-self" heading and put her initials by it.

Debbie continued reading, pausing two more times to think aloud about connections to herself. By the time she finished, the children were staring intently at her, as if she had just surgically opened her head so that they could look inside to see how her brain works. They were captivated by this simple demonstration. They had just glimpsed the thinking processes of a proficient reader.

In the next few days, Debbie was explicit with the children. She used the word *schema* so they could develop a common vocabulary for discussing their reading comprehension. She told them that the purpose of activating schema is to help them better understand books they listen to and read. She also began to demonstrate through thinking aloud that what they already know will change because of what they read.

Referring to *The Two of Them*, she told them that, by thinking about her own grandfather, she could imagine how the little girl felt when her grandfather held her on his lap for stories, and how the little girl must have felt later when the grandfather died. Debbie told the class, "By remembering my own feelings, I could imagine what the little girl in this book might have felt. Because I understand her feelings, I understand the story better. It makes more sense to me and means more to me. When you go back to your own reading today, remember to think about things the book reminds you of in your own life. When the pictures or the story remind you of your life, you're making a text-to-self connection. Happy Reading!"

Debbie's think-aloud on text-to-self connections wasn't over after reading *The Two of Them*. She conducted short (ten- to fifteen-minute) crafting sessions (see Chapter 5) each of the next eight days. Most days she thought aloud with an unfamiliar book or poem, but other times reread some well-loved books as a way to prod the children to activate their own background knowledge and use it to probe the meanings of a book they had read many times. Each day she added the title of the book she read to the chart paper under the heading "text-to-self" and put her initials next to it. The list included several picture books; *Koala Lou* by Mem Fox; *Amber on the Mountain* by Tony Johnston; *The Relatives Came* and *When I Was Young in the Mountains* by Cynthia Rylant; *Nana Upstairs, Nana Downstairs* by Tomie de Paola; a poem, "Yellow Sonnet," by Paul Zimmer; and a piece about the playground written by one of the children in the classroom.

In each crafting session, Debbie focused on thinking aloud about her text-to-self connections. She made two clear points each time:

exactly how her own knowledge or experience helped her understand the book better, and how her schema was changed by what she read.

For crafting sessions early in a strategy study, Debbie usually doesn't invite the students' participation. At the outset she wants the demonstrations of her thinking to stand alone, to be clear, precise, and fairly high level examples of a proficient reader's thinking process. She tries to use as few words as possible in think-alouds, letting those she does choose tell the specific story of her thinking. Gradually the children become directly involved. After a few demonstrations she invites the children to share their experiences and knowledge as she stops to think aloud while reading.

When the crafting session is over each day, the children return to the spots where they read what they've chosen independently or with Debbie's guidance. Debbie confers individually with the children, asking them to talk about their prior knowledge or experience, and asks them to focus on how it helps them make better sense of the books they are reading.

Phase 2/Early—Kathy's Classroom

The day before Kathy's launch of her schema strategy study, she and Ellin put the finishing touches on their plan to coteach the opening lesson. Her district provided a basal teachers could use, but after looking at the selection, *Dragon Gets By*, she and Ellin decided it wouldn't do. They knew that they could do a more effective job of the all-important, first-day think-aloud if the text they used struck a deep chord for both of them. They chose Robert Coles' *The Story of Ruby Bridges*, a book about one of the first black children to go to a "white" school in New Orleans, a book that is moving and meaningful to both of them. They knew that to set the right tone in the early think-alouds, it's important to have a text the teacher loves.

The next morning Kathy and Ellin took their seats on opposite sides of an easel as the children gathered on the floor in front of them. They wanted to build a sense of anticipation, so they waited for absolute silence before they began.

Ellin started. "In this school, all the way back in kindergarten, when you were really little, you learned about metacognition." Kathy wrote *metacognition* on the chart paper. "You know *metacognition* means you can think about your own thinking *while* you're reading, and there are really seven ways—called strategies—that great thinkers can be metacognitive.

"Today, Mrs. Powell and I are going to show you how you use your background knowledge, or schema, to understand more challenging text than you read when you were little kids in kindergarten and first grade." As Kathy wrote *schema* on the chart, two dozen hands shot straight up. Obviously the kindergarten and first-grade teachers had done a good job addressing schema.

Ellin resisted the temptation to let the children talk. Instead, she taught the children her "silent signal."

"When I lift my hand and slowly lower it to my knee, it means that though I really, really want to hear what you have to share, it would not be good teaching for me to stop and listen. My job is to do the best job of teaching that I possibly can. Right? So this means lower your hands and continue to think with me."

The kids nodded.

"And I promise you'll get a chance to talk later."

Ellin tested her silent signal. The children's hands went down and the room quieted.

"Remember when a great reader uses schema, she thinks about the things she already knows that will help her understand the book better. That's what Mrs. Powell and I are going to show you this morning. Your very important job is to watch carefully and see what you notice about how we use our schema to understand this book better. We may have schema that doesn't help us understand the book better, and that's something you second graders are really old enough to learn. If you think of an experience you've had while you're reading, but remembering that experience doesn't really help you understand the book better, you know to just keep reading."

Ellin began *The Story of Ruby Bridges* and paused (about eight pages in) where six-year-old Ruby makes her way through a crowd of screaming white protesters to enter William Franz Elementary. Because Ellin and Kathy were coteaching the lesson, Ellin turned first to Kathy and said, "Mrs. Powell, I have to stop right here and tell you about my schema. I have several examples of background knowledge that helped me understand this story better. First, I know that there was a sad time in this country when African American children could only go to school with other African American children and white children went to school only with white children. The problem was that the "black" schools weren't as good as the "white" schools. The buildings were worse. They had fewer books. More kids were in each class.

"Second, I know that keeping people of different races separate is called segregation. I know people disagreed violently about whether segregation was right or wrong, but today we know it was wrong to segregate people on the basis of their skin color. And third, I know people from the army and the National Guard had to come to schools like this to make it safe for kids like Ruby to go inside."

As Ellin spoke, Kathy quickly listed the three points on the chart paper, then added, "Mrs. Keene, I have more schema. I know many African American families were determined that their children receive the same quality of education that white children received. I'm going to add that to the list."

Ellin asked, "When you just shared your schema about African American families wanting the same quality of education for their children, did that help you understand this book better?"

Kathy nodded. "It did. When I thought about what African American families wanted for their children, I could understand why Ruby's parents would decide it was okay for her to be one of the first black children to go to a white school, even though there were so many prejudiced people protesting. As a mom, it would have been hard to send my kids to a school where so many people didn't want them, but understanding that black families knew how important it was that their children receive an equal education helps me understand Ruby's parents."

Throughout the lesson, Ellin and Kathy lobbed ideas back and forth, demonstrating their use of schema and questioning each other about how using schema helped the other understand the book. Because Kathy's students had had strategy instruction in earlier grades, they could move right into thinking aloud about their connections and how those connections helped them better understand the book. Coteaching early think-alouds, while not essential, is helpful and gives a valuable chance to "role play" the use of the strategies, so children see the interactive nature of the process.

In the first two weeks of Kathy's schema study, she concentrated on thinking aloud, not only about her text-to-self, text-to-text, and text-to-world connections, but on how each enhanced her understanding of the books she read aloud. The class revisited *The Story of Ruby Bridges* several times and during each subsequent read-aloud, Kathy did less thinking aloud and the children shared more of their connections. Initially, she asked them to "turn and talk" on the rug, giving partners about a minute to share background knowledge that helped them better understand the book. The children were familiar with the turn-and-talk procedure in which they sit cross-legged with their knees nearly touching and look at each other. It is a quick and effective way to involve all children in early attempts at using a strategy.

Because most of Kathy's children were familiar with schema, she was able to move quickly to more difficult texts and genres. Soon after

The Story of Ruby Bridges, she used *Through My Eyes*, a book Ellin gave as a gift to her class. *Through My Eyes* is Ruby Bridges' own story, complete with photographs of her experiences at William Franz Elementary. Though it was a more difficult book and one most of Kathy's kids couldn't read independently, because they had read the simpler account and discussed their connections and insights, the children became entranced with *Through My Eyes* and paid attention to long segments Kathy read aloud.

One of the students, Max, asked Kathy if he could read *Through My Eyes* during independent reading time. It was a major "reach" for Max, but Kathy decided to give him a shot at it, with conditions. She copied the two pages she had already read aloud, gave him his own copies, and told him he could read it for fifteen minutes before returning to the "just right" book he'd been working on. She also asked Max to jot his thoughts on sticky notes at places in the text where his schema helped him better understand it.

Max beamed.

To Kathy's surprise and relief, Max read the two pages out loud—probably because it was a very challenging text for him. He even paused to do his own think-alouds for the rapt listeners at his table. Destiny said she had no idea Max could read something that hard and even reminded Max to record his connections on sticky notes. Before long the other children were recording theirs and plastering Max's pages with a blizzard of sticky notes. On the phone that evening, Kathy said, "Ellin, if only Max's mom or one of the other teachers had seen it. No one in the teacher's lounge is going to believe me!"

Neither Kathy nor Ellin would encourage children to read books that are too demanding for them for long periods each day. But in our zeal to ensure kids are in "the right level text," we should never forbid a highly motivated child from reading a difficult text that has been read aloud or is of significant personal interest. Kathy was smart. She copied an excerpt, limited Max's time, and asked him to record his thinking—all means to ensure that he wasn't floundering. The bottom line was that Max actually read a text that was significantly above his assessed level. Interest and engagement were powerful motivators.

Phase 3/Middle—Debbie's Classroom

On a snowy morning four weeks into the study of schema, the children were restless. They popped up and down out of the gathering place during the morning rituals of greeting each other and reading the lunch menu. Elan somehow found his way into a corner behind the rocking chair in which Debbie sat to teach crafting sessions.

Almost in a whisper, Debbie began, "I think you're ready to learn something new about schema today, something most readers don't know until they are much older than you, but I think you're ready."

The room grew still. The children had learned to take Debbie seriously when she challenged them. The accelerating snowstorm was forgotten. Debbie pulled out Patricia Polacco's *Just Plain Fancy* and *Mrs. Katz and Tush*, class favorites that had figured prominently in several minilessons.

"We've read *Mrs. Katz* and *Just Plain Fancy* a bunch of times, you guys. We've talked about Patricia Polacco until we know her style as an author very well. You tell me, what does she like to write about? What is she like as an author?"

Silence.

Roxanne finally ventured a guess. "Well, she likes to write about people from other countries."

Kent interrupted, "Not other countries, Roxanne, people in this country who come from other countries. Mrs. Katz is from Poland, and I know some people who came from Poland. They had a war there."

"You know, Kent and Roxanne, you're both right," Debbie clarified. Patricia Polacco comes from a family of Russian immigrants and she does like to write about families from other cultures who live in the

United States. We're going to read another of her books today. It's called *The Keeping Quilt*. Before we read it, let's list some predictions or expectations we have about this book based on what we know—our schema—about Patricia Polacco."

The list began on the chart paper under a new heading: "Schema for Authors." The children decided that not only did this author like to write about people from other cultures who live in the United States, she also liked to write about older people, often grandparents and their families—or their adopted families, as in the book *Mrs. Katz and Tush*.

Debbie began reading *The Keeping Quilt*. During the first reading, she stopped where the characters Anna and Sasha become engaged while sitting on the quilt.

"You know what?" Debbie looked up, placing the book in her lap. "I'm thinking that since Patricia Polacco comes from a family of people who immigrated from Russia, this might be a story about her own great grandparents."

Elan, out from behind the chair and now fully engrossed, shot up a hand. "Yeah, I thought that too. It's not like some authors who write like it was their family, but really it's not. She is from Russia, so this probably really is her family."

Debbie laughed. "Okay, Elan, what do you think Patricia Polacco is likely to do next in this book? Can you use what you know about her to predict what the rest of her book is likely to be about?"

Elan hesitated. "Yeah, she's going to be in it because she likes to write about kids and old people, like in *Mrs. Katz*. She'll probably be in it only as a little kid."

"Do you mean the author, Patricia Polacco, is going to be in the book?" Debbie asked.

"That's my prediction," Elan announced.

"Let's read it and see." Debbie returned to the book and smiled as she read the page where Elan's prediction was confirmed.

The discussion that followed brought a number of additions to the "Schema for Authors" chart. Based on the three books they'd read, the children added to their list of expectations for Patricia Polacco's books. Debbie talked with the children about how it was much easier for her to predict what would happen next in *The Keeping Quilt* once she had thought about Patricia Polacco's style.

During the two weeks that followed, Debbie and the children brought in books and poems written by a number of different authors: Mem Fox, Charlotte Zolotow, Judith Viorst, Thomas Locker, Nancy White Carlstrom, and Bill Martin Jr. Next to each author's name on the chart, the students listed expectations and predictions based on their schema for that author. During each lesson, Debbie emphasized how schema for an author helps us understand the book more fully by predicting how the author might write her ideas and how our schema for that author changes slightly with each new book.

Phase 3/Middle—Kathy's Classroom

Two weeks later, Kathy's students were making different kinds of connections, creating anchor charts, participating in book clubs focused on their use of schema in a variety of books, and beginning to be able to describe how using schema actually helped them understand more deeply. Kathy was thrilled with the progress, but not sure where to go next.

Ellin suggested she introduce schema in a new genre. "They're moving so quickly and so well, we're going to have to figure out how to stay ahead of them—a delicious dilemma to have, isn't it?"

Kathy seized on the idea and looked for books that would complement their study of solids, liquids, and gases in science. With the help of the library media specialist, Sharon Grimes (author of *Reading Is Our Business*), she found Walter Wick's *A Drop of Water,* a stunning book of photographs and short nonfiction descriptions with fairly sophisticated material about the properties of water. The text was difficult and Kathy was skeptical at first, but the content was perfect, so she decided to give it a try.

She introduced this new phase in science rather than literacy block so her students would see the comprehension strategies as thinking strategies that were used across the curriculum.

"Ladies and gentlemen of the second grade," Kathy began ceremonially. "Your work in making connections and using schema to better understand what you read has been wonderful. We're ready to move forward and use schema in other subjects. This is going to be hard, but I know how smart you are. I can't wait to see what you do. When I think aloud today, I want you to see how using schema can be different in different types of books.

"We've been studying solids, liquids, and gases in science. Let's see how we might use schema in this nonfiction book, *A Drop of Water*. Let's start by looking at these photos." She showed the kids close-ups of the drips, ripples, and frozen forms of water.

"I'm intrigued with this picture of an egg being dropped into a glass of water. It reminds me of when my kids were little and they'd play in the tub. The best part was throwing toys in the water to see what floated and what sank. Look at this. I'm sort of surprised that this pin is floating on the water in this picture. My schema for metal would tell me that a pin would sink. The photograph contradicts what I thought I knew about which objects would float and which wouldn't."

Kathy continued, focusing only on the photos, concentrating on how her existing knowledge helped or hindered her understanding of them. She asked the children to share what they had noticed during her think-aloud and listed their responses on a chart she had labeled "Using Schema in Nonfiction."

For the next week, Kathy moved her schema lessons to science and social studies and concentrated each time on how readers use schema differently in nonfiction than in fiction. Kathy and her kids noticed these differences:

- Readers use schema to predict what might happen when they read books about historical events.

- Readers add many new facts to their schema even when they thought they knew a lot about a topic.

- Writers use what they know (their schema) when they're writing about an experiment.

- Sometimes your schema is wrong and you have to change your mind if you learn new facts that contradict your schema.

- You have to stop reading more often to think about your schema when you're reading nonfiction; with fiction you only have to stop occasionally.

- The harder the book, the more you have to stop to think about schema.

- It helps to talk or write about your schema before you start to read something hard.

Several days after thinking aloud about the photographs, Kathy returned to *A Drop of Water*. She read the very short sections to her class, stopping frequently to think aloud about her schema and the activities related to liquids they had done in science. The children readily understood concepts such as displacement, surface tension, and freezing.

"They're more likely to remember some of these science and social studies concepts," she told Ellin. "When I've taught these units in the past, they just didn't seem to remember from one day to the next what we'd talked about. By applying what we knew about schema to the solids, liquids, and gases unit, I'm doing more than teaching the concepts. I'm teaching them *how* to understand them, *how* to remember them, and *how* to use their knowledge in new contexts. Schema is about way more than reading!"

Phase 4/Late—Debbie's Classroom

It had been five weeks. Debbie was beginning to feel anxious, wondering whether they should move on to a new strategy. The children were becoming more comfortable using the strategy in their own reading and had filled the chart with titles and connections. Crafting sessions had incorporated fiction, nonfiction, and poetry pieces, as well as the children's writing.

The language of the strategy had permeated every facet of the classroom because Debbie had devoted five weeks of instruction, in-depth thinking aloud, and many conversations with each child to the study. But she wondered how she would know when it was time to move on.

It wasn't until Laura was reading Bill Martin Jr.'s *Knots on a Counting Rope* that Debbie realized her class needed more thinking aloud related to their schema, not for text content, but for *text structures*. Laura told the class that she got "stuck" in a section in which dialogue is represented not by the traditional quotation marks and references to who is speaking, but with indentations and few references to the speaker.

> Once there was a boy child . . .

No, Grandfather.
Start at the beginning
Start where the storm
Was crying my name.
> You know the story, Boy.
> Tell it.
No, Grandfather, no.
Start, "It was a dark night . . ."

Debbie realized how readers use schema not only to understand text content, but for the text structures themselves. She collected a number of Byrd Baylor books, including *I'm in Charge of Celebrations* and *Everybody Needs a Rock,* to show how readers develop and use schema for a text's layout as well as its content. She compared how traditional text is laid out, how books like *Everybody Needs a Rock* are different, why the authors may have chosen a different format for the book, and how she goes about solving comprehension problems that are due to text structure.

Debbie and her class had similar discussions about the structure of nonfiction text. She modeled her thinking process using books like Tomie de Paola's *The Cloud Book,* focusing on his use of bold print, headings, and drawings. They talked about how quickly new ideas are introduced in nonfiction text and how readers' expectations need to be different when they read nonfiction. They talked about how proficient readers read more slowly and do a great deal more rereading when they read nonfiction, especially in areas where they don't have a lot of knowledge or experience. And once again, they talked about how understanding different kinds of text structures helps them to understand the book better, and how their schema for nonfiction text had been changed by what they had read.

Their discussions moved from nonfiction to text structure in poetry, newspapers, and magazines. Debbie modeled with a poem, "Elephant Warning," from Georgia Heard's book *Creatures of the Earth, Sea, and Sky,* talking about how authors like Heard write poems differently than they write stories.

In the final days of the strategy study, Debbie focused on integrating different components of schema when reading independently. Debbie modeled the kind of flexible, adaptive thinking used by proficient readers with *The Trumpet of the Swan* by E. B. White, which she read aloud each day after lunch. She moved fluidly from text-to-self connections to author schema, to creating new schema for unfamiliar content in text, to using schema for different text structures.

In her later demonstrations the types of schema blended together. The components of schema were taught separately initially, but in the final stages of the strategy study, they were used interchangeably. Debbie also incorporated monitoring for meaning, which she had taught earlier that year, into the later minilessons.

There was no defining moment that told Debbie it was time to move on to another strategy. Some children still struggled with text structure and author schema. Together, though, they had taken a complex thinking journey. The eight weeks devoted to schema left the children with a kind of independence, a kind of power in their thinking that engaged them in reading more thoughtfully, critically, and enthusiastically.

Phase 4/Late—Kathy's Classroom

Kathy's students moved from using schema to better understand science and social studies texts to thinking about how scientists use schema in their everyday work. They talked about how scientists, ready to test a new hypothesis, would use schema from earlier tests to create a new hypothesis. Then one afternoon, Sarah asked, "What if the scientist doesn't have schema—doesn't know anything?"

This caught Kathy off guard and she lobbed a question back to Sarah. "What do you think the scientist would have to do if he wanted to build his schema?"

As Sarah was thinking, Regina raised her hand. "No scientist doesn't know anything."

Despite the double negative, Kathy wondered if Regina might be on to something. "Say more, honey. How does that answer Sarah's question?"

Kathy had taught her students to take time to think before answering. Regina and Sarah were visibly trying to find the words to describe their thinking. Finally, Sarah said, "Even if a scientist knew something about something that was kinda like the thing he didn't know anything about—"

Cassie interrupted, "Or she—scientists can be shes."

"Or she," Sarah resumed. "Even if she knew something that was kinda like that one thing she wanted to learn, wouldn't it help a little?"

Regina had given it enough thought to pop in. "Yeah he—or she—would really have to get some very easy stuff to read about first, just to figure out the easiest parts, and then they could just read harder and harder and harder stuff until, POOF, then she knows!"

The kids seemed to be talking about how a learner has to build schema in order to learn in greater depth about complex topics. Kathy and Ellin talked about the value of "way in" texts as a way to get started in building schema. "Way in" texts:

- include facts that are woven into a more narrative text structure and so are more storylike

- include factual material for which the reader *does* have schema

- may include more photographs and have fewer words on each page

- may be shorter

- have fewer concepts introduced less quickly (lower concept load) than their more didactic counterparts

- include less new terminology on each page (lower vocabulary load)

Ellin recommended that Kathy have the kids build a library of "way in" texts to support a concept they were studying in science or social studies. By the end of the week, Kathy's second graders had created a "way in" table filled with short pieces, photos, kids' writing, and picture books that supported their study of solids, liquids, and gases. Kathy knew that the key is to build increasing independence so that students can identify times when they don't have adequate background knowledge on a topic and then know what to do to create it.

In the week prior to moving on to a new strategy study, Kathy repeated the schema questions from *Assessing Comprehension Thinking Strategies* (Keene 2006). Each of her students had made at least a one-point, or 20 percent, gain. Many had moved from a 2 to a 4 or 5, a 40 to 60 percent gain.

"My only concern," Kathy told Ellin, "is thinking ahead to ways in which future teachers will challenge these kids to use schema in tougher text."

"Not to worry," Ellin replied. "There's always *War and Peace!*"

~ ~ ~

When Ellin and I read those early paragraphs of Maya Angelou's *I Know Why the Caged Bird Sings*, we made ourselves actively aware of our thinking. We were deliberately *mindful* as we read. As a result, we wandered down numerous rambling mental paths, lined with memories and experiences. Because we had a purpose—to watch our minds at work and to jot down our connections to those paragraphs—we could focus more carefully and critically on the text. By making those connections to our lives, we created a tapestry of memories that will anchor the piece more permanently in our minds.

We have come to believe that this hyperawareness may be a necessary and inevitable stage in coming to know oneself as a reader. It may be that as we reintroduce ourselves to our own reading processes, we need to make conscious the strategies our minds have used subconsciously for so many years. It may be that, in order to empathize with the frustrations of our developing readers, we must spend a few extra hours lost in the words, considering, simultaneously, both the stories we read and the way we read them.

Using Relevant Background Knowledge, or Schema

- Proficient readers spontaneously and purposefully recall their relevant prior knowledge (schema) before, during, and after they read and learn (text-to-self connections).

- Proficient readers use their schema to make sense of new information as they read and to store that new information with related information in memory.

- Proficient readers assimilate information from text and other learning experiences into their relevant prior knowledge and make changes in that schema to accommodate the new information. Linking new understandings to other stored knowledge makes it easier to remember and reapply the new information.

- Proficient readers adapt their schema as they read, converse with others—they delete inaccurate information (naive conceptions), add to existing schema, and connect chunks of knowledge to other related knowledge, opinions, and ideas.

- Proficient readers can articulate how they use schema to enhance their comprehension in all forms of text and in all learning situations.

- Proficient readers capitalize on six types of schema when comprehending text and learning new material:

  - memories from particular experiences and emotions that shed light on the events, characters, and so on in a book (text-to-self connections)

  - specific knowledge about the topic; general world knowledge (text-to-world connections)

- specific knowledge about text topics, themes, content, structure, and organization (text-to-text connections)

- their knowledge of potential obstacles to comprehension (particularly in nonfiction text or text with completely unfamiliar content)

- knowledge about their own reading tendencies, preferences, and styles

- specific knowledge about the author/illustrator and the tools he or she uses to create meaning

■ Each type of schema permits students to monitor for meaning, pose questions, make predictions, draw conclusions, create mental images, synthesize, and determine importance as they read and learn.

■ Teachers assist readers in activating their schema (giving students the necessary tools to recall relevant prior knowledge).

■ Teachers help readers build schema (create background knowledge on a given topic, author, text structure, etc.) if they lack adequate schema for a particular reading situation.

CHAPTER 5

The Art of Discovery

Questioning

Edward Hopper, *Nighthawks* (1942, oil on canvas, 84.1 x 152.4 cm, Friend of American Art Collection, 1942.51. Photography © The Art Institute of Chicago. Used with permission.)

Inventing My Parents

After Edward Hopper's *Nighthawks*, 1942

They sit in the bright café
discussing Hemingway, and how
this war will change them.
Sinclair Lewis' name comes up,
and Kay Boyle's and then Fitzgerald's.
They disagree about the American Dream.
My mother, her bare arms
silver under fluorescent lights,
says she imagines it a hawk
flying over, its shadow sweeping
every town. Their coffee's getting cold
but they hardly notice. My mother's face
is lit by ideas. My father's gestures
are a Frenchman's. When he concedes
a point, he shrugs, an elaborate lift
of the shoulders, his hands and smile
declaring an open mind.

I am five months old, at home with a sitter
this August night, when the air outside
is warm as a bath. They decide,
though the car is parked nearby,
to walk the few blocks home, savoring
the fragrant night, their being alone together.
As they go out the door, he's reciting
Donne's "Canonization": "For God's sake
hold your tongue, and let me love,"
and she is laughing, light
as summer rain when it begins.

      —Susan Ludvigson

Susan's Reflections

Years ago, Ellin gave me a little book, *The Poetry of Solitude: A Tribute to Edward Hopper*, that is a collection of writers' responses—in poetry and prose—to various paintings by Edward Hopper. For several paintings, multiple responses are included, showing how varied reactions can be to the same painting. The poets capture brush strokes in words, creating moods and anecdotes from Hopper's works, which in turn create new moods and anecdotes. A deepening understanding results as images are transformed into words and words into thoughts.

I pull out *The Poetry of Solitude* and land on "Inventing My Parents." As I read my mind fills with questions. Who are "they"? Where is the café? What led to their conversation about Hemingway? What war are they talking about? I notice the subtitle of the poem is "After Edward Hopper's *Nighthawks*, 1942," and immediately answer that question. It's during World War II, fairly early in the war. Perhaps they are talking about Hemingway, because he wrote about the First World War in *The Sun Also Rises* and the Spanish Civil War in *For Whom the Bell Tolls*. War books that lead to war talk, I think.

They are a well-educated couple having an intellectual conversation about literature against the backdrop of a terrible war. Does this animated conversation keep them from thinking of the horrors that are going on across oceans? What is their disagreement about the American Dream? What *is* the American Dream? The United States is a country of immigrants. Is it that if you come here and work hard, you can better yourself, you can create a good life? How true is that today?

"Says she imagines it a hawk flying over, its shadow sweeping every town." Is "it" the war, a hawk casting a nightmarish shadow over the land, leaving everyone downcast and afraid? It is an ominous image. Are they so engrossed in their conversation they don't notice the coffee cooling or are they sad, worried, distraught about the war? When will it end and what price will be paid in destruction and loss? Have they eaten and are they now buried in conversation, oblivious to everything except each other? "My mother's face is lit by ideas." Is she always that way or is it this connection, this moment with her husband, sitting in a quiet café, that lights up her face? I want to know more about their relationship. I wonder what her background is, where she was raised, educated. "My father's gestures are a Frenchman's." Is he actually French or are his gestures like a Frenchman's, quick and expressive? Has he conceded a point here? About the American Dream? I see the shrug, his hands raised and open in front of him, the tilt of his head, the smile of accepted defeat.

"I am five months old." Wait a minute. Where did this character come from? Why did the author make the narrator a five-month-old baby? Is a five-month-old picturing this scene? No, I'm guessing the narrator is much older now. She's looking back, imagining her parents, or perhaps imagining the parents she wished she had. Is this time alone together something they rarely have? Is that why they come across as romantic? What is their love like five years hence, twenty-five years? Were they real people? How did their lives unfold? Are they still alive?

They leave their car and walk home. Can they do that and just pick it up the next day? Are there lots of parking spots and is it no problem to abandon a car for a night? Are they desperate to lengthen this sweet moment together and is that why they chose to walk?

I'm at the reference to Donne's "The Canonization." They seem so well educated. Are they college professors, writers themselves? The quote "For God's sake hold your tongue, and let me love"—is he using it to further seduce and delight her? If so, he is accomplishing that well. She laughs, "light as summer rain when it begins."

I interact with the words, moving from trivial questions about parked cars to questions about the nature of love, to questions about war and human nature that can never be answered. Questions lead me to unexpected places and keep me intrigued. For me, questions are the glue of engagement.

The Quest

The weight of an early September snowstorm has snapped trees all over Denver and left fifty thousand people without power for more than three days. Ellin and I sit, afghans tucked around our legs, thankful that the power outage on Lookout Mountain, where I live, was brief. Our fingers fly over computer keyboards. We take a coffee break in my writing room, watching the snow fall. It's a Friday afternoon and we are working on Chapter 5—a chapter about questions that form in the mind while reading.

"For years, I've been reading the research, Susan, and it's very interesting. It shows that children who struggle to read don't consistently ask questions as they read—not before, during, or after. It confirms what I've seen so many times in classrooms, particularly with upper-elementary and middle-school kids. They're passive as they read. They read—or they submit to the text—never questioning its content, style, or intent. They come to school as five- and six-year-olds filled with questions. What happens to those questions? Do they keep the pressing questions in their lives away from school? We've talked again and again about that passivity that creeps in by later elementary years. I wonder why. Why some kids and not others?"

We shake our heads. The question floats between us, swallowed by the silence of the snow falling. One more question. We've reveled in a continual flow of questions over the course of our friendship and our work together. We've learned more about each other from our questions than from any answers we've stumbled upon. We ask the same questions over and over, puzzling and laughing at the searches and the journeys we've taken together. "Just tell me one thing," Susan will begin, "why do I . . . ?"

~ ~ ~

Of all qualities, questioning is fundamental to being human. It is how we dispel confusion, probe into new areas, strengthen our abilities to analyze and deduce. It is how we learn about other people and deepen friendships. We all know people who never ask us questions. At some level we feel they don't really care about us, don't want to know us better. They remain acquaintances, never friends. Those who take the time to ask thoughtful, provocative questions are those who help us learn about ourselves. Through their questions we learn, also, about them.

Questions weave through the fabric of each day: Why are you sad? What would you like for dinner? How can I fit everything I need to do into my schedule? Why do wars persist? Why do I have such a hard time understanding the issues in countries an ocean away? Some of our questions are insignificant, get-through-the-day questions; others go to the fundamental underpinnings of our society and our lives; still others to issues about what motivates people to love, hate, kill, preserve, or destroy.

Playwright Arthur Miller is quoted as saying, "The job is to ask questions—it always was—and to ask them as inexorably as I can. And to face the absence of precise answers with a certain humility." We can never underestimate the importance of questions, *real* questions, not the prepared questions at the end of the story or chapter, but questions that arise from a true desire to know more, to probe deeper. After all, the root of *question* is *quest*. We must think of setting out on a quest to learn more, to better understand friends and family, to pursue passions and interests, to make sense of our worlds. Many questions don't have clear, direct answers, and these are often the most intriguing ones—questions worth lingering over. Most important is the quality of the question itself, because the act of questioning leads us deeper into our thinking.

Questions also help explain our ever-changing understanding of children and teaching. Why do some learn to read so effortlessly, while others never do? Why do they choose certain books? Why do some choose to reread books so frequently? How does language develop?

How can we help children who come to us with underdeveloped language? Our questions help us formulate our beliefs about teaching and learning, and those beliefs underlie our instructional decisions.

Questions lead children through the discovery of their world. They want to know everything: "Why are there clouds, Mom? What happened to the dinosaurs? Why do leaves fall in the fall? Is that why they call fall fall? Why are flowers all different colors? How does a lightbulb make light?" Children offer an endless stream of questions that delight us and drive us to distraction. Children are natural questioners. It is how they work to make sense of the complex world around them. They want to know the "why" for everything. They are, by nature, curious. And we do them a great disservice if we ignore, belittle, or disregard their questions. We do them an even greater disservice if through our educational process we extinguish their need to question.

Ellin remembers Susan's early questions at the PEBC. "Why isn't public education working for so many kids? Why aren't more of our children reading and writing well? We all know how naturally curious kids are; why do so many lose that curiosity in school? Why are some teachers less than competent? Why don't university teacher-training programs work as well as they might? Why can't we just go around the country and see what works and model it here? Does it really matter how a child learns? Does it matter which educational philosophy we use to teach children? Isn't there research on all sides of every question? Can our work really make a difference for children?"

Initially, Ellin was a bit defensive. Maybe as a lawyer Susan didn't understand the complex realities of working with children. Perhaps she didn't realize that people all over the country were trying to address those issues and that change takes a long time. Susan's questions needled Ellin. They crept into her thinking at odd moments: driving between schools, under the nozzle of the shower. She began to realize that asking the tough questions and providing the venue for conversation about them may be our most important work.

Into the Classroom—Middle School

Julie Melnyk sat in the front row for a two-day workshop Ellin conducted in Hinckley–Big Rock School District west of Chicago in the summer of 2005 and again in the summer of 2006. Each day she asked questions that made Ellin think about aspects of reading comprehension instruction she'd never before considered. Ellin is convinced that if she'd had Julie for junior high English all those years ago, she'd have been engaged in learning (instead of engaged in writing notes to Michael Voeltz).

Several days into a strategy study on questioning, Julie shared Chris Van Allsburg's *The Wretched Stone* with her middle schoolers. A picture book written in the form of a ship's log, *The Wretched Stone* tells of disturbing events on the *Rita Anne* after the discovery of a mysterious, glowing stone on a deserted island. Julie knew the book raised provocative questions for all ages and wanted to focus on how her questions helped her get more deeply into the story. She knew her students might need to hear the book more than once before asking the ultimate question—what *is* this stone?—and coming to an understanding of what Van Allsburg had in mind.

After Julie read the first page, she stopped to think aloud. "I'm really curious about the format here. The way it says May 8 and May 9 and then has entries for those days reminds me of a diary. I wonder why it's set up that way. I also wonder what this means: 'It is a good omen that our voyage has begun with fair winds and a clear sky.'"

"I'm thinking about the word *omen* and all it implies. I wonder how Van Allsburg wants us to think about that word, in the particular context of this book," she muses, not wanting her students to answer but wanting them to linger with her speculation for a moment.

"I'm just starting to realize that when I ask these questions, they play a very specific role. They help me get grounded in the story. The questions pull me right into the story and make me want to find out more."

From the beginning, Julie shared her questions through her think-aloud, but also went the next step—to think out loud about how her questions affected her evolving understanding of *The Wretched Stone*.

She stopped again on the second page. "I'm wondering about these sailors: where they came from and where they're going. I'm wondering if all sailors are like this, singing, dancing, playing instruments, telling stories. What would make someone decide to become a sailor? Are they running from difficulties in their lives? Are they intoxicated by the sea? Why would someone choose to leave his home and spend months or even years on the high seas? When I ask those questions, I start to sink into the minds and hearts of the sailors. Though the text may never answer that question, I can understand a bit, through the questions I ask, about what drives the sailors."

Because of the book's unusual format (the captain's log) and the transformation of the sailors that occurs later, Julie stopped more frequently at the beginning of the book, so her students could grasp the unfolding events clearly, without her being overly explicit about them. She knew that when text deviated from a straight narrative structure, students needed more support as they thought simultaneously about content and text structure.

"When I read this, I get really concerned. Something has changed since they went to the island and brought the stone on board. 'I miss the music and storytelling that had become part of our ship's life.' I'm wondering why they don't tell stories and have music any more. Time is passing more slowly. You know how it is when you don't really have anything to do and you're bored. Time goes really slowly, but if you're doing something you like to do, time flies. That's what this seems like to me, but I'm not sure why." Julie paused.

"This is interesting: 'When not needed on deck, they are down below, gazing in silence at the peculiar light it gives off.' Is there something sinister about the light from the stone? It's like they're under its spell, entranced by it. What is the power of the stone and is it good or evil? Remember when we worked on schema earlier this year? I'm connecting to another text right now. The stone reminds me of the ring in *The Lord of the Rings*, how it is so powerful that it casts a spell on all who come in contact with it, even Frodo and Bilbo."

Julie went back and pointed out the specific passage that caused her to ask the question. She also used a strong verb, *entranced*—a great way to build vocabulary in context—and she wove in a prior strategy that they'd studied, reinforcing the use of background knowledge and reminding her students that when readers grow accustomed to using the strategies, they will call upon several simultaneously as they read.

She read on: "'They rarely speak, and though they swing through the rigging more quickly than ever, they walk the decks in a clumsy, stooped-over fashion.' Why are they changing so much? I'm fascinated by how Van Allsburg changes the mood of the story here. There is a gloomy feeling and I want to remind myself to study how Van Allsburg does that. I may have to reread this book to understand how he did it. What words does he use to create the morose tone? I want to be able to do that in my own writing. Sometimes a question like this will cause me to sense something that isn't stated directly in the text. That's what's happening here. Is it in the words he chooses, the pacing, the illustrations?"

Something ominous has crept on board the ship and into the story. Julie wants her students to experience questions that relate less to the content than to the author's style and technique. She wants to show that her questions add to her engagement.

"This voyage started out with fair winds and a clear sky. With this new information, it feels scary and foreboding. I've changed my view of the story. My questions helped by focusing me on the tone, not just the characters and events."

When the captain goes down in the hold where the sailors spend all their time with the stone, he finds the whole crew has turned into apes. At that point, Julie says, "This is really disturbing. Did the stone somehow cause them to regress to a lower form of life? What would cause that to happen? Were the men so weak or was the stone so powerful?"

Ultimately the *Rita Anne* survives a ferocious storm. The captain, by reading and playing music for the sailors, helps them revert back to human form.

"This story has so many layers. I'm wondering how the captain knew that reading and playing music could save the crew. I'm wondering what ultimately happened to the stone. I know it sank to the bottom of the sea when the captain set the *Rita Anne* on fire, but I wonder if it was ever found and could cast its spell again. I don't know the answers. They're rhetorical questions, big questions that don't have a specific answer, but just thinking about them helps me to imagine a range of different outcomes, maybe even some that Van Allsburg never imagined.

"You know, rhetorical questions are my favorite kind. I love to share them with other readers and hear their big, unanswerable questions. When I was in school, teachers wanted us to either answer questions or pose questions that could be answered right there in the text. Sometimes readers have to seek answers, but I want you to experience the pleasure of rhetorical questions now—I don't want you to have to wait until you're older, as I did. Let's try it. I want you to take a moment now and turn to the person sitting closest to you—groups of three are fine—and share some of the questions—especially rhetorical ones, though any kind of question is okay—that were floating through your minds as you listened to *The Wretched Stone*. Perhaps some of your questions will be similar to mine, but I imagine most will be different. When you're done sharing, I'll be interested to hear if your questions were different from mine."

Julie gave the kids a few minutes to share, then interrupted them, saying, "Okay, I overheard some rhetorical questions. I'd love to have some of you share with the whole group." More than a dozen hands shot up. "No, wait!" Julie laughed her frequently used infectious laugh, "I want you to share if your partner had a rhetorical question. Share questions your partner asked—I'm sure your own were just brilliant, but I also want to know how well you listened!" Only a few hands remained, and after the kids had shared briefly, Julie sent the class off to independent reading (in books that were largely self-chosen and complex enough to apply the comprehension strategies). "When you do your independent reading today, I want you to be hyperaware of your questions as you read. Pay particular attention to how those questions help you better understand the books you're reading. I'll be around to confer, and you can be sure I'm going to ask not only about the questions you have, but how they lead you more deeply into the text. When I'm in between conferences, feel free to hand me a note if you think you've had a rhetorical question while reading. I'm probably going to want to confer with you right away."

Julie may want to return to *The Wretched Stone* after her students have had a chance to record the questions they have about their own books. She may use it and other well-loved short texts to introduce different types of questions as she moves into the middle and late stages of the strategy study (see Chapter 4). She may teach a series of crafting sessions on clarifying questions (those that are likely to be answered in the text); speculative questions (those that are predictive or exploratory about text yet to be read); rhetorical questions (larger questions that have no specific answer); and questions about the author's intent or style. She might hold crafting sessions that show how different kinds of questions are asked in different kinds of text. For example, questions students have when doing research are different from questions of a more rhetorical nature in response to literary texts.

As the strategy study continues, Julie will give her students more responsibility for asking questions and describing how those questions enhance their understanding. Whenever possible, Julie will ask students to assume responsibility for "teaching" the other students, particularly when they stumble upon an untried type of question. Ultimately, the goal is to have them generate questions independently and for a wide range of purposes, including zooming in on facts throughout the content areas, exploring fiction and poetry, and thinking critically about events and issues that affect their lives.

Into the Classroom—Primary

Char Mize and Ellin met after school in Char's first-grade classroom at Sabin Elementary. Char walked her students to the bus as Ellin wandered around her room, darkened by half-closed roller shades and a gray winter sky. Hands-on science materials were stacked in plastic tubs and stored neatly in a learning center at the back. The children's desks sat in clusters of four, with their chairs resting upside down on top and their books and folders piled neatly within. Organization and order permeated the room. It reminded Ellin of the sense of satisfaction she has when her house is dusted, cleaned, counters wiped, and dishes stacked neatly in the cupboards.

Several minutes later Char returned, breathing heavily after a sprint down two long hallways. She collapsed into a first grader's chair. In her warm, gravelly voice, she dove in. "Where do I start, Ellin? What do I do? How do I do it? I've been going to our study group for six months. I hear all the great teachers talk about the things they're doing in their reader's and writer's workshops. I've observed in Ann's class. She's so good. I just don't know if I can make mine that good. I know I want to do things differently, but I want to make sure the kids have the skills they need. I don't know how to cover everything to get them ready for second grade and still help them learn to love to read and write. I've always thought of myself as a teacher with high expectations. What do my expectations look like now? I think I may be too old and rigid to do this."

Char laughed, and as her laughter faded, she paused. Her face grew more solemn. "I have a really tough group this year. A big group, too. I need a change. They need a change. It's overwhelming, Ellin. I have so many questions."

Ellin thought back to the hour earlier in the day when she had observed in Char's classroom. She did have a big group—around twenty-eight. As Ellin circled the room and looked over shoulders, she saw children with a wide range of needs. Kevin's volatile temper intruded frequently, disrupting the class. It took Char five minutes to move Mary in and out of her wheelchair and set up her communication board or a new activity for her every time there was a transition. The PA system cut harshly into the children's hushed work too many times. Six children were pulled out for work in special ed or Title I classrooms just during the hour Ellin had observed.

The classroom had all the hallmarks of a well-organized ship. The room was immaculate and uncluttered. The schedule ran down to the minute. The desks were neat. The classroom was organized in a way that permitted Char to manage an array of variables. She was acutely aware of, and annoyed by, the stream of disruptions and children who were off task. And there was an edge to her interactions with the children that suggested a restless dissatisfaction with the status quo.

During Ellin's observation time, she jotted in her notebook: "In her zeal for a well-managed, efficient learning environment, has Char put in place structures that ensure order but necessarily limit the children's ownership and participation in this classroom? When do children ask questions? What are they curious about? How to begin to tackle the issue of control here? How can I directly, but respectfully, ask questions that will help her see the need to share responsibility for learning with the children?"

Study Groups and Conditions for Success

Ellin had started at Sabin the year before by forming a voluntary study group open to all teachers. They had read and discussed professional literature and talked about classroom practice. They had

Figure 5.1

Conditions for Success in Reader's and Writer's Workshops

- Teachers create a climate of respect and civility using rituals, a predictable schedule, and well-defined procedures for meeting routine needs. They trust children to become increasingly independent and to work together to solve problems.

- Teachers create a warm, inviting environment with soft lighting, work areas defined by rugs and bookshelves, readily available materials, and an abundance of children's work and records of their thinking on display.

- Teachers ensure that the classroom includes a variety of work spaces— comfortable places for children to work independently and talk with each other, an area for the whole group to gather, and a place for the teacher to meet with small groups.

- Teachers create a culture of rigor, inquiry, and intimacy by continually expecting more, probing ideas further, and pressing children to explore their intellect.

- Teachers create a culture conducive to in-depth study of books, genres, topics, authors, and comprehension strategies.

- Teachers provide equal access for all students to the materials and expertise needed by readers and writers.

- Teachers serve as lead learner by living literate lives and modeling how literacy plays an important role in their lives.

---

shared the Conditions for Success in Reader's and Writer's Workshops (Figure 5.1) and spent time thinking about and discussing each of the elements and how they could be incorporated into their classrooms. Some of the teachers had taken off, transforming their classrooms with garage sale castoffs of overstuffed chairs, lamps, and area rugs. They committed to spend time observing in each other's class-

- Teachers think aloud to reveal the ways that proficient readers and writers think during reading and writing and to show how to use comprehension strategies and writer's tools.

- Teachers model what readers who comprehend think about and how they create a literate life.

- Teachers model what writers who write convincingly think about and how they observe the world to feed their writing.

- Children have daily opportunities to participate in large-group, heterogeneous lessons (crafting sessions) focused on comprehension and writer's tools.

- Children choose most books and topics and the ways in which they share thinking and knowledge.

- Children confer with their teachers individually about their work as readers and writers. Teachers use conferences to understand children's present performance level and to suggest new directions for their reading and writing.

- Children have daily opportunities to read and write for long periods of time to apply what has been taught in small- and large-group settings.

- Children have opportunities, as needed, to participate in more focused and intensive small-group instruction (invitational groups) to meet specific learning needs.

- Children engage in in-depth discourse about books, writers, and ideas every day in groups of varying sizes.

- Children have regular opportunities to share ways they have applied what they learned in new contexts. Often children take responsibility for teaching each other (reflection sessions).

rooms and to give constructive criticism, identifying strengths as well as areas that needed attention. They learned from watching one another in action. The mood of exploration and rigor at the adult level was trickling down to the classrooms.

Char had been involved in the study group, but she had stood back, hesitant to make changes and lose control of her ship-shape classroom. Ellin feared that Char's rigid daily routine was going to make it difficult for her to give her students more responsibility for their own learning and to become a learner alongside them. But her honesty, her obvious frustration, her beseeching look made Ellin want to dig in and work with her to create a new home for the readers and writers in her classroom.

Using Writing to Kick Off a Comprehension Strategy Study

Ellin suggested they start with questioning and involve the other primary teachers who were in the study group. "Char, I don't have the answers for you, but I have a thought about where we might start. We've talked a lot about creating the right classroom environment in our study group. That's key. But it's also vital that kids are true participants in the classroom. Kids are great natural questioners. It's a good strategy to start with. I think it might work really well in your class. Let's involve the other primary teachers who are involved in the study group."

Char was nervous about opening her classroom to the other team members, but she was game. They met in Char's classroom before school one morning

"You all wanted to see the children more engaged and excited about writing," Ellin began. "Let's show them how writers use questions to choose writing topics. First graders are a volcano of questions. If we can get them to ask their own questions, they'll be on their way to imaginative writing. They'll also see how important their questions are so when we introduce questioning in reading, they'll get it. "

As they came in, Ellin gathered the children around her for their first crafting session (see Figure 5.2) and pulled out her notebook.

"I've been recording so many questions in my notebook lately," Ellin told the kids. "And you know what? Often my own questions

Figure 5.2

What Is a Crafting Session?

A crafting session is different from an ordinary large-group literacy lesson. It provides

- A time to study reader's and writer's craft in a serious and thoughtful way.
- A time when all class members gather to experience the beauty of written language and the magnetism of story or to observe the teacher composing his or her own text.
- An opportunity to become an apprentice to the finest readers and writers.
- A time for students to observe the teacher model, think aloud, and demonstrate and to share those observations with others.
- A time when children can experiment with their emerging ideas by sharing with a partner in a "turn and talk" or with the whole group.
- A time for intimacy, rigor, and ritual. Children are given the opportunity and the support to think at high levels and to experiment with new forms of thinking before trying them independently.
- An opportunity for explicit teaching (thinking aloud, modeling, and/or demonstrating) that focuses, not on a skill, but on a strategy students can use in future reading and/or writing tasks.
- A charge from the teacher to return to independent reading or writing to apply what has been taught.
- A time when all children are treated as scholars and expected to use a more formal oral language, worthy of their study of readers and writers.

Use these key ideas for successful crafting sessions:

- Thinking aloud helps children peer into the mind of a proficient reader or writer.
- The literature you choose is fundamental to the success of the lesson. Select text that is conducive to thinking aloud and select authors whose craft you can scrutinize.
- Clarity about the teaching intention, or objective, leads to precise and elegant language in the lesson, and precise and elegant language leads to a tone of rigor and intimacy.

Continues on next page

- Modeling from your own experience grounds the lesson in the real world—read and write as the children observe.
- Help children see connections beyond today.
- Use silence to help children understand the gravity of certain points.
- Limit the focus of the lesson to one teaching intention unless the goal is to link to previously learned material.
- Send children off with a specific charge to apply what has been taught or discussed in their independent work.

lead me to write my best pieces." Ellin opened her notebook. "I've been wondering what will happen to this cat that has been roaming around our neighborhood for a couple of weeks. Does she have a home? How does she eat? Where does she sleep? Should I feed her or will that keep her from finding her way back home? Did someone abandon her? Should I take her to the Dumb Friends League? All those questions could become a piece of writing—a story, maybe, or a poem."

Char recorded Ellin's questions on a large sheet of chart paper. As the children watched, Ellin wrote a couple of lead sentences in her notebook that formed the beginning of a first-person piece about the cat.

"I wonder about other things, too, and I want to write them down in case I want to write a different piece later. Our friends told us recently they've decided to divorce. I have so many questions about it I may write a piece that I won't share with anyone else, just to help myself understand this. I wonder what will happen to their son. Who will he live with? Will they sell their house? Will they ever get back together? Why did they decide to separate? Will they remarry?"

Ellin and Char switched roles. Char generated questions for her own writing while Ellin recorded them for the children to see. They paused frequently to talk about how the questions could become pieces of writing—stories, nonfiction, or poetry.

When they sent the children off to share questions with a partner and later to write, ideas flowed. Some began by simply writing the questions. Others were able to take ideas inspired by the questions and write longer pieces. Others drew pictures related to their questions. No one had to be told what to write.

By sharing questions about things in her environment that made her wonder and then asking the children to do the same, Ellin showed how questions weave throughout the day. She also provided the foundation for a strategy study on questioning.

Later, as they debriefed with the rest of the team, Char told Ellin, "I've tried hard to ask good questions, but I never once stopped to think about whether I let them generate questions. They have a million. I realize I haven't heard their questions. I've asked ten thousand questions so far this year. After we read a story from the basal, I skip the literal questions because they bore me, but I ask all the inferential questions, pause, and then tell them what I think. They must know by now they don't have to think, because I'll answer! But really, I have no idea what their questions are—about their lives, their writing, or their reading."

"Char, you don't need questions out of the manual," Ellin responded. "These kids have loads of real questions. And you have your own questions. How about letting those questions guide your discussions in reading, as well as in finding writing topics?"

The observers from Char's primary team could hardly contain their excitement about what the kids were doing. One of them jumped in. "I had Ramon in kindergarten and I have to tell you, he never, ever spoke up in the group and I struggled all year to get him to put anything on paper. Look at him. He's writing—not drawing—writing, and wait until you read his question. I can't believe I'm looking at the same kid!"

The group talked about how Char's reading instruction would differ from the weekly routine of working through stories in the basal. Instead of teaching a series of skills in an order determined by a publisher, she would teach one strategy—asking questions—in real depth over a long period of time (see the Gradual Release Planning Template in Chapter 4). She would model her own use of questions with a variety of texts and confer with the children to monitor their developing use of questioning. She'd form small groups to provide more intensive instruction, either because some kids were struggling or because they were ready to tackle new applications of the strategy. As the team ran back to their classrooms, they committed to try the changes Char was describing and agreed to reform their study group to share their successes and challenges.

Crafting Sessions

Ellin and Char wanted to create an aura of mystery, curiosity, and wonder around the concept of questioning during reading. They wanted the children to experience the insight that comes from questions, and to learn to love unanswerable questions. They wanted the children to experience the absorption they felt when reading a text that filled them with questions. They discussed the concept of crafting sessions and decided to use the term to describe whole-class, heterogeneous lessons that set the tone they hoped to create.

Thinking aloud about their questions was vital if the children were to become aware of the questions they naturally ask as they listen to or read text. Through much trial and error, Ellin had learned that she didn't need to "dumb down" her questions. If she asked simple, literal questions that were easily answered later on in the text, those were what the children mimicked. If she asked probing, challenging questions that went to the heart of the matter, the children followed suit. She also knew that part of her job was to help the children be aware of what went on in their minds as they read so they created an ongoing dialogue with print.

Char dimmed her classroom lights as Ellin opened *The Way to Start a Day* by Byrd Baylor. The illustrations, poetic language, and unconventional diction immediately seized the children's attention. Ellin read all the way through the book slowly, quietly trying to capture a sense of awe in the words. She wanted the first reading of the book to reflect a sense of sweeping light, space, and wonder.

Without a word she closed the book, paused, went to the chart and wrote, "What did Byrd Baylor want me to feel as I read her book?" Then, instead of inviting answers or rereading the book from the beginning, Ellin sat down and started from the middle of the book: "People have always known that. Didn't they chant at dawn in the sun temples of Peru? And leap and sway to Aztec flutes in Mexico? And drum sunrise songs in the Congo? And ring a thousand small gold bells in China?" Ellin closed the book. She and Char had prepped these first graders enough that she didn't need to say anything. Hands shot up and their questions started flowing.

Char laughed as she struggled to record the avalanche of questions. "We're going to need more chart paper!"

The children's questions were as diverse as they were. Maria, usually a silent presence in the classroom, listened to a question about why Byrd Baylor wrote her words more vertically than horizontally on the page, then raised her hand tentatively and said, "She likes questions."

"Tell me more about that." Char pushed.

Maria looked as if she might not respond at all, then paused and said, "and ring small gold bells in . . . ?"

It took them a moment to realize Maria was referring to the author's use of questions as a way to tell this story. As Char recorded Maria's insight, Ellin reread Byrd Baylor's questions about morning rituals from cultures around the world.

Char turned on the overhead lights. Ellin asked the children to return to their desks for their independent reading. "Listen to your minds at work. Do you have questions before, during, or after you read? We'll be around to confer with you about your books, and we want to hear the questions your mind creates about your books."

Gathering Baseline Data

At the outset Ellin and Char gathered data. They used the Major Point Interview for Readers (updated as *Assessing Comprehension Thinking Strategies*, Keene 2006) to identify the children's present use of questioning. For children who were reading very predictable or controlled vocabulary books, they used *The Way to Start a Day* and asked them to share questions related to it rather than to the book they were reading independently. They asked questions like these:

What did you wonder about before I (you) started to read this book?

What questions did you think about while I was (you were) reading this story? (When necessary, Char or Ellin reread part of *The Way to Start a Day*.)

What questions do you have about this book now?

Does it help you to understand the book when you ask questions like you asked just now? How do those questions help you understand the book?

After the crafting session, Ellin and Char sent the children back to their seats—Char wasn't yet comfortable with the idea that they could read in other places around the room—to apply what they had learned. As they got their books out, Char and Ellin stood back to observe. When a child approached them with a problem ("I'm done with my book—which book should I read next?"), Ellin stepped in before Char could answer the child's question. "Honey, what have you been taught about how to find a book in the classroom?" These kids knew the procedures. "Okay, then, I think you have just solved your own problem. I'm so impressed with kids who can solve their own problems. You're amazing, I wish all the kids would solve problems just like you do!" Too often, teachers jump in to address a problem when, in the same amount of time, we could remind them that they know how to solve it. In so doing, we're teaching them to be independent.

When everyone was settled in, Ellin and Char began to confer. For the few children who were reading books complex enough to make in-depth questioning possible, Char and Ellin conferred by inviting them to share questions they had about either *The Way to Start a Day* or their independent reading books.

Jotting the children's responses was *not* a time-consuming process. Many merely repeated questions from the think-aloud and others made declarative statements about their books or *The Way to Start a Day*. Char and Ellin were discouraged by the small number and mediocre quality of questions. "We have to remind ourselves of the great questions they've written and what they're coming up with during crafting sessions," Ellin said. "These will improve."

Once they had the baseline information, they pored through it and identified a clear direction for instruction. Most of the children weren't aware of any questions they asked as they read and couldn't say how questioning helped them understand a book better. The children needed to observe proficient readers generating questions during thinking-aloud lessons and talking about how asking questions before, during, and after reading helped them understand better.

Char and Ellin provided think-alouds in a wider variety of texts. To integrate the social studies unit into the study, Char used books like *I'm in Charge of Celebrations* by Byrd Baylor, *The Girl Who Loved Wild Horses* and *The Friendly Wolf* by Paul Goble, *The Rough-Face Girl* by Rafe Martin, and *Doesn't Fall Off His Horse: A Cherokee Tale* by Virginia

Stroud. They also created an anchor chart listing ways questions helped them and made the first contributions:

Asking questions . . .

helps me focus on the parts of the text that are most important to understand—Mrs. Mize

makes me aware of the parts of the text that are toughest for me to understand—Ellin

helps me to stop reading long enough to see pictures in my mind about the book—Ellin

Keeping Track of Thinking

By the third week of the study, the children were generating more diverse and interesting questions in the daily crafting sessions. Char used more complex books than most of the children were able to read independently. Some of the most insightful questions came from children Char *didn't* expect to contribute much. Children who lagged behind in decoding and fluency work frequently asked questions that revealed they were thinking at high levels. It became clear to Char that teaching fluency and decoding alongside comprehension instruction was not only appropriate, but dramatically enhanced struggling children's confidence as readers.

The next big step would be to help the children focus on applying the strategy in their own reading. Reading conferences and small-group instruction became increasingly important. Char taught the children to use sticky notes, write a question mark on them, and place them in books wherever words or an illustration caused them to ask a mental question. They loved this scheme, and for a few days a hurricane of yellow notes whirled around the room. Soon the novelty wore off and they began to use the notes more judiciously.

During reading conferences, Char asked the children about their question marks, but realized the sticky notes didn't always do the trick. She laughed as she described conferences with children whose books were filled with question-marked notes, but who couldn't remember their questions.

To spark the children's memories, Ellin and Char used the "turn and talk" procedure: They interrupted the class several times during independent reading time, asked the children to share questions with their nearest neighbor, and then had them mark their questions in their books with sticky notes. Talking about their questions helped the kids remember, and Char was better able to focus her conferences on their real questions.

Within a week the room became a hive of questions. The process of generating questions about books became a routine part of reading—before, during, and after. Many children spontaneously shared questions about their books with each other. Large-group sharing time frequently turned into small-group sharing time because so many children had questions they wanted to share.

Invitational Groups

"I'm still frustrated, Ellin," Char said when the study was well under way. "I don't really know whether all the kids are aware of the questions they have as they read. Some see how their questions help them understand, but there are six or seven kids hovering out there. They don't share much during large-group sessions or when I confer with them. Sometimes I think they're just mimicking what I say in the crafting sessions."

Char ran a hand through her short blonde hair. "Manuel is a good example. I say, 'Manuel, what questions do you have as you're reading *William's Doll?*' and he'll say something like, 'Why did the author write this book?' or 'What would have happened next in the book if the author had kept on writing?' Those are questions I or other kids have asked during crafting sessions or sharing time. Brian asked the question about what would have happened next if the author kept writing, and I made a huge fuss over it because I thought it was such a great question. The problem is I don't know how to tell if Manuel really has that question. He doesn't seem excited about his questions and they don't seem authentic for him. How can I find out?"

Char's question was one that had troubled PEBC staff developers and teachers for some time. What if the children were merely echoing the language they'd heard their teachers using in crafting sessions and think-alouds? What if they didn't have a real understanding of the strategy and weren't using it automatically as they read?

Ellin suggested they try a technique used masterfully by a colleague, Colleen Buddy. In her first/second-grade classroom, when faced with similar concerns, Colleen calls for an invitational group meeting. *Invitational group*s are needs-based groups that meet for a specific instructional purpose (see Figure 5.3). Children are invited to join the group for a short, intensive crafting lesson that reinforces or extends a concept they've discussed in large-group instruction. Invitational groups enable the teacher to gauge a child's use of the strategy more quickly and tailor instruction for a group of children with similar needs.

A group may disband after one session or meet several times during the course of a comprehension strategy study. Occasionally, children who already understand and are adept at applying the strategy are invited to join the group. Sometimes several children who are adept at using the strategy call their own invitational group to work on it with more difficult text or in a more in-depth way.

Other times, when a teacher tells the whole class that an invitational group will meet, she names those who will be part of the group, and also announces that there are two or three open positions. If children other than those she's named believe they would benefit from more in-depth instruction on the strategy, they too are welcome to join

Figure 5.3

What Is an Invitational Group?

An invitational group is different from an ordinary small-group lesson. It offers

- A time during independent reading and writing when the teacher identifies and meets with small groups of children based on a shared need for intensive instruction and discussion.
- A time to read instructional-level texts in order to experiment with or reinforce deep and surface structure strategies and skills recently taught.
- A time to write short pieces in which children can experiment with or receive more intensive instruction on skills or strategies recently taught.
- A time during which a small group of children explores ideas with an eye toward sharing them with others later in crafting or reflecting sessions.
- A time when children have an opportunity to practice, with teacher support, strategies and skills taught in crafting sessions. Children have an opportunity to observe the teacher model in a more controlled, focused setting than in a large-group crafting session and to try the skill or strategy immediately, often in a simpler text, with teacher guidance.
- An opportunity for the teacher to think aloud or model a skill or strategy again and to observe children closely as they begin to apply it.
- An opportunity to introduce a skill such as a writing convention or decoding skill that the rest of the class already demonstrates independently.
- A time for students to read and write silently and discuss problems they encounter immediately.

Effective invitational groups share certain characteristics:

- Invitational groups are short, focused, and active.
- Children are actively and enthusiastically involved because they have been effectively prepared; their teacher has created a learning environment conducive to enthusiastic student involvement.
- The group has a spirit of support for other group members.

Continues on next page

- The teacher is free to focus exclusively on the invitational group, having taught the rest of the class to read and write independently for long periods of time.
- Students and teachers plan to share what they've discussed with other children in the reflection time.
- Invitational groups are not static—the same group of children may meet one to three times to focus on an area of need, then disband.
- Invitational groups are not necessarily homogeneous.
- Invitational groups are designed to offer instruction in a group's zone of proximal development. In other words, instruction closely matches a clearly identified need for each child in the group and presses them to move forward.
- Invitational groups are not used as an opportunity for the teacher to listen to children read aloud in a round-robin style.
- When the teacher is working with an invitational group, the other children are reading and writing.
- When working with an invitational group, the teacher does not permit interruptions from other students or initiate an interruption to manage other children.
- The teacher creates a sense of anticipation and excitement for those invited to a group.
- Children who have participated in an invitational group are often invited to teach or demonstrate to others what they have learned during a reflecting session.

the group. The teacher convenes several invitational groups during a given strategy study, each with a different purpose.

Invitational groups meet for a short (ten- or twelve-minute) period during the workshop or independent reading time—the time when a teacher typically would confer with individual students. The teacher models or thinks aloud about a specific instructional need and the children talk about their understanding and use of the strategy. The teacher scaffolds the instruction more specifically than she does in a large group. For example, she may read aloud, share one question, and then ask each child to share a question they have had so far in the text. The teacher can monitor each child's responses more closely and provide on-the-spot, individualized instruction.

Char and Ellin started out by convening an invitational group of five. They offered two open spots, which were quickly filled by children eager to join the group. They discovered that the children Char had invited didn't seem to be fully aware of the questions they asked while they were reading. They were able to generate questions before and after reading, but seemed not to pay attention to their questions during reading. The children could read independently in predictable, rhythmic books with controlled vocabulary. But those books, while appropriate for them to use in practicing their newfound decoding skills, had little story development that inspired genuine questions.

In the invitational group Char read aloud, asking questions as she read using books more likely to inspire questions. She focused on the questions she had during reading, particularly those that helped her clarify portions of the text that were more difficult for her to understand. Then she asked the children to write a question on a sticky note and share it with the small group. She sent them off to do the same in their independent reading. After two short invitational groups in which Char thought aloud, the same children were asked to come back to the group with sticky notes marking questions they had collected while they read independently. As a group they generated possible answers to the questions, but the reader was always left to make the final determination about the meaning of the piece.

Delia was typical. "I brought *Just Me and My Babysitter* [by Mercer Mayer] today," she announced. "And I have a question. Why does Lil' Critter say, 'I always eat all my dinner' when right here he's pouring his food out on the floor?"

Char immediately knew that the answer to Delia's question was critical to understanding the book. "Delia, that's the kind of question great readers ask. While you were reading this page, you had a question, and you stopped and thought, 'This doesn't make sense. The picture shows Lil' Critter throwing his food on the floor, but the words say he always eats all his dinner. How can both be true?' If they're really confused, great readers have to figure out some answers before they can really know what the book is about, right? Let's tackle Delia's question together."

The group read the pages before and after the page that confused Delia. The children concluded that the text and illustrations differ throughout the book and that the author intentionally created the contrast to make the book funny.

Through a series of meetings this invitational group solved a variety of comprehension problems that they had identified by asking questions. Gradually, the group members generated their own questions before, during, and after reading. They continued to ask more relevant questions about the more complex texts used during crafting sessions, but each became more aware of his or her own questions and began to use questions to clarify the meaning of a text if they were confused.

Students as Teachers: Reflection Sessions

One afternoon in the fourth week of the study, Char and Ellin met to debrief and review the children's questions on sticky notes. All of the students were asking more questions. Many were asking questions that went beyond mere clarification. Char was thinking about her changing role as the children took more and more responsibility for asking questions about a variety of texts. "What would you advise for the large-group crafting session?" Char asked Ellin. "I feel like I'm doing the same thing over and over each day."

Ellin knew teachers needed to revise their roles as the strategy study moved forward and the children became more independent. "Why not have the kids teach some of the crafting sessions? Have them share their thinking with the group; and instead of just having them share, ask them to reflect on their own learning and teach others to do what they've learned to do. If one child is asking questions in nonfiction texts, why not ask him to prepare a 'lesson' on how questioning is different in nonfiction than in fiction?"

Char's students jumped at the opportunity to teach each other. The class called these new lessons "reflection sessions" because kids were asked to reflect on their own learning as well as share something others could try. (See Figure 5.4.) Char reminded them they needed to plan for their instruction just like teachers. They needed to have a short written plan that included what they would teach, provide time for their classmates to discuss what they had learned, and follow up to see if they were using it.

"This is gratifying," Char told Ellin after a week of children's reflection sessions.

"We understand concepts so much better if we have to teach them, Char. It's the same with kids. They really take ownership when they're in charge!"

Six weeks after the chaotic day when they began the study, Char and Ellin sat together after school. Char marveled as they reviewed the interviews they'd given at the beginning and end of the study. "They're using questioning to solve problems on their own and for each other all through the day. They talk about asking questions in math and science."

Ellin looked around Char's room. The roller shades were tossed away, letting in a stream of natural light; floor lamps lit reading and writing areas; the burnt orange chair had become the heart of the classroom. More important, asking questions had become part of the culture of Char's classroom, which looked very different from the too-organized room Ellin had walked into that winter day months before. Char had more work to do, but she had made a vital shift. She had nurtured the engagement that occurs when the students "own" the classroom along with the teacher. A transformation had begun when the children were allowed to ask their own questions.

Figure 5.4

What Is a Reflection Session?

Reflection sessions are different from ordinary sharing sessions:

- A reflection session is a time for readers and writers to share what they have learned with others in a way that makes their learning more permanent and applicable to other learning situations.

- A reflection session can be any size, from the whole class to pairs, trios, or quads.

- The child conducting a reflection session begins by describing his or her own learning, specifically answering the questions: "What did I learn about myself as a reader or writer? What can I 'teach' that will help other readers and writers?"

- Children have been taught how to explicitly teach their peers. Children gradually take responsibility for planning reflection sessions and for ensuring that their "students" understand.

- Before asking students to use them, teachers model various forms of reflection sessions—that is, sessions in which partners share, whole-class sessions, and sessions that include teaching students outside the immediate class members.

- Children conducting reflection sessions emphasize ways in which their "students" can apply what they learn in their own reading or writing.

- Children who are in the role of learner while their peers are teaching are taught to ask the "teacher" questions, to challenge what is being shared, to argue diplomatically, and to push the "teacher" to expand his or her thinking.

- Reflection sessions are concluded with a challenge to the learners to apply what has been taught in their own reading and writing.

- All class members need regular opportunities to conduct and learn from reflection sessions.

~ ~ ~

Asking children questions and awaiting their quick responses has become habitual for many teachers. Children's ability to fire back an answer somehow affirms for us that they are learning. Of course, we want children to be able to answer questions in some circumstances, for certain purposes. But we also want children to ask *real* questions. Just as we pose questions that push us deeper into life and living, that awaken us to other people's conditions, that disclose practical and ethical dilemmas, and that force us to reflect about how we treat those around us, children can, from the earliest grades, do the same. Questions tend to be generative, leading to more thinking. Answers frequently bring thinking to a full stop. Questions reveal far more about children's thinking than do pat answers, hastily delivered. Questions slow us down and help us focus on what is truly important. They launch us into studies of areas of great interest. They propel us to pursue our passions. Einstein once said, "Learn from yesterday, live for today, hope for tomorrow. The important thing is not to stop questioning." For the good of us all, we must nurture our children's curiosity gene so that they never stop questioning.

Key Ideas for Comprehension Strategy Study

Asking Questions

- Proficient readers spontaneously and purposefully generate questions before, during, and after reading, depending on their purpose in reading.

- Proficient readers ask questions to
  - clarify meaning
  - speculate about text yet to be read
  - show skepticism or a critical stance
  - determine an author's intent, style, content, or format
  - locate a specific answer in text
  - consider rhetorical questions that will take their understanding deeper into the text

The types of questions differ based on the type of text (genre) and the reader's purpose.

- Proficient readers use questions to focus their attention on ideas, events, or other text elements they want to remember.

- Proficient readers understand that many of the most intriguing questions are not answered explicitly in the text but left to the reader's interpretation.

- However, when an answer is needed, proficient readers determine whether it can be answered by the text or whether they will need to infer the answer from the text, their background knowledge, and/or other text, or whether the answer is explicitly stated in the text.

- Proficient readers understand how the process of questioning is used in all areas of their lives, both academic and personal.

- Proficient readers understand and can describe how asking questions deepens their comprehension.

- Proficient readers are aware that as they hear others' questions, new ones—called generative questions—are inspired in their own minds. In some cases, a reader's own question causes him or her to generate more.

CHAPTER 6

Creating Meaning

Inference

Celebration of the Human Voice

Their hands were tied or handcuffed, yet their fingers danced, flew, drew words. The prisoners were hooded, but leaning back they could see a bit, just a bit, down below. Although they were forbidden to speak, they spoke with their hands. Pinio Ungerfeld taught me the finger alphabet, which he had learned in prison without a teacher:

"Some of us had bad handwriting," he told me. *"Others were masters of calligraphy."*

The Uruguayan dictatorship wanted everyone to stand alone, everyone to be no one: in prison and in barracks and throughout the country, communication was a crime.

Some prisoners spent more than ten years buried in solitary cells the size of coffins, hearing nothing but clanging bars or footsteps in the corridors. Fernandez Huidobro and Mauricio Rosencof, thus condemned, survived because they could talk to each other by tapping on the wall. In that way, they told of dreams and memories, fallings in and out of love; they discussed, embraced, fought; they shared beliefs and beauties, doubts and guilts, and those questions that have no answer.

When it is genuine, when it is born of the need to speak, no one can stop the human voice. When denied a mouth, it speaks with the hands or the eyes, or the pores, or anything at all. Because every single one of us has something to say to others, something that deserves to be celebrated or forgiven, by others.

—Eduardo Galeano, *The Book of Embraces*

Ellin's Reflections

I have read "Celebration of the Human Voice" many times. Each time, it takes me to a different place. Earlier today, sitting on my patio with the *Denver Post* and a cup of coffee, surrounded by the gardens I've spent so much time tending, I wrote,

> "Celebration of the Human Voice" brings to mind poverty I've seen firsthand in this country. When I read it, I see the faces and hear the voices of children I've taught at low-income schools. I feel a type of despair that links the prisoners in this essay to the children I've known, their sense of being trapped by something beyond their control. I feel outrage on behalf of the prisoners, whose only crime was to disagree with their government. I feel a sense of impotence when it comes to dealing with the despair born of poverty in this country.
>
> I hear the litany: housing problems, low-wage jobs, immigration, declining test scores. I hear friends express angst about children who have so much when many children have so little.
>
> There is a silence—a thundering silence of missing voices—those most affected by the cycle of poverty. I can't help but wonder what our policies might look like if the people they are designed to help had a larger voice in creating them. That would be a celebration of the human voice. Those voices seem eerily silent, absent from the national dialogue about the best solutions.

The doorbell rang. The UPS man interrupted my writing. I never went back to it. There were breakfast dishes to do, laundry to fold.

Hours later, when I reread what I had written, it sounded bitter, like I was trying to blame someone. I wish I could. It would make my anger easier to channel. Struck by the tone of outrage in this response and certain that it had come, in part, from reading poverty and crime statistics in the *Denver Post* moments before, I dug out an old notebook where I had written a response to the same piece months before:

It's exquisite and inexplicable—the hope that compels people such as these prisoners to invent a way to communicate when they must have known how desperate their situation was and how unlikely it was that they would walk out of that prison alive. Strength from deep in the human soul rose up to embolden them to create a communication system, one for which, if discovered, they would surely be punished, perhaps by death. I wonder how they created it. I don't think it mattered if they actually understood what the others were saying; though perhaps they did. They expressed their deepest thoughts and someone responded with taps on a wall. The connection with another human being kept them alive; the knowledge that someone was listening.

What is it in the human heart and mind that must feel a connection to others, especially in the most dire circumstances? This essay reminds me of *Man's Search for Meaning*. Something permitted Viktor Frankl to find small joys and purpose in his life in a Nazi concentration camp and ultimately to survive. There is such courage demonstrated here and by Frankl. Ingenuity born of courage. When we face circumstances less grim, but certainly complex, in our own world—curing cancer, creating jobs, educating children, providing health care, dealing with a world fraught with conflict and hate—will we have the necessary courage? Perhaps strength like that comes only from the harshest adversity, the ultimate test of the human spirit.

I'm struck by how different my responses are several months apart and realize that each time I read "Celebration of the Human Voice," my response will change, depending upon current events, what I'm reading, what has been happening in my life. In workshops when teachers read "Celebration of the Human Voice," they often talk or write about Helen Keller, about special needs students who "speak" with a smile or a look even if they don't have a voice, about kids in their classrooms who *always* figure out a way to communicate even if that's the last thing they should be doing. They picture themselves hooded, able to look down just enough to see the movement of another prisoner's communicating hands. They hear the tap, tap, tap of the dancing fingers. They imagine with horror what it would be like to be confined to a coffin-sized cell. Though none of them has experienced life in a Uruguayan prison, they make a personal connection to the piece. They talk of the evil of a dictatorship that wanted "everyone to stand alone, everyone to be no one." They remark about the extraordinary ability of human beings to find ways to communicate no matter how dire their situations, no matter how limited their actual facility to talk. They rejoice in the dignity embedded in the line: "Because every single one of us has something to say to others, something that deserves to be celebrated or forgiven, by others." They read and reread, talk and write until the piece holds a powerful meaning for them.

When I read "Celebration of the Human Voice," I inferred. I trusted that listening to my inferences would help me understand. I didn't always read this way. I have had to work hard to make myself a more aware reader, one who thinks about her thinking as she reads. I have moved from a passive to an active stance. When we're considering the most effective ways to teach inference, we must begin by scrutinizing how *we* infer. We need to be aware of *our* thinking, so we can be as explicit as possible when describing to children how we infer in lessons. We need to help them gradually learn to listen to—and trust—their inner voices and the inferences they generate. They need to know that they aren't "wrong" if their inferences are different from those of their teachers or classmates. They need to know they can create more detail and depth from listening to those inferences than even the author might have imagined.

I write out "Celebration of the Human Voice" and jot:

> It feels good to hand-write poems and essays. So much of my writing is done on a keyboard. I can hardly read my own writing anymore, but I love the physical sensation of looking back and forth from a book to my paper, watching my hand write the words that give me pause. It slows me down and helps me understand pieces better. I realize now that my heart leaps to the children I've known in poverty when I read "Celebration," in part because I think nations have always tried, in one way or another, to silence the people who make leaders most uncomfortable. Some twisted logic leads those in power and privilege to believe that if we muzzle those faced with the greatest challenges (or those who challenge us most) we can turn our backs on the problems. It is that systematic silencing that haunts me from the Galleano piece and leads me to wonder how much we silence children in schools. A disquieting idea, because so much learning comes from conversation. For me, discourse is the lifeblood of the creative process.

I ask Susan to read "Celebration."

"I think of so many things when I read this, Ellin. Mainly I think of Katherine, of how she has been unable to speak all of her life, but has found a way to communicate that is amazing. People who don't know her don't understand. They ask me if she can talk and I say no, but she lets us know what she feels and wants through her smiles and facial expressions. She shows gratitude. She shows love. Though her situation is very different, it gives me a deep appreciation of those prisoners' need to communicate."

Katherine is Susan's oldest child. Now twenty-seven, she has Rett syndrome, a debilitating condition that has left her profoundly handicapped, though she developed normally until her first birthday. She is one of the most helpless people I've ever met; but, because of her family's response to her, one of the most powerful. Susan has written a book about her journey with Katherine, *Keeping Katherine* (Zimmermann 2005). Searching for meaning in her confounding life experience, she wrote of the sorrow, the shattered dreams, and the intense efforts she and her family undertook to help Kat recover. She wrote of periods of despair and helplessness, of the heroic strangers who came into their lives to work with Katherine, of how, after great struggle, she came to understand Kat's gifts, and of how Kat's unpredictable and life-altering condition gave added meaning to the rest of the family.

For twenty-seven years the reality of feeding, bathing, changing, and carrying Katherine from room to room provided a sobering backdrop to Susan's life. Slowly, by acknowledging that Katherine has a profound and powerful effect on those who interact with her—an ability to "speak with the hands or the eyes, or the pores, or anything at all"— Susan began to extract a larger meaning from her daughter's life. Through the process of her own writing, a new interpretation evolved—one that did not in any way match the hopes and dreams parents have for their children, but one that permitted a deep understanding of the power of love and the dignity of all human life.

So it is with inferring. We are bound, to an extent, by the print on the page, as Susan and her family are bound by the constraints of Katherine's life. Katherine will never walk, talk, or feed herself. That is the literal reality. Yet her gifts are significant, and the interpretation of her life through *Keeping Katherine* is a contribution to all who have experienced loss. Through it, we learn how a family has come to understand Katherine's "language"—a lifetime of inferences that have led them to know someone who will never speak.

Susan tells her story through the images of her life with Kat, those things she could not forget: a floppy blue doll Kat once loved, a plastic activity center, a potty high chair, their first camping trip, Kat's thirteenth birthday. Between the images, she weaves her learnings from Kat, at one point writing:

> When we are in the depths of pain and everything around us has become tasteless, we try to bury the images that remind us of our loss, to force them back into the box that holds our sorrow, but they erupt at unexpected times and leave us shaking. If we help them out, if we bring them forth and make them a part of our stories, finally, with time's passing, we are able to see the drama and beauty of our lives.

I read "the box that holds our sorrow" and my eyes landed as if for the first time on a small wooden chair that has been in my bedroom for years. My eyes followed the curves of the chair and I recalled pulling it to the side of my mother's bed where she lay in the final stages of her battle with leukemia. The funny little chair that came from my grandparents' home, found its way to my parents' home and later to mine, is part of the image of sorrow I carry. Susan's words opened that box.

When I read "the box that holds our sorrow," a flood of visual images and prior knowledge caused me to remember the tone and substance of my final conversations with my mother. That recollection linked back to Susan's words, "the drama and beauty of our lives," which made me realize I had created an entirely new interpretation for the short passage she had written. There was a sort of drama in those final days with my mother. The conversations we had would be our last and we knew it. That knowledge added intensity and strangely slowed the pace of the conversations.

My memories are of sitting in that little wooden chair with my feet propped on my mother's bed, talking for hours or listening to her halting breaths as she drifted in and out of sleep. Those memories bring to my reading of this passage an entirely original interpretation—one that no other reader will create.

If my reading of "Celebration of the Human Voice" had been limited to a literal interpretation, chances are good I wouldn't remember the passage. But my thoughts, winding around the little wooden chair and *Keeping Katherine*, took me far beyond the literal and made both texts unforgettable. Susan's words permitted me to recall the intimacy, the humor, the joy, even the hope I had felt during those last conversations. I realize now that I didn't hold out hope she would survive the cancer, but came, slowly, to believe I would have a life after she died. I knew I was learning the most important lessons of my life.

Inference is part rational, part mystical, part definable, and part beyond definition. Individuals' life experiences, logic, wisdom, values, creativity, and thoughtfulness, set against the text they are reading, form the crux of new meaning. Because each person's experiences are different, the art of inferring takes the reader beyond the text to a place only he or she can go. When we read, we can choose to limit our interpretations to the literal words of the text, but by doing so we greatly limit understanding. It's like calling paint-by-numbers kits (where the object is to stay within the lines) art. They don't expand, but contract, our creativity. In "Celebration of the Human Voice," we are inspired to overcome petty frustrations when we hear about the reality of those prisoners' lives, as well as the lives of many people in the world who live in war-torn countries or under the thumb of tyrants. We are reminded of the power of the human spirit to overcome the most grueling and cruel conditions and find a way to make their "voices" heard, because "everyone has something to say."

Inferring gives the reader an opportunity to sense a meaning not explicit in the text, but which derives or flows from it. Knowing this about my own reading leads me to wonder if we create adequate opportunities for children to infer and, therefore, better learn the lessons of their lives. Not everything that is read can or need be remembered. The reader makes judgments about what must be remembered and what can be forgotten—she determines importance. As a society, we may disagree about what we want children to remember, but all would agree that there is critical content to be learned, recalled, and reapplied in new situations.

When I visit classrooms and observe teachers who ask children to recall endless literal detail from what they've read, I wonder what the consequence is when children read or listen only for the literal meaning or "just the facts." The price may be nothing less than the inability to recall important concepts. We wring our hands over children who seem to remember and reapply little of what they've read. Yet how often do we create classroom environments in which they discuss, evaluate, ponder, argue, restate, reflect, persuade, relate, write about, or otherwise work with the information we consider critical for them to recall? It may be true that the reader has more latitude to infer in fiction, memoir, and poetry, but we must infer when reading nonfiction text as well. To push beyond a dry, literal understanding, to add our own opinions, knowledge, and ideas— *that* is to infer.

Reflecting on Instruction: Thinking Aloud

Thinking aloud is the single most important teaching tactic at our disposal. It is different from modeling or demonstrating. Thinking aloud provides direct access to the reader's (or writer's) mind, allowing children to observe how understanding comes about. The best think-alouds are clear, concise, and explicit illustrations of what we think when we read. Ideally, they evolve into a give-and-take between the teacher and students and then between students. The teacher stops to share her thinking using one or more strategies, then invites the students to share their thinking, first in pairs, later in different configurations of peers. The purpose of think-alouds is to show students the process a proficient reader uses to make sense of text, with the goal of having them do the same type of thinking independently as they read (see Figure 6.1).

Figure 6.1

Teaching Tactics:
Day-to-Day Instruction in Comprehension

By thinking aloud, teachers show how readers and writers think:

- Teachers read aloud, pausing to make their thinking explicit.
- Teachers are clear about how the strategy they're using helps them comprehend more than they would have comprehended without the strategy.
- Teachers work to ensure precision in their think-alouds, focusing on the most probing, high-level use of the strategy. They do this even at the beginning of a strategy study so that children apply the strategy at a higher level.
- Teachers clearly describe how students can apply the strategy independently.

By modeling, teachers show how readers and writers behave:

- Teachers describe their lives as readers and writers—they relate their preferences and areas of passionate interest, describe how they select books, reflect on why they gravitate to certain authors, describe what they do when they encounter problems, and explain how they share their work to solicit feedback from others.
- Teachers create a classroom environment conducive to in-depth learning—an environment that is comfortable and encourages conversation and reflection.
- Teachers ensure that learning experiences are authentic—they don't ask children to do assignments readers and writers outside of school are unlikely to undertake.

By demonstrating, teachers show how readers and writers interact and work with the ideas they understand:

- Teachers demonstrate or help students demonstrate a variety of ways readers and writers deepen comprehension, solicit feedback on their writing, extend comprehension, and share insights (e.g., book clubs, rituals and routines, book selection).

Into the Classroom—Primary

In many states, high-stakes assessments include "inferential thinking" questions. Students tend to struggle most on those items. At Stemley Road, a low-income school near Talladega, Alabama, the data showed that students were flummoxed by the inference questions. Principal Janet Cumbee, Literacy Fellow Becky McKay, and Ellin decided to tackle the issue with a couple of days of demonstrations in a third-grade classroom.

"Children's difficulties on inference-related items often correlate to teachers' lack of clarity about what good inference instruction looks like," Ellin reminded them as they met over lunch before working with the children. "If we're not sure how to describe inference, our instruction tends to be less explicit, less frequent, and less than memorable. Have you ever heard teachers telling kids to 'read between the lines'?"

"You bet!" Janet laughed.

"Yep, and I bet you've also seen kids holding books close to their eyes, trying to read between the lines and pulling their teachers' chains by saying, 'There's nothin' there!'"

"Many times," Becky related.

"Well, reading between the lines doesn't mean much to a kid and it sure doesn't help them learn *how* to infer. We need to show them how proficient readers create inferences. That's what I'm aiming for today."

That hot spring afternoon, they began their work on inference with a class of thirty third graders and a dozen teachers observing. With the children gathered on the floor around her, Ellin held up Jon Muth's *The Three Questions.* "This is a child's version of a story by a famous Russian writer, Leo Tolstoy. Today I want to show you how I infer. I'm going to pause as I read and I'll share my inferences. Inferences are really important and great readers make them all the time. An inference is something a reader knows from reading, but the author doesn't include it in the book. It helps you understand the story more deeply and helps make books mean something very personal to you."

In *The Three Questions*, a young boy, Nicolai, hoping to be a better person, seeks the answers to three questions: When is the best time to do things? Who is the most important one? What is the right thing to do? His friends, a heron, a monkey, and a dog, try to help him answer the questions, but to no avail.

Ellin stopped to share on page 4. "I'm inferring that the boy has a special kind of power that allows him to communicate with these animals. I've always wished I could do that. I infer these animals are his friends and that it doesn't matter that they're animals and he's human." As soon as the words were out of her mouth, she regretted them. She realized it would have been far better to keep reading and trust that a more probing or insightful inference would come to mind. Instead she inferred about something obvious to the listeners, something she works hard to avoid.

She went on, stopping again on page 7. "As I read the first few pages of this book, I'm inferring that Nikolai is overwhelmed and confused about the advice his friends are giving him. I know that's an inference because I'm using evidence from the text as well as knowledge from my own life to conclude that Nikolai feels very overwhelmed." Again, Ellin was disappointed, aware her inference was hardly profound. The ideas in the book were worthy of more. She tried, on the fly, to think of another inference or a better way to articulate the inferences she'd already shared, but came up short as a sense of quiet desperation seeped in.

Sometimes teachers experience a moment of inspiration in an otherwise hopeless situation. With a blank mind, Ellin looked at the children and said, "I'm going to need a moment in silence to think. The inferences I've shared with you are not yet helping me to understand this book as well as I know I can. I'm going to take just a moment to listen to the voice in my mind."

She looked at her lap and closed her eyes, momentarily picturing what might happen in the classroom while she paused to think. The two images that came to her were less than comforting: an airport the day before Thanksgiving and then news images of the wild anarchy that erupts in some developing nations after a botched presidential election. She kept her eyes closed and forced her mind back to the book. She took so long she was sure darkness had descended on Alabama and the buses had left without the third graders. When she finally looked up, she found everyone in the room indulging in their own silent reverie, many with their eyes closed. The observing teachers' pens were at rest and the third graders were actually quiet and calm. Just as Ellin was about to share a more thoughtful inference, she bit her tongue, enjoying the silence. When Ellin broke it, she realized it had been well worth the wait.

A hand shot up. Though she had planned to share more of her inferences before asking the children to do the same, she couldn't resist calling on Remy.

"I just know, just then I knowed what I thought!" His voice was this side of exuberant.

"I just known that boy Nik—"

"Nikolai," Ellin offered.

"That boy Nikolai just knows he's asking a whole big question about life and that the question might be one—what do they call that kind of question—that makes you only think of more questions, not really the answer." Remy was out of breath. "You know how some of those kinds of questions make your life just come out different. That kid is—I mean the reason he is trying so hard to come up with answers to those questions he's asking is that he knows that knowing the answers will make him a better person. It's like if he can *really* know the answers to questions like, ah, I forgot . . ."

"One of the questions he asked is 'what is the right thing to do?'" Ellin said.

"Right, yeah, if he knows what is the right thing to do, it will be a part of everything he does from now on until he dies. And if you think about how many other people will be in his life, he can do a lot of good for them if he just can know those answers."

Again silence. Remy's inference deserved to be mulled over for a moment.

Finally, Ellin spoke. "You know Remy, I'm just so interested in your inference. I want to know two things. First, how did that inference come into your mind, and second, how did that inference help you better understand this story?"

Remy immediately said, "I don't know."

Ellin sensed that was a defense against saying something wrong and used her favorite line, "I know you don't know Remy, but if you did know, what would you say?" Her experience told her that when children say "I don't know," they are often really saying, "I need more time to think about your question."

"Well, okay, I was thinking about it when you were thinking."

"You mean your inference came into your mind when I was taking quiet time to think about my own inferences?"

"Yeah, then, and then the more I said out loud the more I knew I knew." He looked at Ellin with a face that said, "Do you get that?" She did.

"So you're telling me that while I was thinking about my inferences, you were doing the same thing and you realized that the questions Nikolai was asking in the book were questions of huge importance, because the answers, if he could find them, would affect the rest of his life?"

"Yeah, important, like, if he knows the answers, he's gonna be able to be better and help other people be better, too."

"Hmm," Ellin said, "and Remy, how do you think that inference helped you to better understand this book?"

This time Remy didn't say "I don't know." He looked up. "Because now I get why Nik is working so hard to find the answers to his questions. I get why he's asking all his friends to help him because it's not just little questions he wants to know. He wants to know stuff that will make him a certain kind of person, like a more helpful person."

Ellin reminded herself that children's responses are nearly always worth the wait, and that silence, though uncomfortable for the adults, can lead to great thinking. Insightful inferences often don't come quickly. If someone asked you to say something brilliant, really fast, you would most likely freeze. That's what we do to children when, in large- or small-group lessons, we're too quick to move on to the next child who has a hand up. Too often we leave a child who pauses or blurts "I don't know," saying, "I'll come back to you if you remember what you want to say." Often we never get back to them, or by the time we do, they've forgotten their train of thought. We've probably also given them the subtle message that going deep with their thinking isn't valued.

Lessons Along the Way

The two key lessons Becky, Janet, and Ellin learned as they debriefed that afternoon went beyond a new direction for instruction at Stemley Road and fell into the lasting-lessons-for-teaching category. The first was that we should work to create an ethic in the classroom that *values longer periods of time for reflection,* not just on inference, but on all the strategies and across the curriculum. If a child says I don't know, we need to resist the temptation to move on to someone else. We should instead encourage the child to take the time needed to consider the ideas from the book. We can quietly reread a portion of the book or restate what the child has already said in order to help him refocus. Given time, most children will share interesting inferences or thinking that encompasses many of the strategies. When we create a norm that values time for reflection, children quickly adapt to that norm and become accustomed to taking time to think more deeply.

The second lesson was that we should *raise the level of our strategy use* during think-alouds even when we're not certain that the children are getting all the literal details. Often, if we share higher-level inferences (or questions, syntheses, mental images, etc.), the literal details fall into place without our having to discuss them explicitly. The result is that more of the children's time is devoted to observing—and eventually undertaking—more sophisticated thinking. Granted, it's tough just to tell ourselves to think at higher levels during think-alouds, but when we put our minds to it, we *can* do it.

In trying to raise the level of her think-alouds, Ellin keeps in mind a quote from her philosophy professor in college: "I would not spend my life in conversation with people who talk about people or people who talk about things, but rather with people who talk about ideas." In teaching inference, she asks herself, "Am I inferring primarily about *things* (the events in a story, for example), *people* (such as the characters), or *ideas* (the prevailing concepts, the lessons and direction for our lives we take away from reading)?" By focusing on the following three principles, she works hard to make sure she includes a healthy dose of inference about ideas worthy of children's consideration:

1. **Trust children to pick up on more obvious points in the text, and take time to think and focus on inferences that go beyond the literal and obvious.** In my experience teaching comprehension strategies, I've learned that if I take a moment in silence and carefully consider the weight of the content I'm about to use in a think-aloud, I can usually avoid the more obvious, even cliché inferences (or connections, questions, important ideas and images) and move on to an idea with greater merit. If I pause right in the middle of a think-aloud or conference, even for a brief moment, I can reshape what I say to focus more on the subtle, higher-level ideas adult readers are likely to have about the text. When I do, I've noticed that children are far more likely to share more sophisticated inferences when it is their turn to apply the strategy.

2. **Think aloud about reading strategies and ideas that have broad applications, beyond today's book.** I'm working to focus my think-alouds on the kind of thinking that applies beyond the immediate text and assignment. I try, for example, to pause and consider whether the

inference I'm about to share is important to students for any book besides this one.

3. **Use books rich in ideas that inspire think-alouds about content that matters in the world, that causes students to respond with passionate attention or even action.** I try to ask myself if the inference I share in a think-aloud has implications for how children might think, believe, and act in their world. For example, if I read books that address issues of general social concern, such as those by Eve Bunting, Patricia Polacco, Jacqueline Woodson, and Cynthia Rylant, I find that children respond more fervently and focus on ideas rather than only on events and characters. These topics correspond to issues children face in their lives and in the world.

Figure 6.2 shows contrasting think-alouds based on *The Three Questions*—Ellin's first-day think-alouds and those she used on the second day, when she focused on using more sophisticated inferences and vocabulary.

Finally, we need to stress that there is no one right way to do think-alouds. For example, teachers can be equally effective making completely different inferences from the same book. In fact, since we are all different, our responses will and should be different. The more variety children are exposed to, the more apt they will be to infer broadly in their own reading. When we raise the level of the think-aloud so that meaty ideas are presented and children are given time for reflection and discussion, children have an opportunity to reach much further with their inferences and to be challenged and inspired by ideas.

Thinking About Instruction: Conferring

Conferences are lifeblood to comprehension teaching. It is through conferences that we come to understand each child's strengths and needs. In conferences, we tailor instruction to promote new learning

Figure 6.2

Less-Developed and More Highly Developed Think-Alouds

Less-developed think-aloud

After reading to page 2 where Nikolai first poses his three big questions
I'm inferring that the boy has a special kind of power that allows him to communicate with these animals. I've always wished I could do that and I infer that these are his friends and that it doesn't matter that they're animals and he's human.

More highly developed think-aloud

After reading to page 2
When I first started to read about Nikolai, I realized that he has certain qualities that I wish I had. When I read about how serious and pensive he is, how focused on trying to understand the most important questions in life at such an early age, I realize that there is something in his serious manner that we might all learn from as we try to understand the world. I realize that Nicolai is providing a model of being a thoughtful person interested in important questions in the world.

After reading to page 7 where Nikolai's three friends generate answers to his questions based on what is happening to them in the here and now
I'm inferring that Nikolai and his friends Gogol, Pushkin, and Sonya have been friends for a long time and trust each other.

After reading to page 7
When I read about Nikolai's friends' hasty responses to his important questions, I conclude that, even though we have good friends whom we trust, sometimes the answers to the most important questions in our lives come from ourselves. I infer that the reason Nikolai is dissatisfied with their responses is that he knows that the answers to such important questions should come from himself and his experiences rather than from his friends, no matter how much they mean to him.

Continues on next page

Less-developed think-aloud

After reading to page 13 just before Nikolai rescues the panda

I'm predicting (a type of inference) that Nikolai will be the one to save the panda and her baby and that he will begin to think about the answers to his questions when he does.

More highly developed think-aloud

After reading to page 17 after the panda and her baby are reunited in Leo's home

I'm predicting that because Nikolai played such an important role in the rescue of the panda and her baby that he will begin to realize that his questions may be unanswerable or, if there are answers, they will have to come from him thinking about his actions and how those actions help him understand *When is the best time to do things? Who is the most important one?* and *What is the right thing to do?*

I also infer that, though our questions may be different from Nikolai's, this author and Leo Tolstoy, the author of the story that inspired this book, are trying to tell us that it is very important that we have big questions about how the world works and that it is one of our jobs in life to consider the elusive answers to those questions. I think that when we ask those questions and seek the answers, we may be more able to help others, just the way Nikolai did.

and new levels of comprehension at the moment a child demonstrates a need. Much as we might like to believe that small-group instruction can meet individual needs, there is no substitute for one-on-one conversation. Conferences are far more than nice chats about the book the child is reading. Because they help identify specific needs, they are a vital tool to help children become increasingly independent in using everything from skills like decoding or use of quotations to more abstract concepts like inferring. Effective teachers use conferences to assess a child's use of what has been taught and to lead them to explore new applications and challenges. Teachers conclude conferences with a discussion about exactly what the child will attempt next in her reading or writing.

Into the Classroom—Primary

Back the next day in the third-grade classroom at Stemley Road School, Ellin again pulled out *The Three Questions*. This time her primary objectives were to have the children begin to infer in their own reading and to weave conferences into the forty-five-minute period set aside for independent reading.

After Ellin's second think-aloud with *The Three Questions*, she lowered her voice to the children around her on the rug. It never hurts to increase the drama. "You all are so smart and you've done so well paying attention to my use of inferring. I think you're ready to work on inferring in your own books. What d'ya think?"

There were lots of enthusiastic nods, punctuated by a few defiant "Nopes!"

Ellin chose three children who had indicated they were ready and had them come up to her. "Okay, you guys are ready to focus on your own inferences, but what books are you going to read? Are you going to read the easiest book you have at your table? I don't think that's the kind of book that's going to inspire a lot of inferences. Maybe you can choose the book you're reading that has the most interesting ideas, one that different readers would interpret differently."

After sending the first three back to their tables, Ellin had the rest of the children move closer to her on the floor. "Now watch them! I think they're going to choose books that are particularly good for inferences, books where the authors leave a lot for their readers to decide. I think you're going to see them go back to their tables and read with real focus."

Of course, the first three could hear Ellin. They self-consciously chose their books, then settled down to read, becoming the perfect models for how to get started independently.

"Look at them," Ellin whispered loudly. "They're showing us what great readers do when they are about to try something new and challenging. Did you notice how Tiffany got out sticky notes? That's amazing. I think she may be getting ready to mark the places in her book where she infers. I love when that happens. I didn't even think to tell them they could do that, but Tiffany figured that out and she's ready to roll."

The other two quickly grabbed pads of sticky notes from the materials baskets in the center of the tables.

"I wonder if anyone else thinks they might be ready for independent reading. I don't know," she teased. "You may not be ready yet and that's okay, just let me know." About twenty enthusiastic hands shot up. "Okay, if you really think you're ready, you can go back to your tables."

Ellin deliberately injected a bit of ceremony into this first "send-off," wanting the children to take seriously the task of focusing on their thinking in a new way. Though the ceremony differs across grade levels, she always wants to raise the anticipation about using a new strategy to increase excitement and concentration.

When all the children were reading, she stood back to observe who was working well independently, who might need a little boost, and who had sharpened a pencil five times in the first three minutes. Ellin asked the children not to interrupt while she was observing. If someone forgot, she raised a hand to indicate she wasn't yet available. She wanted to give the kids time to get settled and avoid jumping right in and responding to their questions. Often they solve small problems on their own. Then the conferences are more purposeful and focused.

On this day, Ellin spotted Chrystal, a tiny girl with white-blond hair reaching down her back, as she moved around the room searching for a book. She was one of the last in the group to say she was ready to begin inferring on her own.

When Chrystal finally took her seat, Ellin went over and knelt beside her. "Chrystal, I noticed that you were working hard to find the perfect book to read today. Can you tell me a little about that?"

"Just lookin' for a good book."

"Okay, what did you come up with?"

"This." Chrystal pointed to the picture book *The Other Side* by Jacqueline Woodson.

"Great, I love that book, Chrystal. Why did you choose it?"

"Well, I think because Ms. McKay loves it and she has read it to us a bunch of times."

"How do you usually choose books?" (See Figure 6.3 for tips on book selection.)

"Just if I like the look of them," Chrystal responded candidly.

"Chrystal, you know the last couple days we've been talking about how readers infer when they read; how they know more in their minds and hearts than the author puts on the page?"

"Yeah."

"You've heard this book before and you chose it because Ms. McKay likes it so much. I'd love to see how you're beginning to infer in it. I'm going to read the first few pages to you and as I do, I want you to pay attention to the voice inside your mind and listen to any inferences you may have."

(In conferences focused on comprehension strategies, I usually don't ask the children to read aloud to me. Often, the book they're reading to practice comprehension strategies is challenging, at least at the idea level, and I'm concerned that if children read aloud, my focus will start to shift to helping them identify words and read fluently. On other days, I begin with a child reading aloud and focus on issues related to word identification and decoding. I find that if I try to do

Figure 6.3

Helping Children Make Thoughtful
Book Selections Independently

Teachers should provide explicit instruction to guide children in their book selections throughout the year. When creating lessons on book selection, it's important to model and use demonstrations to emphasize the following points.

Text is most readable when children

- Have schema for text content and author.
- Have schema for text format, print style, layout, density, and illustrations and graphs.
- Can apply a comprehension strategy to leverage more meaning from both narrative and expository text.
- Have had prereading experiences, such as hearing a read-aloud from the text and/or discussion about the text content or format.
- Have a need and/or desire to comprehend.
- Have a history of or passion for reading.

Variety is critical if kids are to develop a wide range of interests and the capacity to move seamlessly from genre to genre.

- Children need to read in a variety of genres.
- Children need to read text that challenges them in different ways, in both surface and deep structure learning.
- Children keep track of their choices to ensure variety and enable teachers to see at a glance whether they are reading high-quality text that crosses a variety of genres and levels.
- Teachers need to ensure that children gradually assume responsibility for selecting appropriate texts, then continue to interact with students about their selections throughout the year.
- Modeling is critical—at repeated intervals throughout the year, teachers should model ways in which they select and recommend books.
- Teachers can ask children to "field test" text—try a page or two, or a section; think aloud; use the five-finger rule (remembering to put a finger down not only if they come to a word they don't know, but also if an idea is confusing).

both, the conference runs long and is less effective—there is simply too much for the child to take in.)

Ellin read several pages, then paused to give Chrystal time to think. Chrystal rotated the book so she could see it better, took a breath, then let out the breath and shook her head. "No inferences."

"No problem. Sometimes readers don't infer until much later in the book," Ellin said, concerned Chrystal might not know what an inference was, especially since she was familiar with the book.

Ellin read three more pages, stopping at the point in the story where Annie, the white child, sits on a fence that divides the African American and Anglo sides of town and invites Clover, the black child, to sit next to her on the fence both have been forbidden to cross.

"Chrystal, as you listened to the voice inside your mind just then, did you become aware of anything you knew about this book that the author or illustrator didn't even put into it? Did you have any inferences?"

"Yep, she's going to get up on the fence and they're going to be friends."

Ellin faced a dilemma. If Chrystal had been unfamiliar with the story, this would have been a legitimate inference (in the form of a prediction), but she knew the story and was merely retelling what she knew would happen later.

"Okay, Chrystal, I remember the girls become friends in the end, too. I love to reread books because I get to think again about all the great things that happen to the characters. But, I also like to challenge myself and I have a challenge for you. When I reread, I work hard to listen to my inner voice tell me ideas about the book that I've never thought of, even if I've read the book before. I also like to think about ideas that even the author hasn't thought of. Here's your challenge: I'm going to go back to the beginning of the book and just slowly turn the pages without reading it because I know you know this story so well. You can stop me at any point and tell me an idea, an inference, that you never thought of before and that you think even the author or illustrator might not have thought of. Okay?"

Chrystal nodded. Ellin slowly turned the pages until Chrystal placed her hand on the page where Clover and Annie are seen with their mothers who are pulling them in opposite directions down a sidewalk.

"Here," Chrystal said. "I thought of a thing I never thought of before. I thought that lots of times it's the kids who get in trouble and do stuff wrong, but here in this page, it's the moms. Those moms are *making* their kids afraid of each other. They're making them hate each other. Ms. McKay said this book was from a long time ago when black and white people weren't liking each other, and I think the moms made it worse."

"Great, Chrystal! Now let's test it. Let's see if it really is an inference. Is the idea you just told me about the moms written on the page or shown on the illustrations?"

"No, I heard it in my head."

"Is it something that the author may or may not have thought about when she was writing this book?"

"I guess she could have thought of it, but I don't know."

"Okay, Chrystal, what just happened?" Ellin asked.

"I did an inference!"

"You absolutely did! Fantastic! Now the tricky part will be to see if the voice inside your mind continues to tell you inferences that are new to you and that the author may or may not have thought of when she wrote this book. Okay, you inferred in this book when I was turning the pages and pausing for you to think about the ideas in it. How did that work for you?"

"I think it was easier to get an inference because I wasn't just thinking about the words. I was thinking about new stuff that was in there," Chrystal said.

"That's really interesting, Chrystal. Maybe other kids would benefit from hearing how you approached inferring in a book you already knew. Would you be willing to share with the rest of the kids during our reflection time today in case that might be helpful to them?"

"Can I bring this book?"

"You bet! Now, what challenge would you like to take on as you continue to be the kind of reader that infers? What will you do when I leave today?"

"I'm gonna keep reading *The Other Side,* and I'll see if my mind tells me any more inferences."

"Great, and what will you do to capture your inferences so that you can remember and share them with other kids who love this book?"

"I'll sticky note them."

"That will work, Chrystal. I'm about to leave now to confer with other children. Is there anything else I can do to help you?"

"Nope." She was already turning the pages.

The conference with Chrystal could have gone in several different, equally productive directions. If Chrystal had continued to struggle, Ellin might have done a think-aloud or two in the conference, which would have allowed her to observe more inferences and possibly try her own. She might have tried a text that was unfamiliar to Chrystal to see if a new text would have inspired inferences or reused *The Three Questions.* Or, if others shared the same problem, she might have called Chrystal to an invitational group to work on the issue together.

When conferring (see Figure 6.4 for key ideas) the teacher's job is to listen intently and understand each child's current use of skills and strategies, and to get to know their passions, needs, and interests. In kicking off conferences, teachers may identify children who are struggling and work with them more intently for the first few days of the strategy study. They may require the most support to work independently, but investing time in them early will pay off down the line. During the course of a four- to six-week strategy study, there will be an opportunity to confer with all the children and to tailor conferences to their specific needs. Ultimately, the

Figure 6.4

Key Ideas on Conferring

Conferring permits the teacher to help a child focus intensively on a skill or strategy and, through conversation, indicate ways the child might use the strategy to reach the next level of understanding.

The teacher

- ensures ample time every day to confer with students

- assesses the child's progress in applying a skill or strategy independently

- avoids the temptation to confer about a number of different teaching points and keeps the conference focused and purposeful

- provides immediate, focused instruction that responds directly to what the child has shared or demonstrated in the conference

- is explicit about how the strategy or skill discussed in a conference can be generalized beyond the current context

- and the child discuss and agree on a new challenge or direction in the child's reading or writing; they decide how the child will demonstrate the new level of skill in the next conference or by sharing in a reflection session

- focuses intently on the child throughout the conference and doesn't permit interruptions from other children or visitors in the classroom

- understands that conference times vary based on the needs of the child— some may be a short as 30 to 45 seconds, others as long as 5 to 7 minutes, depending on the child's needs

- keeps dated records that will help her remember the teaching point and the book the child is reading in each conference so she can follow up to check progress at the next conference

- reviews conference records later to look for patterns of shared need that may be addressed in a crafting session (whole group) or invitational group (small, needs-based group)

- may choose to announce that he will confer, on a given day, on deep structures (comprehension) or surface structures (word identification and fluency), allowing children to anticipate the type of conference and select text as well as skills or strategies to demonstrate in the conference

The child

- knows that conferring with the teacher means sharing his application of the skill or strategy most recently learned or one the teacher has asked to review

- keeps track of her progress and is prepared to share her thinking when the teacher comes to confer

- knows that he will share word identification and fluency skills in a surface structure conference and application of comprehension strategies in a deep structure conference;

- takes notes related to the new challenge he has decided, with the teacher, to work on following a conference, and keeps track of his progress on that challenge

- confers with peers to share application of a skill or strategy as well as to discuss and recommend books

- meets with peers who have similar needs to work on the application of a skill or strategy between conferences with the teacher

- works to solve problems independently as she reads or writes

teacher's role is to be agile and responsive to the insights gained from the conversation and to create personal horizons toward which each child can advance.

~ ~ ~

Teaching children to infer often begins with a journey into our own reading, stopping ourselves when we infer and analyzing our process as we do. We should pay attention to the conditions in which we infer and go about creating classroom structures that permit children to discuss, ponder, argue, restate, reflect, persuade, and write about what they read. And we must think about the most effective ways to entice children—especially those whose oral and written language is just developing—to express their inferences.

When Ellin read "Celebration of the Human Voice," she wrote about it, shared it in her workshops, and talked about it with Susan. She saw how her inferences changed over time and how through the process of thinking about it, the piece became woven into other life experiences such as her mother's last days. It took on a unique and personal meaning for her because she slowed down and took time to ponder.

We build meaning by doing something with the text, as Ellin did. Whether that something is a quick, almost subconscious prediction, a conscious sense of outrage and indignation, a vigorous discussion in a book club, a quiet conversation with a friend, or a letter to the editor, to infer is to make text our own—to create our own meaning.

Certainly much that children read in classrooms is never sculpted and shaped, discussed and written about. Much of what we read passes through the lenses of our eyes to our brains, is comprehended superficially, and never considered again. However, as teachers we need to make sure children have the cognitive agility to consider what is worth savoring, what portion of a text has the potential to change a life, what merits discussion, and what should be lingered over, argued about, and anchored in memory, because to comprehend only literally would be too great a loss.

Key Ideas for Comprehension Strategy Study

Drawing Inferences from Text

- Inferring is the process of creating a personal and unique meaning from text. It involves a mental process that combines information gleaned from the text and relevant prior knowledge (schema). The reader's unique interpretation of text is the product of this blending.

- When proficient learners infer, they create a meaning that is neither stated explicitly in the text nor shown in the illustrations. The process implies that they actively search for or become aware of implicit meaning.

- Inferring may cause the reader to read more slowly, reread sections, converse, write, or draw to better understand the content.

- Inferences may be more thoroughly developed if the reader pauses to reflect and consider multiple interpretations and perspectives.

- When they infer, proficient readers:
  - draw conclusions from text
  - make reasonable predictions as they read, then test and revise those predictions as they read further
  - create dynamic interpretations of text that they adapt both while they read and after they read
  - use the combination of background knowledge and explicit information from the text to answer questions they have as they read
  - make connections between conclusions they draw and other beliefs or knowledge, and use the inferences to extend and adapt existing knowledge
  - arrive at insight after struggling to understand complex concepts
  - make critical or analytical judgments about what they read

- When proficient readers infer, they are more able to remember and reapply what they have read, create new and revise existing background knowledge, discriminate and critically analyze text and authors, and engage in conversation and/or other analytical or reflective responses to what they read.

- Proficient readers revise their inferences based on the inferences and interpretations of other readers.

■ A wide variety of interpretation is appropriate for fiction and poetry; a narrower range of interpretation is typical for nonfiction text. Teachers should allow great latitude for inferences, provided that the readers can defend their inferences with a description of relevant, prior knowledge and specific text they have read.

CHAPTER 7

Bringing Text to Life

Using Sensory and Emotional Images to Enhance Comprehension

The Cough

Our young father walked Ash Alley whistling "Rescue the Perishing," but already he carried mine tunnels home in his black-streaked breath. It was like first sleet against an attic window. My mother would look at him, her lips a line of impatience and fear. "Your lungs will soon be stone," she said. "It's good money, Dorse. It's our only money."

Some of the men who stopped at our house to see my father had tongues like fish that stuck out between words. Gray-faced, shoulders bony, they all seemed to cave in. My mother would leave the room, her lips thinner than ever, but the cough followed her across the linoleum, down the cellar steps, hunkered close when she planted sage and primrose. The cough was like a child. It was always hungry. It demanded attention. It woke us up at off times and sat in the good chair by the window. In the winter, it trailed behind my father like a peacock feather on a woman's hat.

One summer he told us we were on a planet going nowhere fast. He made a model he called an orrery, and showed us how the heavens worked. The center was bright and hung there like one of my mother's peony blossoms. "That there's what pushes it," he said. "And that's what made the coal."

We looked at him and nodded, but we had our own ideas about what made it go. We could hear it behind the least little thing.

— Harry Humes, in *Micro Fiction: An Anthology of Really Short Stories*

Susan's Reflections

Scenes unfold in my mind. I see a good-looking, raw-boned man, whistling as he walks down an alley. Quickly that carefree image changes. At "he carried mine tunnels in his black-streaked breath," the mood shifts from benign to menacing. I want to know what "Rescue the Perishing" sounds like, the tune, the words. At first Ash Alley seemed a lane. Now it is a coal-grimed road, crowded with tired, dirty miners. I picture the big, lumbering elevator, and hear the clank and squeal of metal as it descends into the bowels of the earth, day after day, taking men on an ominous ride into a Hades of heat, darkness, and danger. I imagine a deep mine tunnel, men with headlamps, strained faces blackened with coal dust.

At "my mother would look at him, her lips a line of impatience and fear," I see a tired young mother, growing thinner and meaner from the daily grind of making ends meet and pushing away the fear she feels as she hears the changes in her husband's voice, the coming of a cough that will not go away. She knows where he's headed. She looks at him carefully, worry written on her face, lips tense and tight, wanting a change for him so that she can sleep at night without the fear of having to raise the kids alone. "Your lungs will soon be stone," she spits. I hear her dismay and his unanswerable reply, "It's good money, Dorse. It's our only money." There are no options for this young couple. They are trapped.

Another scene: I picture a small, white clapboard house in grave need of a paint job and old miners who stop by and sit in the kitchen at a metal table with a chipped Formica top. Their teeth are yellow, their tongues sharp. Already they are dying of black lung. Their gray faces are the color of death, their thin, worn-out bodies the shadow of what they once were, of what the father still is. What a price they've paid. Dorse can't bear to see them. She walks away, her lips tighter.

And always there is the cough: "It was like first sleet against an attic window . . . The cough followed her across the linoleum, down the cellar steps, hunkered close when she planted sage and primrose. The cough was like a child. It was always hungry . . . It woke us up at off times and sat in the good chair by the window . . . It trailed behind my father like a peacock feather on a woman's hat." I hear the sharp rap of sleet hitting glass; I experience the discomfort of being weighted down by an inescapable burden; I feel the unending responsibility of caring for a child; I see a beautiful, brightly colored peacock feather on an old-fashioned hat, an odd juxtaposition. Vivid, incongruous. The cough becomes a living thing, an enemy, but also an ally, because "it's our only money." The coarse rasping sound is everywhere.

My father had a cough, too. "Pneumonia picked up in Africa," he was told. It started soft and then became harsher, more insistent. I wouldn't see him for six months and when I did he would be "fine," but the cough would still be there. I wasn't alarmed: just a persistent cold, a remnant of the pneumonia. It would be okay. I think I knew something was not quite right. My mother thinks Dad's leukemia was caused by exposure to chemicals in the plants he worked in over his career. They weren't as careful when he started out in the 1950s. "There was really nasty stuff, Sue," she says. "We'll never know," she goes on, "but his parents lived to be almost a hundred. I just have this hunch." My father, who died at 77, becomes linked by his cough to the young father here.

In the third paragraph, there is a change. I learn more about the father. He is a man of intelligence, curiosity, and some education. He builds an orrery (I had to look up that word), a model of the solar system, for his children to show them "how the heavens worked." There's something wonderfully childlike about his excitement, his wanting to share this with his children. I see pipe cleaners, metal wire, papier-mâché planets, and a bright yellow sun in the center "like one of my mother's peony blossoms." I see the children bend closer to their father and his creation. He tells them all he knows about how the sun makes coal. His story is punctuated by his cough. They are enthralled by what he has to say. Yet they view things differently. They can't buy into his enthusiasm. They know what makes their world go. It is his cough, the cough with which their father pays for their life and home, his quiet heroism and self-sacrifice, the bargain he makes with his own health and vitality to provide for his family. That is "what made it go."

In four short paragraphs, a movie unwinds, a grim, foreboding tale of a man's quiet heroism and the acute observations of a child.

~ ~ ~

On my daily walk on the trails near my house, this story won't leave me. When I read it earlier, it was set squarely in the mountains of West Virginia, a coal-mining area not far from where I lived as a child in southeastern Ohio, where my father worked at an aluminum plant by the Ohio River. It was rural and tough, an area with out-houses and, in many areas, without electricity. As I walk, a different image comes to me. I'm not sure why. Perhaps it is the word *orrery* that takes me to England. That word is unusual for an American to use, especially a miner who probably wouldn't be well educated. Now I picture an English coal-mining town, Birmingham or Leeds. Instead of a white clapboard shack, I see a line of brick row houses blackened by coal dust. I see a large tailings hill outside the town. I hear thick accents. The young father and mother look the same in my mind, but the place feels urban poor, not rural poor. On my walk, my set of images went through a metamorphosis because of the word *orrery*. I look it up again and see that it comes from "Charles Boyle, 1731, 4th Earl of Orrery" (Webster's Seventh *New Collegiate Dictionary*), a British lord no doubt. My images now are set more squarely in the north of England.

I carry an amalgam of images of "The Cough." The story starts to feel like an old friend. I come to know the characters and even to care about them. It is both soothing in its familiarity and heartrending in its personal, yet universal, message of people's willingness to sacrifice for those they love.

~ ~ ~

The sensory and emotional images that surface as we read are a kind of Impressionism of the mind. The images are like dabs of paint on a canvas. Each brushstroke is meaningless unless the viewer stands back to regard the whole painting. In the same way, each image created in the mind while reading has little meaning unless we associate it with words on the page and with other images and memories in our lives.

If we stand very close to an Impressionist painting, we see a blur of dots and abrupt brushstrokes that leave us with no sense of form or character. As we move back, we gain perspective and clear images emerge for our interpretation. When we view the painting for a prolonged time or return for a second look, our response deepens to something more profound and lasting. When we remember it or try to describe it later, the meaning is more fully developed. Similarly, the images that spring to mind as we read are part of understanding the whole text, but the perspective gained from rereading, writing about, or discussing that text enhances the meaning and adds to the images from the first reading.

An image, like a paint stroke, may mean little alone but become a memory associated with a text in the mind of a reader. "The Cough" is multifaceted. I hear my father's cough juxtaposed with the young father's. I feel a double sadness. I see coal-mining towns that I have driven through in Appalachia, as well as early-twentieth-century English mining towns that D. H. Lawrence describes in novels like *Women in Love* and *The Rainbow*. I have not one motion picture in my mind from this piece but two, and I know that other images will form if I read "The Cough" again years hence. My sensory images change and they make this piece my own.

Edgar Degas, *Uncle and Niece* (1875, oil on canvas, 39¼ x 47³⁄₁₆ in., Mr. and Mrs. Lewis L. Coburn Memorial Collection, 1933.429. Photography © The Art Institute of Chicago. Used with permission.)

Ellin's Reflections

I collect museum catalogs—the vast, heavy inventories of exhibits I have seen and want to remember. My collection began in 1982. Jan Dole and I spoke at an International Reading Association conference in Chicago. Jan introduced me to the Art Institute of Chicago and, after that introduction, I saw little of the conference. The book Jan gave me is filled with beautiful representations of Impressionist paintings from the museum's large collection.

It is open on my desk now to a painting, *Uncle and Niece*, by Edgar Degas (Portraits of Henri and Lucy de Gas). The fragments of this painting—a child's ear, papers lying on the table, a window with green just outside it—are indistinct and appear unfinished. The vibrancy and meaning of the painting, like the meaning of a text, become clear only after considering and reconsidering the whole.

The child and her uncle are dressed in black that blends into one garment as the girl pauses behind his chair. They both look toward the viewer, but in different directions, as if their minds are occupied by different thoughts, though they are within a foot of each other. Their dress and mood seem somber. Have they just experienced a loss? Each seems accustomed to the presence of the other, but not completely comfortable with it. There is a resignation in the red around the uncle's eyes and a wistful boredom in the tilt of the child's head. According to the catalog, she is an orphan, he a bachelor raising his brother's child.

In looking at the painting, I hear the rustle of his newspaper, smell smoke from the cigar he holds in his left hand, feel the smooth, curved wood of the chair the child leans tentatively against and the chafing of her neck under her stiff white collar. There is longing implied in both sets of eyes—perhaps that is what occupies them at this moment captured by Degas. There is an acceptance in the still air around them. They define each other's life now.

Creating Sensory Images

Paintings like these conjure images from the senses and from emotions. When we view a painting a second or third time, new images and meanings are added to our existing impressions. So it is with images from text. Images originate in our senses and our emotional fabric. And they are altered each time we read or reflect on a text, extending and animating what we read. Text comes alive through the creation of sensory images. Those images take on a three-dimensional quality in our minds and connect us personally, often permanently, with the text.

Teachers know that students who struggle are often disengaged and don't choose to read outside school (or within, for that matter!). Creating images can be the conduit to student engagement and is, therefore, especially important for students who struggle. Yet, we can't take for granted that students create images spontaneously as they read. Many don't. They don't realize they should. The fact is many children spend a lot of time in front of screens—movie, television, video, and computer—where a vast array of images is provided for them. Unless their image-making capacities have been nurtured as young children (from being read to and told stories), they don't realize they have the ultimate computer between their ears and enormous capacity to create their own images. They need explicit instruction as they develop and trigger their image-making abilities.

You can help ensure that children create images by thinking aloud, early in the strategy study, about your own images and then asking the children to turn and talk to a neighbor or briefly sketch the images they have so far in the book. Then continue to think aloud, describing what you see, smell, taste, touch, and feel as you read. Be sure to include images from all the senses as well as your emotions—what we call "images of the heart." Images can be fleeting, so talk about which images you'll strive to remember. Emphasize that images change as a book progresses. Refer to the text frequently to show that the images are grounded in the book. Go the next step by saying something like, "Okay, now that I've described my images, I want to think about how they help me understand better." Then describe how the image enhanced your comprehension.

The bad news is that many children simply have not had experiences in creating images that they can sustain over the course of reading a book. They are not creating vivid, detailed images in their minds. The good news is that we can do a lot to remedy that problem by thinking aloud about our images and inviting children to talk about, write about, draw, or perform theirs.

Into the Classroom—Middle School

When Ellin was a staff developer in the Douglas County Schools, Enid Goldman, a teacher at Parker Vista Middle School, asked her to conduct a demonstration lesson on evoking images as part of a comprehension strategy study her eighth graders were beginning. Ellin decided to use a picture book, *Where the River Begins* by Thomas Locker, to help the students describe their images. *Where the River Begins* starts with a young boy asking where the river that runs near his house begins. With his brother, father, and grandfather, he explores the question and hikes to the river's source.

The morning of her visit to Parker Vista, Ellin awoke before five, tortured by her own sensory images of a class of eighth graders responding to the oral reading of a picture book. At Parker Vista she watched as twenty-five eighth graders shuffled into the room, dragging their feet over dirty linoleum, and flopped into their chairs, studies in lethargy.

Ellin asked herself, "Am I really going to read a picture book to these kids? Why did I agree to do this?" At the same time, the kids posed their own questions: "Who's she?" "Is she a sub?" The elementary teacher in Ellin marveled at the size of the feet that shot out in front of all those desks in rows. Ellin pulled out her picture book, anticipating the students' comments.

They did not disappoint, but their comments—"That book is for little kids," "C'mon, what's this for?" and "Do we have to sit here and listen to you read? We can read, you know"—lasted only a moment. Ellin removed the jacket from the book and held it close so none of the illustrations, each an original oil painting by the author, was visible. While the students concentrated on looking like they were not listening, Ellin read the whole book; then she reread a few pages before looking up and beginning to think out loud about the images Locker's words had created in her mind. She tried to be as detailed as possible in her think-aloud, and to include images from the hearing, tasting, touching, and feeling as well as seeing realms.

A few pages later Ellin invited the students to share their images. The offerings were pretty meager. Ellin glanced at Enid, who raised her eyebrows dispiritedly. She read on and again asked the students to describe the pictures that came to their minds, knowing that the propensity to create vivid images during reading correlates highly with overall comprehension.

Roberta raised her hand and said, "Well, I see them by the river, they're walking along and they have backpacks."

Ellin paused. "What are they wearing?"

"Ummm. Shorts."

"What color, length? Do they have belts on? Are they wearing hiking boots, hats? Do they have sunglasses on? Are the three dressed the same? Do they have T-shirts or sweatshirts?" As Ellin took a breath, the snickering died down.

"Oh . . ." Roberta said, as if she had never thought about elaborating her image. "Well, the grandfather is mostly bald and he's wearing, you know, those old army pants—fatigues, that's it—and the boys are around twelve and fourteen and the older one is mad at the younger one all the time. They have on shorts and tennis shoes, but their grandfather has told them—this wasn't in the book—that it was dumb to wear shorts and sneakers because their feet will get all wet and their legs will be all scratched up, but they didn't listen and now their feet are wet because the ground near the river is all marshy and stuff."

Roberta's was a perfect example of how images can be used to amplify the meaning in a book. She filled in shape, color, line, and composition. As she elaborated, her images became more detailed and enhanced her understanding of the characters. When she talked about the grandfather's reaction to the boys' clothing, Roberta made an important inference about their relationship. Other students followed with their images as Ellin challenged them to hear, touch, taste, smell, and pay attention to the emotional content of the images.

Mark raised his hand and began a little sheepishly, "Okay, I think that this grandfather maybe took this same hike when he was younger. Now he's, like, getting old and he wants his grandsons to see what he saw before he dies. That's really not in the book, but that's something my grandfather would do. Is that an image?" He paused.

"I'm making this up, you know."

"I know, Mark," Ellin said. "But that's just what you should do. You're taking time and creating images that take you deeper into the book. The more detailed your images, the more the book will stay in your memory. I'm impressed by how you brought the history of the grandfather into the story. Your emotional image allowed us to go back in time and imagine what would have led to the events in the book. Amazing. Do you do that a lot when you read, Mark?" Ellin asked.

"Uh. I'm not sure."

"When you go back to your own reading today, why don't you experiment with this. If it makes sense in your book, create images of the characters' histories, what might have led or motivated them to the place you are now in the book. I'll be curious and I'd like to ask you to share with the rest of the class what you learn by doing that."

The kids at Parker Vista created—some for the first time—images from their emotions as well as their senses. For many this was a breakthrough. They experienced the creative power they have as readers. They saw how words on the page can become recollections anchored in unforgettable images of their own making.

Into the Classroom—Primary

Sabrina Coan is a smart, dynamic, young teacher in Spartanburg, South Carolina. Her classroom is welcoming and functional, perfectly designed to encourage independence among the first graders who inhabit it. Sabrina loves children's literature and has a large classroom library of diverse titles that cross genres and grade levels, and she is undeterred when colleagues tell her that first graders are too young for some of the books she uses in crafting sessions.

One morning Sabrina decided to use Nobel Prize winner Toni Morrison's *Remember*, a book of photographs taken in schools and communities during the transition from segregated to integrated schools in the South, in a crafting session with her students. Writing in the first person, Morrison creates a compelling and intimate account of school desegregation that reads like a personal narrative.

Sabrina lingered over several of the photographs, including some that depicted segregated schools in which black children sit on benches in classrooms with no desks, dim lights, no books, and an old stove in the center of the room. She paused to think aloud about the heat and cold she imagined in those classrooms (too hot in spring and fall, too cold in winter), the gray lighting, the sound of the teacher's chalk on the blackboard, the smell of too many children crowded into the room, and the sadness she felt about the unequal treatment they were receiving.

At the end of Sabrina's crafting session, Ellin noticed that Ciella, a big-eyed girl with pigtails splayed in all directions and clasped with different color barrettes, remained on the floor for several minutes before moving to independent reading. When Ciella finally returned to her desk, a lively conversation about *Remember* was going on around her, but she didn't seem to notice. Ellin wondered if she wasn't feeling well, then noticed that rather than a book, she grabbed her writer's notebook from her desk. Ellin watched. Within moments, Ciella was writing furiously.

After conferring with several children, Ellin saw Ciella was still at work in her notebook, oblivious to anything around her. Ellin went over.

"Ciella, I'm so interested in what you're working on over here. I noticed you stayed on the floor after crafting for a long time. Since then you've been writing so much. What are you working on?"

"A picture," Ciella said without looking up.

"Honey, can you show me what you were writing in your notebook before you started your picture?"

Ciella turned back seven or eight pages, most of which Ellin could not have deciphered. "I just love to hear kids read their writing. Could you do that for me?"

In a tiny voice, Ciella began, "My granma was at that school. There were only blacks. She got cold always. Kids kicked her. She goed to whites' schools. There's where they kicked her. Her legs did get bloody. And she couldn't eat with the whites at the white school. She ate only outside even when it was raining. There was fire in front of the school once and some kids got on fire. Granma says no fires when I be here."

Sabrina joined Ellin. Ciella told them her grandmother had been sent to one of Spartanburg's first integrated schools and that a lot of discrimination went on, especially after black children were moved to formerly whites-only schools. Ciella told them that even now her grandmother refused to be in any building where there was a fire because the sounds and smells brought back the terror-filled days when protesters set fires in front of South Carolina's newly integrated schools. The picture she was working on depicted her grandmother with bloody legs.

To record the vivid images from her grandmother's stories, Ciella broke with the classroom routine and didn't follow her teacher's directions. The images from *Remember* as well as those Sabrina created during the crafting session compelled Ciella to write. It was as if Ciella had placed her grandmother right into the photographs, unearthing a potent mix of history and complex emotion.

When they talked about Ciella's work later, Ellin and Sabrina discussed how to replicate Ciella's powerful experience with the other children. Ciella had made them realize how urgent the need can be to capture images in writing that may disappear if left unrecorded, even for a short time. They resolved to integrate writing more liberally into reader's workshop. They discussed how important it was to let children have flexibility after crafting sessions to read *or* write, and what a breakthrough it was when children, of their own volition, felt compelled to write about something important to them.

They agreed that Sabrina's habit of recording her thinking on chart paper probably led to Ciella's independent writing at a time of day typically reserved for reading. Sabrina wanted to be even more explicit about when and why she recorded her thinking during reading. She decided to talk more about that with the children, and she asked Ciella to share how she had used writing and drawing to capture the images that swirled in her mind when she listened to *Remember*. They also concluded that the quality and quantity of Ciella's writing, which far exceeded anything Ciella had done previously, was because Ciella had *chosen*, rather than been told, to write.

They changed the reader's workshop structure in Sabrina's classroom to encourage children to read *or* write during the independent work time and changed the name from Independent Reading and Independent Writing Time to Composing (see Figure 7.1). Sabrina had two crafting sessions each morning—one for reading and one for writing. Now the children could write or read in the composing sessions that followed each crafting session. Sabrina made a simple, laminated card (kept in a basket at the center of the table) for each child on which they could mark each time they "composed" in reading and in writing with the understanding they needed to do five of each every week, but they could choose when.

This change came about from the simple act of watching and listening to one child. And it made a huge difference. The children began to use writing to explore their thinking about books they read. It didn't take the place of the children's daily writing, but became a natural way for children to capture their thinking about reading and to understand how integrally connected reading and writing are.

Figure 7.1

What Is a Composing Session?

A composing session provides

- A time each day for children to immerse themselves in reading challenging and interesting texts in a wide variety of genres, applying what they have been taught in crafting sessions.

- A time each day for children to write in writer's notebooks, collecting and gathering short pieces they may choose to develop into more formal pieces later.

- A time during which children develop written pieces into published pieces.

- An opportunity for children to select text that is interesting to them and appropriate, given their goals as readers.

- An opportunity for children to select writing topics about which they are passionately interested and that permit them to apply what they have recently learned in writing-focused crafting sessions and invitational groups.

- A time when individual children meet in conferences with their teacher to show their application of deep and surface structure strategies recently taught.

- A time when children read and write independently while their teacher hosts invitational groups.

- An opportunity for children to meet in pairs and small groups to discuss their application of recently taught deep and surface structure strategies in reading and writing.

- A time for children to meet in pairs and small groups to apply skills and strategies from crafting sessions on speaking and listening.

- An opportunity for children to meet in book clubs to discuss books they have read in common and ways in which they have applied deep and sur- face structure strategies in those texts.

- A time to plan (with the teacher in a conference or with other students) what a student will share and teach others during the reflection time.

Effective composing sessions share these characteristics:

- Children are deeply engaged in independent work—they read and write with intensity for long periods of time; they have been taught to do so.

- The classroom is filled with a sense of urgency—children are eager to apply what they have learned in crafting sessions and they work in texts that are challenging to them, at both the conceptual and the reading level.

- There is an atmosphere that supports rehearsal. Children experiment with the deep and surface structure strategies they have learned, taking risks in their reading and writing and spending a substantial amount of time rereading and rewriting.

- Children plan to demonstrate their new strategies for their teachers in conferences and alongside their classmates during reflection time.

- Children feel independent and trusted to make the right choices—they know it is up to them to choose the right text to read and the right writing topics. When they encounter problems, they know to attempt to solve them independently first.

- There is a spirit of camaraderie. Children eagerly share their insights with other children in small-group discussions and book clubs.

- Teachers move around the classroom engaged in a variety of tasks—observing the children at work, taking anecdotal notes and running records, conferring with individuals, encouraging experimentation, helping book clubs get started, and hosting invitational groups.

Into the Classroom—Intermediate

"We've just finished reading *Shiloh* and I'm not sure where I want to go next," Todd McLain told Ellin as they sipped coffee while his fourth graders were preparing for the holiday program with the music teacher. "I really want them to select their own novels and read independently, but I know I can't read all of them and I don't know how I'm going to know if they are comprehending—or even reading them!"

Todd began their first conversation by telling Ellin he was feeling overwhelmed. He was in his second year of teaching, his first year in fourth grade. He had been tucked into an improvised and rather dismal interior room at Cottonwood Creek Elementary in the suburban Cherry Creek school district. No windows and only a flimsy partition separated his class from the next fourth grade. His head was full of creative ideas; his desk was stacked with incomplete paperwork.

As they talked, Ellin learned that Todd's class had read *Shiloh* as a group, taking turns reading orally to the whole group, discussing the book as they went, and completing independent projects from a list of activities at the end of the unit. As he talked about it, he grew more uncomfortable. The whole process had taken too long. Some children didn't pay attention as their classmates read. Others had little personal connection to the book. Others seemed to have a difficult time following the plot. A few shared very sophisticated interpretations. Todd wished more children had found depth and meaning in the book. Those whose final projects revealed thoughtful effort were few and far between. Todd described a lethargy most students had shown toward their projects.

"The worst part of it," Todd began, and Ellin knew what was coming, "is that during *Shiloh*, I didn't feel like I was teaching reading, and I'm beginning to realize these kids really need it. I've always heard that kids learn to read in the primary grades and read to learn in the intermediate grades. Now I realize that they are still very much learning to read, and I've got to teach that. I'm not sure if discussing one novel with the group is the kind of teaching they need. I want them to choose their own books next time, but I've got to have an instructional focus."

Two weeks later, after several crafting sessions and demonstrations about selecting books and a great deal of book selection support from Ann Zimmer, the school's library media specialist, each student had a novel to fly (read) and one in the hangar (a fallback in case the one chosen proved inappropriately easy, difficult, or uninteresting).

They set an instructional focus: Todd decided to undertake a comprehension strategy study on evoking images during reading. He had noticed that too many of his students didn't stick with a book long enough to develop an interest in it, and if they did, didn't notice much more than the most literally stated events. There had to be a way, he reasoned, to help them engage deeply in reading, immerse themselves in language, and create vivid interpretations.

Todd wanted the children to pay closer attention to their reading, to make the characters and events real in their minds, and to be able to share their interpretations with others. He knew he couldn't just tell them to engage deeply and create vivid images; he had to model explicitly how he creates images as he reads. He knew that, over time, they would need to take responsibility for doing the same thing.

The crafting sessions in the early weeks of the strategy study focused on thinking aloud. With the class gathered around him, Todd read from a wide variety of texts: picture books, *National Geographic* magazine, poems, even the social studies textbook. As he read, he paused to think aloud about his mental images, both sensory and emotional. He included lots of detail in his descriptions and emphasized how pausing to stand back and reflect on his images helped him understand the text better. He talked about how his images changed as he read further in each text and how his images helped him create his own meaning for the text.

He thought out loud about how fiction and poetry gave him more latitude in creating images and forming interpretations than the social studies text, but how visualizing events from the westward expansion chapter made it seem more real, almost like a movie in his mind. He talked about how being aware of his spontaneously formed images and purposely forming other images helped him comprehend and engage more fully in what he read. He stopped to think aloud when the images ceased, pondering reasons for the break in comprehension.

During these weeks the children gradually assumed responsibility for monitoring, paying attention to, and elaborating on their own mental images as they read, marking the text with sticky notes when they became aware of an image, and marking again when that image changed as they read further. They began to differentiate between sensory and emotional images and talked in pairs and small groups about the details of the images they saw and felt as they read.

The large-group sharing time at the end of most reader's workshops focused on how awareness of images deepens comprehension and engagement. The students talked about how being aware of mental images helped them experience the detail in the books they read. They told stories about rereading sections with a particular image in mind to see how their comprehension changed. They laughed at how wildly different students' images were about the same text.

One morning, toward the end of the sharing session, Todd looked up from a conference to see Kent with a pencil sketch in front of him on the floor where other class members had gathered around him. Kent seemed to be deliberating about whether to share.

On numerous occasions Kent had declared his aversion to anything having to do with reading. When visiting teachers came to the room, Kent was quick to tell them how much he hated to read. In fact, he had spent many days at the beginning of the school year avoiding reading altogether. Now he actually seemed to want to share.

"Kent," Todd looked at him curiously, "what's that paper in front of you?"

"I don't know. Something I drew." A long pause followed. Kent looked down.

"I can't really see from here. Can you tell us about it?" Todd asked.

"It's from *Where the Red Fern Grows.*" Kent stared at the drawing of one of the dogs from the novel. "I don't like to talk about images, so I drew mine."

"That's cool," Todd replied. "That means you had a really strong image."

When Todd and Ellin huddled after the fourth graders trooped off to lunch, they knew they had to build on Kent's idea. "Is there life beyond sticky notes?" Todd laughed. "There have got to be other ways for these kids to mark and express their images."

Undoubtedly there were others in the room who would love to sketch or paint their images from the books they were reading. Todd was concerned about those who were reluctant to draw and preferred to discuss the images.

"Okay, we know that it's going to help their comprehension if we can get them to stand back and be aware of the images they have while they're reading," Ellin said. "Most of them are really doing that now. We also know that, if we can get them to express the images somehow, they will develop them even further. Kent drew his. Other kids are less comfortable with drawing.

"And I have serious questions about all the projects we ask kids to do. I'm sure I wrote two hundred literature units with all kinds of so-called creative projects for kids when I had my own classroom. At best they were glorified book reports. I was only asking them to retell, albeit in a creative form, what they read. I was asking them to report on the book, not on their thinking about the book. Maybe the kids were slightly more interested in doing them than a traditional book report. We give them this stuff so *we* have something to grade. But I don't think it helps them become better readers or thinkers. We need to get kids creating written, oral, artistic, or dramatic responses that show their thinking about the books they read. So I guess the question becomes, what are *all* the ways we can encourage them to describe their thinking about books?"

They decided to create four "capturing thinking" areas that the children could use throughout the year during all of the strategy studies.

Todd established four small areas near the corners of his classroom: the theater, book talk zone, artist's studio, and writer's den. Each area had limited space and provided different materials students could use to express images (their thinking) that came from reading their own books. Todd set aside a thirty-minute time slot during the composing portion of reader's workshop two to three days a week when the students could choose which area to work in to capture their thinking. (See Appendix B, Thinking Rubric, for a way to have students rate the quality of their own thinking.)

The theater corner was designed for groups of children who had read the same book or poem to dramatize images (or any other strategy, connections, questions, inferences, etc.) from the text. The area included a small staging area and chairs in a semicircle. There were long sheets of chart paper to use for scenery backdrops, markers, and a box of fabric scraps. Copies of poems, allegories, and picture books were available so that small groups could have a common reading experience. The theater corner could accommodate four actors and up to four audience members.

The book talk zone consisted of six chairs clustered around a small, beat-up table Todd found in the school's storage area. A cast-off table cloth was thrown over it and a small lamp provided a softer light. Up to six children could gather there to discuss images from their books. A basket of pretzels and a carton of juice and cups were available as a way to make students' visits to the book talk zone authentic and more intimate.

The artist's studio had different sizes of unlined paper, markers, pencils, crayons, oil pastels, watercolors, brushes, and blank paper. The class easel was set up in a corner and the walls in the area were stripped of everything so that paintings could be hung in the area. Children who did not want to paint at the easel took art materials back to their desks.

The writer's den had all the equipment needed by writers—different kinds of paper, staplers, hole punchers, pencils, pens, lined and unlined paper, and so forth. As written responses to books accumulated, they were framed with construction paper and hung around the den, letting students read the responses of other students, as well as write their own.

Todd introduced each area by dividing the class into four groups and stationing them in each area of the room while he read aloud scenes from Cynthia Rylant's *Appalachia*. He paused and asked each group to begin by sharing images with the other members of the response options.)

erformed a theatrical interpretation of the work to represent their images with paint, k talk group shared and expanded upon the writer's den, images were recorded and process each day for four days until all of f how each area would operate. After the talked about the rough spots: What addi- d in the area, how to involve students who ndle those who tended to dominate, how linked to the book, and whether to share

strategy study, most of the kinks had been thinking" areas. Todd was able to assess nd to draw important conclusions about hension.

s required time and effort at the outset. resources have to be gathered, organized, and introduced, but the procedures for using each area had to be amended several times. The class finally formed committees to draw up procedures for each area, and in time, the four areas became part of the everyday fabric of the classroom—not so much an activity as a means

Figure 7.2

Beyond Reporting on the Book:
How Children Can Record Their Thinking *About* Books

Written means to share thinking about a book:

- Thinking notebooks—children record their strategy use in a notebook and comment on how the strategy helped them better understand the text.

- Sticky notes to show strategy use in the text. These may be lifted so the teacher or other students can review them.

- Double-entry journals containing quotes from the text followed by the child's thinking about the quotes.

- Fluency responses—writing everything the child thinks while reading a short text or excerpt.

- Venn diagrams to show inference or how thinking overlaps (the intersecting area is the inference; the outer circles show the background knowledge and text sources for the inference).

- Column charts to compare thinking for several rereadings of an excerpt. Children may use two, three, or four columns so their thinking on two, three, or four consecutive readings can be recorded adjacent to one another.

- Letters to other readers and authors about a child's thinking/use of a strategy and how that strategy helped the child better understand a book.

- Highlighting text to show where a strategy was used.

- Story maps/webs to show thinking about important themes/topics. The theme may be reported on one "branch" and the child's use of the strategy on "subbranches."

- Transferring a text excerpt to a transparency. A teacher or child can use a wipe-off marker to show strategy use. This can be done in crafting or reflection sessions or invitational groups.

- Coding text to show use of one or more strategies in the text—for example, DI = Determining Importance, ? = Question, IN = Inference.

- Timelines to show how a child's thinking changes over time.
- Bar and line graphs to show changes in frequency of strategy use over time.

Artistic means to share thinking about a book:

- Sketching images and other manifestations of thinking during reading.
- Group depictions of text concepts and use of strategies during reading. These can be on long sheets of butcher paper with children's images recorded in a circular fashion around each side of the rectangle.
- Artistic metaphors—creating a visual metaphor for thinking during reading.
- Artistic timelines to show changes in thinking over time.
- Photographs of the mind—quick images from particular moments in a text.

Oral means to share thinking about a book:

- Four-way share (clockwise share), typically at a table or desk grouping.
- Think-pair-share—begin with pairs, refine thinking in fours, eights, and so on.
- Book clubs and literature circles to focus on strategy use and how it enhanced understanding.
- Turn and talk—a brief oral interchange on a focused topic, usually in the middle of a crafting session or during a composing session.
- Large- and small-group sharing—learning to take time to think in front of a group.
- Notice and share—observing demonstrations, fish bowl, and so forth.
- Strategy study groups in which children gather to experiment with a strategy in a shared text.

Dramatic means to share thinking about a book:

- Any student-created dramatic representations of students' use of a strategy, their thinking about a book, or an excerpt from a book.

for expressing and exploring the meaning of books. The children's work from each area was sent home following each comprehension strategy study, providing parents with a glimpse into the authentic ways children in Todd's classroom represented what they understood when they read.

~ ~ ~

We have all walked into a movie made from a favorite book and been overcome with disappointment. They just didn't get it right. It's hard to stay seated. The visual images are too far from those we carried in our minds—and cherished—as we read.

Boris Pasternak's *Doctor Zhivago* and Katherine Anne Porter's *Ship of Fools* are two of Susan's favorite novels: books that create poignant, tangible, gritty visual images. For Susan, Omar Sharif and Julie Christie were perfectly cast as Yuri and Lara. They captured the passion, the complexity of the characters, and the era depicted in Pasternak's epic work. Her strong mental images were confirmed, even enhanced, by that movie.

In the film version of *Ship of Fools*, however, her images were thwarted. Among other things, the older, too-brittle Vivien Leigh didn't work as Mrs. Treadwell, and the blonde, by then stocky Simone Signoret was miscast as the Spanish Condesa. The movie destroyed Susan's imaginary characters. Its portrayal clashed too much with what she carried in her mind. She couldn't finish watching it.

We all have examples of movies of favorite books that work or don't work for us, some that actually leave us with an "aha" of deeper understanding, others that dampen our imaginations and stifle interpretations. This is one reason why it is best to encourage children to read the book before they see the movie. Then they have a chance to create their own interpretation on their mind's screen before being given one on the big screen that will forever influence how they view the book.

In reading, our images take on a life of their own—a three-dimensionality, a meaning, a vividness—often without our consciously knowing it. The images are evolutionary, changing over time, developing organically like a tree whose trunk thickens and branches spread.

Sometimes we've read a book too quickly or without full attention. Years later we reread it only to be amazed at the depth and range of our response to words that before meant little to us. Or we read something and at first see only one aspect of it, but find our eyes opened through a discussion with others that gives us much more vibrant and profound images.

We have all known students who, as they grow older, begin to censor and limit their images as they read. They focus only on literal meanings—narrow, dictionary-type definitions of each word. It is as if they have been taught to think that only the dabs of paint and brushstrokes matter, though when they were younger, their imaginations were intact and full of vivid images. Too often in school kids have been conditioned to focus only on the literal interpretation of text. When that happens, something critical is lost. Understanding, attending to, and developing a personal awareness of the sensory and emotional images helps get children hooked on what they're reading and gives them the capacity to experience an added depth of interpretation.

When Susan read "The Cough," one image led to another. Scenes leapt into her mind. The word *orrery* caused her to change the setting from Appalachia to England in her imagination. The man's cough led her to her father's cough. That link heightened her sadness at the reality of the young miner literally giving his life to feed his family. If her experiences had been different, her images would have been different. The act of writing about them altered and enhanced them and forced her to slow down and think about the piece more carefully and thoughtfully. Yet meaning is dynamic. If down the road Susan rereads "The Cough," new images will be added onto the old.

For writers, images allow infinite possibilities of expression. For readers, the mental images derived from what they've read connect them personally to the texts, over time coalescing into the self-awareness, complexity, and depth that are at the core of being human.

Evoking Images

■ Proficient learners spontaneously and purposefully create images while and after they read. The images emerge from all five senses and the emotions and are anchored in the reader's prior knowledge.

■ Proficient readers create images to immerse themselves in rich detail as they read. The detail gives depth and dimension to the reading, engaging the reader and making the text more memorable.

■ Proficient readers use images to draw conclusions, to create distinct and unique interpretations of the text, to recall significant details, and to recall the plot/story or information long after it was read.

■ Images from reading frequently become part of the reader's writing.

■ Images from personal experience frequently become part of a reader's comprehension.

■ Proficient readers adjust their images as they continue to read to incorporate new information revealed through the text and new interpretations they develop while reading.

■ Proficient readers understand and can articulate how creating images enhances their comprehension.

■ Proficient readers adjust their images in response to the shared images of other readers.

CHAPTER 8

The Heart of the Matter

Determining Importance

Stockings

Henry Dobbins was a good man, and a superb soldier, but sophisti-
cation was not his strong suit. The ironies went beyond him. In
many ways he was like America itself, big and strong, full of good
intentions, a roll of fat jiggling at his belly, slow of foot but always
plodding along, always there when you needed him, a believer in the
virtues of simplicity and directness and hard labor. Like his country,
too, Dobbins was drawn toward sentimentality.

Even now, twenty years later, I can see him wrapping his girlfriend's pantyhose around his neck before heading out on ambush.

It was his one eccentricity. The pantyhose, he said, had the properties of a good-luck charm. He liked putting his nose in the nylon
and breathing in the scent of his girlfriend's body; he liked the memories this inspired; he sometimes slept with the stockings up against
his face, the way an infant sleeps with a flannel blanket, secure and
peaceful. More than anything, though, the stockings were a talisman
for him. They kept him safe. They gave access to a spiritual world,
where things were soft and intimate, a place where he might someday take his girlfriend to live. Like many of us in Vietnam, Dobbins
felt the pull of superstition, and he believed firmly and absolutely in
the protective power of the stockings. They were like body armor, he
thought. Whenever we saddled up for a late-night ambush, putting
on our helmets and flak jackets, Henry Dobbins would make a ritual

out of arranging the nylons around his neck, carefully tying a knot, draping the two leg sections over his left shoulder. There were some jokes, of course, but we came to appreciate the mystery of it all. Dobbins was invulnerable. Never wounded, never a scratch. In August, he tripped a Bouncing Betty, which failed to detonate. And a week later he got caught in the open during a fierce little firefight, no cover at all, but he just slipped the pantyhose over his nose and breathed deep and let the magic do its work.

It turned us into a platoon of believers. You don't dispute facts.

But then, near the end of October, his girlfriend dumped him. It was a hard blow. Dobbins went quiet for a while, staring down at her letter, then after a time he took out the stockings and tied them around his neck as a comforter.

"No sweat," he said. "The magic doesn't go away."

—Tim O'Brien, *The Things They Carried*

Two Readers' Reflections

My husband Paul and I sit in our library looking out to the Continental Divide. Mid-April, it's the thick of mud season in our mountain neighborhood. The dirt roads have turned to muck; rain in Denver is snow at our 7,500-foot elevation. Daffodils and crocuses bloom down the mountain; not so here until late May.

"Would you mind reading this? I'd love your thoughts on it." I hand him *Stockings* and leave the room.

Ten minutes later, he joins me in the kitchen.

"Powerful piece," he says, handing the paper my way. "I didn't have just one reaction. I thought about a lot of things. I was thinking about Henry Dobbins and how he reflected both bad and good things in America: a bit dumb and fat, naive, but also likable and simple. It was amazing the many different things the pantyhose represented: 'good luck charm,' 'flannel blanket,' 'talisman,' 'body armor,' 'the spiritual world.' It's almost magical that one item evoked so *many* things. There's also a powerful mix of the carnal and the spiritual in his reaction to the stockings. But the bottom line is that the stockings worked. Dobbins was just fine. Anyone else would have been killed, especially when you think he tripped a Bouncing Betty."

"What *is* a Bouncing Betty?"

"It's a type of land mine that jumps up into the air to explode, a real nasty little number. Treacherous. I'm intrigued by the name Henry Dobbins. Maybe it's the guy's real name, but it's a name like you'd give a big old horse. That was curious. It made me think about America being dumb, but lucky in the same way Dobbins is. We seem like a very blessed country, but sometimes I wonder why we're so blessed. This is a short piece, but there's a lot in it. Another thing is that, for all guys my age, there is deep ambiguity about Vietnam. You can't help but ask yourself if you *should* have been part of the defining conflict of our generation. If you didn't go to Vietnam, does that make you less of a man or less brave? In the past, if there was a war, men went and fought in it. That's what men did. With my dad being a general, I really felt that. There was something very courageous about going. The men who didn't would be missing out on something. They weren't part of the brotherhood. I remember a friend telling me about literally standing on the Friendship Bridge near Niagara Falls with a cheap suitcase in one hand and transistor radio in another. He would have kept going to Canada if he had a low draft number. He didn't, but to this day, he wonders what he would have really done.

"In medieval times, the lady would give a handkerchief or scarf to the knight to wear into battle, and he would treasure and prize it in almost the same way Dobbins did. This is a modern variation of that. But here's where it gets really interesting: 'It turned us into a platoon of believers. You don't dispute facts.' The stockings were no longer just for

Dobbins. They became a sacred thing for the whole platoon. The other guys were really worried when she dumped him, because in a way that Dear John letter endangered the whole platoon. Dobbins' reaction was important for all of the men. They relied on him. 'No sweat. The magic doesn't go away' were critical words for all of them."

"What seemed really important to you in 'Stockings'?"

"I suppose the most important thing to me was the sense of magic and ritual that people in dangerous situations create to achieve a kind of peace, to cope with the 'uncopable.' These guys faced maiming or death every day. Dobbins' response, and then the whole platoon's, wasn't based on reason or rationality. It was much more primitive. I can imagine Aztec or medieval warriors having a similar ritual. Deep, deep down, there is a human need to create something that gives protection—hope really—in the most horrible human situations. Also, it gave a sense of control and power over what is essentially uncontrollable—that lurking death."

"Anything else?"

"Yeah, in many ways this short piece is what all great literature is about: love and death. Even though she dumped him, the stockings still worked. People who painted on the caves in Lascaux twenty thousand years ago were doing something similar. They were trying to bring order to the chaos of life, to gain control, to make sense of the unfathomable, to understand or keep at bay the mystery of death."

"Lots to ponder," I said.

"Truly."

Too Much Information

In this information age, every day we are bombarded by options. Turn on the television and there are ninety-nine channels to choose from. Google a topic like teak lawn furniture and you find 62,000 sites you could go to. Google "research-based reading programs" and you have 12 million options to choose from. At the shopping mall, there isn't one clothes shop but dozens. If you go to a grocery store without a list, written or mental, you're bound to be overwhelmed by all the choices you can make. It all depends on what you need. And you need different things if you are planning a dinner party, or just picking up a quart of milk to tide you over until you head out of town. It depends on your purpose; it depends on your mood; it depends on whether you're hungry or not; it depends on whether something is on sale or whether you're attracted by the packaging; it depends on your resistance to impulse.

So it is with reading. And in this age of information overload, how do we read critically so that we separate the essential from the nonessential? How do we determine what's important?

Ironically, when text is well written, it's often more difficult to decide what is most important or essential. Elegant diction and a tight compression of ideas combine to persuade me that everything is equally important. I embark on an absorbing intellectual game. I reread excerpts and ask myself, consciously and subconsciously, what is most important here, what is essential to remember? There is a layering that occurs. What at first appears important might change as I ponder the piece and give my mind space to roam. There is not one important idea, but many, and by thinking about them, I am often led to a synthesis of what the piece means.

In "Stockings," I engage in a tug-of-war. Is the essence of the piece Dobbins' belief in the power of the stockings to keep him safe? Is it the power of smell to elicit memories of someone loved? Is it the changing role of the United States in a world growing more complex? Is it the importance of a talisman to focus one's energy and belief and ultimately, through that, to create some type of protective power? Is that any different from positive thinking? When his girlfriend dumps him, does Dobbins realize how important he has become to his platoon, how much the other soldiers need him to continue on as if nothing has happened, as if "the magic doesn't go away"? Was Dobbins just lucky? Is it the fear of death or bodily harm that creates the need for talismans? At any moment, somewhere in the world, there are soldiers facing the same fear and unknown that Dobbins and his platoon faced. They are searching for something to protect them from death, just as Dobbins did. There is something universal here that links soldiers throughout time. I think of my father and my father-in-law, both West Point graduates, veterans of the Korean War and World War II, who survived the horror, and now our nephew Paul who is stationed in Iraq. I'm hoping that he has a talisman as effective as Dobbins' stockings.

Into the Classroom—Intermediate

Summit Elementary was one of the early schools in the PEBC's Literacy League. Ellin was fortunate to be its staff developer, working with a group of highly skilled teachers hired to open the new suburban school and their top-notch principal, George Mansfield, who had been one of the Literacy League's early architects. Because of the group's luster, at the outset she was more intimidated than usual. The sleek coldness of the new building—not yet broken in with children's paintings and voices— didn't help.

At her first meeting with the staff, they gathered around tables in the stunning new library, which was filled with natural light, an amphitheater, and half bookshelves that allowed the children to reach all the books. Mimi DeRose was the teacher whose direct gaze and sense of humor Ellin most remembers from that meeting. During the session with the staff, Mimi asked a number of challenging questions. Ellin had a slight sinking feeling, unsure of what she'd bring to the already-stellar team.

At the end of the session, Mimi calmed her concerns. "I really look forward to working with you, Ellin," she said. "It'll be helpful to have a fresh pair of eyes and some new ideas."

Weeks later, after the chaos of getting the school up and running, Mimi and Ellin started working together to set up a reader's and writer's workshop in her fifth-grade classroom.

Several years later, after the PEBC's Reading Project was underway, Ellin returned to Mimi's classroom for another round of coteaching and coaching. By then Summit felt more lived-in. Children's pictures and reproductions of great art lined the walls. The carpets had a few stains. The new school smell had been replaced by scents from the cafeteria.

"Something has been bothering me for a long time, Ellin. You know these kids head off to middle school next year, and they're expected to read and write expository text immediately. In the past, I don't think I've done enough to prepare them. Reading textbooks and writing reports are so different from what we typically have kids read and write in elementary school. It's really more of a fiction and narrative focus at the elementary level, so I want to concentrate on helping them develop their expository skills."

"Don't think you're alone with those concerns, Mimi. Our staff developers are struggling with the same issues. Let's see what we can do together," Ellin suggested.

Mimi walked across the room to where she kept the students' writing folders and flipped through them as she talked. "I also want to focus on my reading conferences. My writing conferences are pretty effective and I've seen real growth in the kids, but conferring in reading is tougher. I feel like I sit down with kids and say, 'How is your reading going? What do you like about the book?' and it just doesn't go far enough. The conferences rarely get beyond the superficial."

For several weeks during Ellin's day-a-week visits to Summit, she spent time in Mimi's classroom. She and Mimi stood back and observed the students with Mimi's goals in mind. They watched, took notes, and jotted questions about their reading and about ideas for crafting sessions. To the casual observer, the kids were reading well. They chose books effortlessly. They read and shared in conferences and during sharing times. They were enthusiastic about the novels they read, yet when students read the texts Mimi had chosen to set the stage for social studies and science learning, many struggled to understand and then discuss what they read. Most were competent oral readers. They pronounced words correctly, missed few words, and had a number of strategies to identify words they didn't know. But many were so disconnected from and dispassionate about the meaning of the text, especially expository text, that they were often unaware of the essence of what they were reading.

"Why does this happen, Ellin? These kids are fluent readers and many of them really like to read, but it's as if this fog bank rolls in when they're hit with challenging nonfiction. They're in a kind of daze and for many of them, it's almost impossible to find any clarity. They're going to be eaten alive at middle school."

One morning, after several weeks of observing and conferring with the students, Mimi and Ellin stood to the side, leaning against the room's built-in teal-colored laminate cupboards. They scanned the class, sitting side by side on the countertop, and quietly discussed their two conclusions: First, explicit instruction in reading expository text would be critical if the children were to learn the social studies and science content through their independent reading; second, conferences would become a critical venue for reading instruction because there was such wide variance in the students' needs.

Ellin and Mimi decided to undertake a comprehension strategy study focused on determining importance in text to coincide with a planned quarter-long study of the colonial and Revolutionary War period in social studies. Based on their observations of the children's needs, this linkage made sense. They could provide explicit instruction in determining importance by modeling with expository text written about the revolutionary era. Crafting sessions would focus on how Mimi, as a proficient reader, made decisions about what content was most important, most essential, in a nonfiction passage. She would follow up by conferring with individual students as they made their own way through the expository text they needed to read for the group presentations that would bring the unit to a close. Mimi resolved to teach the kids explicitly how to zero in on what was most important. Mimi and Ellin brainstormed a list of reasons why readers make decisions about what is important. These included the reader's purpose for reading, specific questions that initially directed the reading or arose as the reader progressed, and the need to find specific information. Ellin suggested that explicit instruction on expository text structures should become a part of the plan for the study.

Conferring

One of the first snows of the season distracted everyone one morning. The cooperative learning groups that had met to plan their presentations were gradually disbanding, with students pausing at the window to see if there was any hope of an early dismissal. That hope dashed, some of the fifth graders were reading and taking notes while others worked on the early stages of their colonial projects.

Mimi and Ellin leaned against the counter and watched, looking for a place to begin their conferring for the day. Mimi's goal was to infuse conferences with more instruction based on the child's needs as a reader. They watched as Jeremy took an extra-long gaze out the window, his longing to be somewhere else clearly written on his face.

"A perfect victim for our first conference," Mimi laughed. As they pulled alongside Jeremy, he refocused on a printout on the Revolutionary War. Mimi leaned toward him. "How's it going Jeremy? Are you starting a plan for your part of the presentation?" she asked.

Jeremy's reply wasn't inspiring. "Not really." He stared at the page.

"How can we help?" Ellin asked.

"Not sure," came the reply.

"Why don't you read to us a little bit and let us get the gist of this text," Ellin suggested. With no reluctance, Jeremy launched into reading the page.

The first armed encounter of the American Revolution took place in Massachusetts, where the British force in Boston numbered some 3500 men. General Gage was aware that the militia members of the outlying towns were being trained and reorganized into active elements known as Minutemen, ready for immediate service. Ammunition and military stores were being gathered under direction of a Committee of Safety acting for the provincial assembly. (Microsoft Encarta Encyclopedia)

Jeremy pronounced every word accurately. His inflection was good. He paused appropriately at the end of sentences. Mimi and Ellin glanced at each other over his head, silently puzzled by his lack of direction. He certainly was *reading* this text.

Mimi interrupted Jeremy, who stopped, hunched over the page. "Thanks, I think we're getting the picture. Tell me, Jeremy—" She paused, long enough that he turned his head to look at her. "Tell me what, if anything, you are going to use from that passage in your group's presentation." The silence that followed became uncomfortable for Ellin, but Mimi was wiser. She waited patiently, knowing Jeremy needed time to collect his thoughts.

Finally, he said, "I really can't decide. It seems like I should use everything, but Mr. Ricker told us in fourth grade we had to put things in our own words for reports and I don't want to put everything in my own words . . . you know?"

"What parts do you think are most important here, Jeremy?" Ellin ventured. "Can you show us in the text you just read what you believe are the most important ideas? Look back over this section. See if you can decide what is most essential to you."

Jeremy looked over the page and, lackadaisically, pointed to the sentence that began with the words *ammunition* and *military stores.*

"Can you tell us why you decided that was most important?" Ellin asked.

"I like guns and stuff. My brother wants to go into the army after high school." Mimi shot Ellin a knowing glance.

Ellin said, "Thinking about how the text reminds you of your own life is one way to decide what's important. Great readers often do what you just did, Jeremy. They let their own interests and experiences come into their minds as they read. They focus on certain parts of the text they believe are most important to understanding the whole piece. Very often great readers decide something is most important because they have background knowledge in that area. That's one way to decide what is most important or essential in a text." Ellin paused and reminded herself that Jeremy might need to hear what she'd said a number of times before really understanding it. "Let's try something together, Jeremy," Ellin suggested. "We're going to break this passage down a little to make it easier to decide what's important. You need to decide what's most important for two reasons: so you don't have to put the whole thing into your own words, and so you can choose what you're going to put into your part of the presentation. Great readers are thinking all the time as they read, 'What's most important in this part, what's most important in that one?' I'm going to read that sentence you just pointed to. You listen, and I want you to tell me what you think is most important in that one sentence, okay?"

He looked at her quizzically, but said, "Sure."

Ellin read slowly, "'Ammunition and military stores were being gathered under direction of a Committee of Safety acting for the provincial assembly . . .' What d'ya think, Jeremy?" Silence. Ellin resisted the urge to pose another question.

"I don't understand anything after this word." He pointed to *committee*. Ellin reminded herself that when he first read to them, he had read each word perfectly with the exception of *provincial*, which he had sounded out adequately. Then Jeremy said, "But I think this thing about gathering is really important, because if they were gathering, that's like stockpiling weapons, then they had a plan of attack."

"Stockpiling, wow, I didn't think of that." Mimi's response led to a visible change in Jeremy. He launched into a short monologue on stockpiling for Mimi's benefit.

Ellin slipped in as he took a breath. "Jeremy, let me tell you something I've noticed about people who are trying to understand text like this—text that is trying to teach the reader something. It's hard to decide what is most important when there is a new idea or two in every sentence, and that's how nonfiction is often written."

"Yeah, and it is borrring," Jeremy said, rolling his eyes.

"Yeah, sometimes there's a voice in your head that says, 'Ugh, this is boring' or 'I don't get this' or 'I love reading about this,' you know?" she asked.

Ellin got a little nod from him.

Then she said, "When great readers are reading this stuff that has so many ideas in it, they have to listen to that mental voice tell them which words, which sentences or paragraphs, and which ideas are most important. Otherwise they won't get it. Great readers really listen to the voice saying, 'I think this sentence or this paragraph is most important.' Then they're able to decide which ideas are most important in the piece."

Ellin reached into her bag and retrieved a highlighting marker to hand to Jeremy. "Try something for us, okay? Take this marker and highlight the words or phrases in this passage that you really think are most important to understanding what the whole passage is about. Be sure to use it only on the words or phrases you think are essential for you to understand the whole thing. Deal? We'll stop back in a few minutes."

Mimi and Ellin moved away. "I don't know, Mimi, whether that was the right direction to go with him. His stockpiling interest was a good step. But, in general, he isn't discriminating important from less important ideas too well. If other kids are struggling like this, I think we're going to have to do a lot more thinking aloud in that kind of text during crafting sessions."

She agreed. "I can definitely incorporate more borrrrring (to use Jeremy's word) text in think-alouds and try to be more precise in articulating how I make decisions about what's important. But with Jeremy, this isn't the first time I've had that kind of conference with him. It's like pulling teeth. I'm a little surprised that he isn't comprehending more than he is, because he reads so fluently orally. There are so many unfamiliar concepts in that passage that somehow the ideas seem to run together for him, and he isn't able to sort out what is important."

"I gave him the marker to make it easier for him to focus on identifying important words or sentences before he tries to identify important concepts, though he might highlight everything the first few times he uses it."

"That could happen," Mimi laughed. "I'll buy a bunch of them."

Determining Importance at the Word, Sentence, and Whole-Text Levels: Unique Challenges in Expository Text

There are at least three levels at which proficient readers make decisions about what is most important in any text: the whole-text or idea level, the sentence level, and the word level. After we read, we make rational judgments about what was most important, but even as we read, we make continual decisions about what sentences or phrases are most essential in a paragraph and even which words are most important in any given sentence. These decisions are influenced by our background knowledge, our purpose for reading, what we find aesthetically pleasing in the piece, the degree to which an author focuses on an idea or repeats information, and the text features (bold print, italics, etc.).

At the word level, eye movement studies show that the eyes of proficient readers focus longer (by milliseconds) on words that carry the weight of the meaning in any given sentence. Linguists call those key words *contentives*. Sometimes they are nouns and verbs, sometimes not. Contentives are words that hold the meaning—the content—in a sentence, depending upon the overall meaning of that sentence in the passage.

For example, in the sentence, "Even now, twenty years later, I can see him wrapping his girlfriend's pantyhose around his neck before heading out on ambush," the words *pantyhose, girlfriend,* and *ambush* are important to understanding the sentence. Those three words would be considered contentives. The words *can, him, his,* and *out* are functors. In effect, they hold the sentence together—are functional—but have little impact on the meaning.

At the sentence and paragraph levels, writers use devices such as repetition, text features (bold print, italics, graphs, figures, and photographs), and longer passages to emphasize information or ideas they consider most important. Ultimately, what's critical is determining importance at the whole-text or idea level. As they read, children need to be aware of what's important at the word and sentence levels so they will be able to understand the overall meaning at the whole-text level. Students who are less aware about what is important *during* reading will flounder at the whole-text level, because they haven't been making critical decisions about what is important as they read.

Often there is more than one important idea, especially in complex material. Because of this we do children a disservice by teaching them to identify *the* main idea. "Main idea isn't found in nature—only on standardized tests!" Ellin often jokes. Children benefit from knowing that in many test-taking situations, they should concentrate on the one most important idea, but in most reading situations, they will come away with a number of key ideas.

It can be useful to teach students about contentives and functors. They love the words! Have them identify important words (contentives) and functional words (functors) and get them to talk about their choices. Have conversations about which words, sentences, and ideas carry the weight of the meaning. If there is disagreement, ask them to back up their opinions with evidence from the text so they learn how to support their position and to focus more carefully and critically on their reading.

Ellin thought if they encouraged Jeremy to identify important words and sentences first, he might start to monitor his own understanding more and work toward identifying important ideas in longer passages and text.

"It's interesting, Ellin," Mimi said, turning serious, "but I think Jeremy and the majority of kids in this room, from what I've been able to tell so far, are much better able to decide what is important in fiction or even in nonfiction that is written in a less didactic way, but they seem to lose that ability to discriminate when they pick up a textbook."

Mimi's concerns are common among intermediate-grade teachers. Reading theorists distinguish between considerate and inconsiderate text. Text is *considerate* when it is written in such a way that its content and format (text structure) are familiar or predictable to a particular reader. When writers take the intended audiences' probable background knowledge into consideration, the text is usually more considerate. Text is *inconsiderate* when it is written in a way that is difficult for its intended audience to understand.

For Jeremy and many others like him, fiction is more considerate. In fiction, characters interact in a setting and encounter some conflict. The action rises and falls around that conflict and their actions until some sort of resolution presents itself. Those fiction plot elements and sequences allow the reader to make reasonable predictions. This helps make the text considerate or readable.

In American schools children generally learn to read in predictable storybooks and other fiction, making these more considerate forms of text for most learners. Nonfiction that is more narrative or storylike tends to be more considerate than pedantic, expository text.

Jeremy had encountered text that, for him, was inconsiderate. The paragraph from which he read was long. There were no characters. There was no bold print to draw the reader's attention to important ideas. Words such as *militia* and *provincial* weren't defined contextually in the passage. It was a far cry from Beverly Cleary's *Dear Mr. Henshaw*, which Jeremy had recently read and loved.

It wasn't inappropriate for Jeremy to read that challenging text. We all must tackle inconsiderate text at times. But Jeremy needed some specific instruction to help him pay attention strategically, to help him focus on the most important ideas.

Back to the Classroom

"I don't think I've ever seen Rachel wear the same hair bow," Mimi whispered as she and Ellin passed Rachel's corner desk, stacked with organized piles of paper, open books, and spare pencils, sharpened and resting in the crevices between her desk and those on both sides of hers. She didn't even look up when they walked past to confer with other students. All they saw was her long blonde ponytail and her head bent over the neat array of tools on her desk.

Rachel was a fifth grader with a mission. She didn't want to be interrupted. Later, they overheard her open a meeting with her presentation team members: "Okay, you guys, here's the plan . . ." Ellin and Mimi didn't worry too much about Rachel. She was engaged and conscientious. Children with more pressing needs generally drew them.

After some time moving around the room, conferring with several children, Mimi and Ellin pulled back and stood near the door to observe the interactions and activity. They wanted to be sure they didn't solve problems for the students but allowed them to use their knowledge of the strategies to solve problems for themselves.

"Look at Rachel," Ellin said, shaking her head in awe and relief. "She's amazing. What organization! I can't wait to hear what she's going to present."

"Didn't I tell you her idea?" Mimi asked. "She's going to relate the Revolutionary War to modern military conflicts. She's researching patterns and similarities between the Bosnian and Revolutionary wars. I overheard her tell her group that she'd try to make all the research they'd done on colonial times more relevant to the audience by comparing it to Bosnia."

Rachel read for a couple of minutes, then jumped up and scurried to a nearby corner where she'd stashed a storyboard—three large pieces of tagboard bound together by clear tape so that the board can stand alone. On the storyboard Rachel had taped newspaper clippings, sketches, poetry, and envelopes that said "Open Me."

"That's her part of the project," Mimi told Ellin. "It's starting to look a little crowded on that storyboard. It represents all Rachel's research on Bosnia."

"Let's confer with her," Ellin suggested.

As we moved in her direction, Rachel looked up with her index finger tucked into *I Dream of Peace,* a book written about the war in the former Yugoslovia. "Mrs. DeRose, I need to make a copy of this poem for my storyboard."

"Hmmm," Mimi glanced at the book and then at Rachel. "Why?"

"It's a great poem and it makes me feel what it's like to live in a place that's in a war. Listen." She read from a poem written by a child Rachel's age whose experience with war allowed her to write in a painfully accurate way.

"It's so sad and so real and the girl was about my age, so I can really understand how lonely and worried she would have felt. I hope her dad's okay."

Mimi and Ellin agreed the poem was powerful. Ellin made a mental note about the importance of using primary sources in the research process.

"You're welcome to make another copy, Rachel, but you've made a lot. You can't use every poem in this book, so you're going to have to make some tough choices," Mimi told her.

"Yeah, I really like all of them, or almost." Rachel twisted her finger through her ponytail and squinted in concentration.

"Maybe you need to ask yourself why you're using them, Rachel. What do you think your audience is going to learn from them?" Mimi paused. "We've been working on this research for over five weeks now. During that time we've also done a comprehension strategy study on determining importance. Maybe we're talking about the same process in reading and in putting together a presentation. Let's think out loud a bit. How do you decide what's important enough in your research to include in your presentation?"

Rachel answered quickly, speaking with energy and confidence. "Well, I've read all these newspaper articles. I've read these two books by kids. You really get to feel what it's like to live there. And I've interviewed our neighbors whose grandparents live in Sarajevo. They worry all the time if they're okay, especially if they don't get any phone calls or letters for a while. I've read lots and it was all really important, you know? It was all about the war in Bosnia and that's my part, you know, to connect it to the Revolutionary War." She hadn't taken a breath so far, but she went on. "The presentation is two weeks from Thursday and I really think those fourth graders need to know how kids in war feel—waiting and watching all the time for something bad to maybe happen."

"Whoa, Rachel!" Mimi laughed and put her hand on Rachel's shoulder. "You've found so much that's important. You've found out so much about Bosnia. Let me ask you again, though, what exactly is your role in this presentation?"

"To compare the Revolutionary War to wars today."

"Okay, if that's your purpose, how do you decide what to leave in and what to leave out of your part of the presentation? How did you decide what to include on the storyboard, for example?"

"Well, not much more stuff will fit." Rachel's statement turned into a question right around the word *fit*.

"Let's talk about your presentation, Rachel," Ellin offered. "Who's going to see your storyboard and listen to your presentation?"

"The fourth graders, right?" She shot a glance at Mimi, who nodded.

"You were in fourth grade once a long time ago, Rachel! What did you know about the Revolutionary War, and how wars in this century compare, when you were in fourth grade?"

"I don't think I knew anything," Rachel said.

"And now you know a lot, right?" Ellin whispered as if they were, at that moment, surrounded by fourth graders. "Rachel, they're not going to really learn everything you know about these two wars. Look at your storyboard. It's crammed full of information. Your presentation notes are, how many, six pages long? Think about the fourth graders and what they know. Think about what Mrs. DeRose just asked you about your role in the presentation. If you could have your audience remember just two really important ideas, what would those be? Are there two ideas you think are most important when you compare these two wars?"

"I don't know," then her voiced revved to full throttle. "I really want them to know . . ." and she was off again.

When the litany had concluded, Ellin said, "Rachel, we're going to leave you for a while so that you can identify what two things you think are most important to your part of the presentation. Take some quiet time, look over your great work so far, read through your notes, but when we check back in, say, fifteen minutes, I want you to tell us the two ideas here that you think are most important for the fourth graders to learn."

"Two, not twenty-two, Rachel," Mimi winked at her as we left. "And we're going to ask you to defend your choices."

"I figured that," she said.

Ellin and Mimi retreated between conferences to our place on the counter. "You know what I just realized? She doesn't discriminate, Ellin. She comprehends all kinds of text, including the newspaper, beautifully. But she thinks everything is important. You know, we've been in this comprehension strategy study for weeks. I've really modeled, thought aloud about how I make decisions about what is important in narrative and expository text, but she's not following through on any of it. She doesn't seem to have any criteria in her mind to help her select a few key themes and leave the rest out. She has an incredible memory. She remembers everything, and she must figure if she can remember it, it must be important to include."

Ellin agreed with Mimi, saying, " I think Rachel and probably a few others in here need to understand that it's the purpose for the reading, as well as personal beliefs, experiences, prior knowledge, and knowledge of the audience, that governs our decisions about what is important in any text. Rachel has a lot of background knowledge, and she has a clearly stated audience and purpose. The problem is that she isn't really considering her audience and purpose as a way to discriminate between important ideas and interesting but unimportant facts that don't match the purpose or the needs of the audience."

"That's right," Mimi nodded.

"I think they may need some crafting sessions on how proficient readers actually use purpose, beliefs, prior knowledge, and audience to make decisions about what is important in text."

"Yeah," Mimi said. "I've done so many crafting sessions in this strategy study where I read aloud and pause to think out loud about what I think is important, but I don't think I've been explicit enough about how I decide, why I decide—you know, what criteria I use to make those decisions. I guess I wasn't consciously aware of it before now. Just when you think you're done," Mimi joked. "But I know that's right. If we have a kid like Rachel who is comprehending so much, but can't prioritize, I worry that she'll have a tough time in middle school doing assignments like writing a summary or a persuasive piece. I also worry that she'll believe everything she reads. Through this comprehension study, I've discovered better what I mean when I talk about determining importance. I want them to develop the ability and propensity to read critically, to mentally throw out propaganda or stuff that is just plain inaccurate according to their background knowledge, opinions, and beliefs. When you focus on what's important, you're also deciding what isn't worthy of being remembered. These kids need to discriminate in that way, too."

The Importance of Determining Importance

Determining importance is a more critical life skill now than it was ten years ago when Ellin sat in Mimi's classroom. So many of the dilemmas Jeremy and Rachel faced remain common, but the complexity of the situation has been compounded by the excess of information available on the Internet. Today instruction on determining importance must include a focus on maintaining objectivity so we can differentiate between solid facts and exaggerated, or just plain inaccurate, information. By thinking aloud, we need to show kids exactly how we include a healthy dose of skepticism as we read; how we keep an eye out for propaganda and commercial motives that underlie some "nonfiction" on the Internet. We need to spend more time with kids in conferences discovering how they approach different types of nonfiction and noticing the degree to which they corroborate questionable information with data from other sources, including good old nonfiction books!

Given the rapidly changing world in which today's students operate and given the plethora of information at their fingertips, the importance of modeling how we determine importance has increased dramatically. While we hope kids will be able to determine importance simultaneously as they use other strategies in fiction and nonfiction, we also want to emphasize that in some circumstances, determining importance will be the key strategy kids need to focus on. In fact, they may need to do so to the exclusion of other strategies. For example, in very concept-laden nonfiction material, readers often don't have a lot of latitude in terms of inferring or creating vivid mental images. They are called upon to extract factual information from the text and to do so in the most efficient way possible. In such circumstances, determining importance is an invaluable tool—one that we want kids to be able to use in a focused way. In effect, we're teaching kids that sometimes they need to "turn up the volume" on a particular strategy and "turn down the volume" on others. This requires clear, explicit instruction and the use of conferences to follow up and monitor the degree to which children are successfully identifying what is most important.

~ ~ ~

In *The Things They Carried*, Tim O'Brien writes:

> How do you generalize? War is hell, but that's not the half of it, because war is also mystery and terror and adventure and courage and discovery and holiness and pity and despair and longing and love. War is nasty; war is fun. War is thrilling; war is drudgery. War makes you a man; war makes you dead . . . To generalize about war is like generalizing about peace. Almost everything is true. Almost nothing is true. At its core, perhaps war is just another name for death, and yet any soldier will tell you, if he tells the truth, that proximity to death brings with it a corresponding proximity to life . . . And in the end, of course, a true war story is never about war. It's about sunlight. It's about the special way that dawn spreads out on a river when you know you must cross the river and march into mountains and do things you are afraid to do. It's about love and memory. It's about sorrow. It's about sisters who never write back and people who never listen. (81–85)

It is the paradox of war that O'Brien writes about, how it brings out the best and the worst, how it makes people into heroes and monsters, how in war there is an intensity that is both more beautiful and more horrible than at any other time. There is a heightened awareness about the preciousness and inconsequence of life. There is a heightened awareness of what is important.

~ ~ ~

In our lives, we determine importance every time we shop, drive, read a newspaper, or listen to a friend. As parents, we make judgments hundreds of times a week as we consider which issues to take on directly and which advice is better left unsaid. When facing a decision about whom or whether to marry, how to nurture our children, the best care for a dying loved one, we are determining importance in the most profound way. We continue to struggle with those types of decisions throughout our lives, and most of us do so without any specific instruction. We learn from the models around us, and we eventually jump in and start making our own decisions.

In classrooms, we have an opportunity to teach kids explicitly how to focus on what's most important. We can help students to sort out ideas that may inform them for a lifetime from a curriculum that is already bloated and growing more so every year. When we teach kids to determine importance, it means that we initially become aware of our own processes for determining importance—when we read, when we converse, when we shop, when we make profound decisions—and then we reveal our thinking. They may, like Jeremy, have difficulty identifying anything of importance, or they may, like Rachel, need to learn about the criteria we use to discriminate among a myriad of facts and ideas. They may find focusing on the essence effortless in some texts only to be confounded by the process in others. Our task is to sharpen their ability to grasp what is essential.

Key Ideas for Comprehension Strategy Study

Determining Importance in Text

- Proficient learners make purposeful and spontaneous decisions about what is important in the text at each level.
  - **Word level:** Words that carry the meaning are contentives; words that connect are functors. Contentives tend to be more important to the overall meaning of a passage than functors.
  - **Sentence level:** There are usually key sentences that carry the weight

of meaning for a paragraph, passage, or section. Often, especially in nonfiction, they may contain bold print, begin or end the passage, or refer to a table or graph.

- **Text level:** The text contains key ideas, concepts, and themes; our opinions about which of these are most important change as we read a passage. We typically make final conclusions about the most important themes after reading the passage, perhaps several times and/or after conversing or writing about the passage. Clues, such as repetition for emphasis, illustrations or diagrams, symbolism, foreshadowing, character and setting prominence, and conflict all point to importance at the text level.

■ Decisions about importance in text are made based on:

- the reader's purpose

- the reader's schema for the text content—ideas most closely connected to the reader's prior knowledge will be considered most important

- the reader's sense of the aesthetic—what he values, considers worthy or beautiful

- language that surprises or otherwise captures the reader's sustained focus

- the reader's beliefs, opinions, and experiences related to the text

- the reader's schema for the text format—text that stands out visually and/or ideas that are repeated are often considered most important

- the reader's understanding of text structures—for example, in a cause-and-effect text structure, the reader should direct her attention to causes and effects described in the text

- concepts another reader mentions prior to, during, or after reading

- Frequently, pointing out nonexamples (what is unimportant) helps students to distinguish importance more clearly.

- Interesting discussion emanates from dispute about what is most important. Children need to work toward defending their positions, but there is rarely one "right" set of important ideas.

- Students should be able to articulate how they make decisions about what is important in a given context and how those decisions enhance their overall comprehension of the piece.

CHAPTER 9

The Evolution of Meaning

Synthesis

The most dramatic moment in subsequent European–Native American relations was the first encounter between the Inca emperor Atahuallpa and the Spanish conquistador Francisco Pizarro at the Peruvian highland town of Cajamarca on November 16, 1532. Atahuallpa was absolute monarch of the largest and most advanced state in the New World, while Pizarro represented the Holy Roman Emperor Charles V (also known as King Charles I of Spain), monarch of the most powerful state in Europe. Pizarro, leading a ragtag group of 168 Spanish soldiers, was in unfamiliar terrain, ignorant of the local inhabitants, completely out of touch with the nearest Spaniards (1,000 miles to the north in Panama) and far beyond the reach of timely reinforcements. Atahuallpa was in the middle of his own empire of millions of subjects and immediately surrounded by his army of 80,000 soldiers, recently victorious in a war with other Indians. Nevertheless, Pizarro captured Atahuallpa within a few minutes after the two leaders first set eyes on each other. Pizarro proceeded to hold his prisoner for eight months, while extracting history's largest ransom in return for a promise to free him. After the ransom—enough gold to fill a room 22 feet long by 17 feet wide to a height of over 8 feet—was delivered, Pizarro reneged on his promise and executed Atahuallpa.

Atahuallpa's capture was decisive for the European conquest of the Inca Empire. Although the Spaniards' superior weapons would have assured an ultimate Spanish victory in any case, the capture made the conquest quicker and infinitely easier. Atahuallpa was revered by the Incas as a sun god and exercised absolute authority over his subjects, who obeyed even the orders he issued from captivity. The months until his death gave Pizarro time to dispatch exploring parties unmolested to other parts of the Inca Empire, and to send for reinforcements from Panama. When fighting between Spaniards and Incas finally did commence after Atahuallpa's execution, the Spanish forces were more formidable.

—Jared Diamond, *Guns, Germs, and Steel*

Susan's Reflections

A shameless fiction addict, I make a commitment to read more nonfiction. A friend recommends Jared Diamond's *Guns, Germs, and Steel*, a Pulitzer Prize winner that explores why human history unfolded so differently on different continents. Diamond's thesis is that the environment where different cultures took root profoundly shaped their ability to create the institutions needed for more complex societies. Hunter-gatherers spent their time hunting, gathering, and moving from place to place. There was no time to develop societal institutions beyond the level of a roving tribe. But, in some locations—because of climate, soil, access to water, and the presence of wild plants that could be domesticated—conditions were ripe for staying put and raising crops. Not until farming and domestication of animals occurred was there the stability in habitation and extra food that permitted differentiation of societal tasks. Only then could there be kings, priests, scribes, bureaucrats, and inventors.

A statement in Chapter 3, "Collision at Cajamarca," piques my curiosity: "The most dramatic moment in subsequent European–Native American relations was the first encounter between the Inca emperor Atahuallpa and the Spanish conquistador Francisco Pizarro at the Peruvian highland town of Cajamarca on November 16, 1532" (68). I don't know anything about Cajamarca, but I'm drawn in by "the most dramatic moment." As I read the first paragraph, my thinking evolves. I understand that this is a clash between two extremely powerful men and that Pizarro is the serious underdog. I'm blown away by 168 "ragtag" Spanish soldiers defeating an empire of millions of Incas and an army of eighty thousand. Pizarro takes Atahuallpa captive, then renegs on his promise and executes him after receiving the largest ransom ever given.

At first, I summarize to keep the events in my mind. But I start wondering how this could have happened. It is inconceivable. Pizarro's was an act of incredible audacity, as well as utter ruthlessness. I need to make sense of this event. Is this the nature of conquest, murdering those who previously held power? If memory serves, that is exactly what Machiavelli recommended in *The Prince*: Conquerors should exterminate the leaders of conquered lands in order to prevent later revolts and to cow the populace into submission. That is certainly what Pizarro did here, thus helping to guarantee Spanish conquest of the vast Inca empire.

I remember a conversation with my friend Luke, who lived for years in Chile and Uruguay and was a student of South American history. We were talking about what motivated the Spaniards to leave all that was familiar and set forth to conquer South America. "We came to serve God and make ourselves rich," Luke quoted one of the conquistadors with a twinkle in his eye. That conversation pops into my mind and helps me understand their motivation: God and greed. The Spaniards had absolute faith in the rightness of their cause—for God and their king—and, of course, for their own self-interest. They stood to gain enormous riches if they won. That helps explain Pizarro's behavior, but what about Atahuallpa? I read on to an eyewitness account of the meeting.

> First came a squadron of Indians dressed in clothes of different colors, like a chessboard . . . Next came three squadrons in different dresses, dancing and singing. Then came a number of men with armor, large metal plates, and crowns of gold and silver . . . Among them came the figure of Atahuallpa in a very fine litter with the ends of its timbers covered in silver. Eighty lords carried him on their shoulders, all wearing a very rich blue livery. Atahuallpa himself was very richly dressed, with his crown on his head and a collar of large emeralds around his neck. He sat on a small stool with a rich saddle cushion resting on his litter . . . These Indian squadrons began to enter the plaza to the accompaniment of great songs, and thus entering they occupied every part of the plaza. In the meantime all of us Spaniards were waiting ready, hidden in a courtyard, full of fear. Many of us urinated without noticing it, out of sheer terror. (71–72)

Why did Atahuallpa go to Pizarro in full ceremonial splendor, but unarmed? What would have possessed him to be so naïve? A Spanish friar approached Atahuallpa and presented him with a Bible. Atahuallpa had trouble opening the book, but when he did, he looked at the script, turned crimson, and tossed the Bible on the ground. That gave the Spaniards all the excuse they needed to attack. They created a cacophony of sounds—booming guns, blowing trumpets, loud rattles on their horses—to terrify the Indians. In the resulting melee, the Indians panicked; they climbed into mounds, suffocating one another; and the Spaniards proceeded to cut the Indians to pieces. The images from this eyewitness description outdramatize Hollywood in its most extreme Ben Hur or Cleopatra moments. The Spaniards literally scared them to death.

My synthesis is changing. At first I thought it was Pizarro's ruthlessness and belief in the rightness of his cause that allowed this rout to occur. Now I believe an equal factor is that Atahuallpa saw himself as a god. He went forth unarmed because he assumed his grandeur and presence would subdue Pizarro, that the Spaniards (like his own subjects) would perceive him as godlike and omnipotent and treat him accordingly. After reflecting, I conclude this incident at Cajamarca is really about the power of belief systems to shape—or distort—reality. Atahuallpa simply could not contemplate, much less anticipate, the treatment he received from Pizarro. Pizarro had a very different belief system. He saw Atahuallpa as an ignorant heathen. In Pizarro's view, God and right (and greed!) were on his side and authorized him to do anything to crush the Indians. Though this conclusion isn't stated anywhere in the text, I come to view religious belief as playing a large role here, for both the conquered and the conqueror.

As I read, then read further, then reread, my synthesis changed. My process was an evolutionary one that allowed me to shift my thinking and change my conclusions as I pondered this extraordinary event that led, on that November day in 1532, to a decisive turn in the history of the world.

Synthesis: How Readers Create a Mosaic

Even after years of studying reading comprehension instruction, observing children as they struggle to create meaning for themselves, and talking to hundreds of teachers about what proficient readers do to make sense of text, our thinking about each strategy continues to evolve. This has been especially true as we have come to understand how readers synthesize.

Synthesis is the mind constructing beautiful mosaics of meaning. Susan remembers seeing ancient Byzantine mosaics while traveling in Turkey, and being awestruck by the artist's ability to conceptualize a complex and splendid whole while holding only a tiny fragment of colored glass in his hand. So it is with synthesis.

Synthesis takes place during and after reading. It is the process of creating a mental plan—a blueprint—for what we're reading, experiencing, or learning—and then continually revising the plan as we recall or encounter new information. When we amend our initial understanding as we read further, our synthesis evolves. When we combine conclusions we drew in the early paragraphs with later ideas, our synthesis continues to change. We synthesize when we think about what we have finished reading, bringing in additional concepts, beliefs, emotions, and texts that affect our understanding. We synthesize when we go back to reread sections to clarify or deepen our understanding, combining our new ideas with our earlier interpretations.

Synthesis involves ordering, combining, and recreating into a coherent whole the mass of information that bombards our minds every day. It is the uniquely human trait that permits us to sift through a myriad of details and focus on those pieces we need to know and remember, to collect a disparate array of facts and opinions and connect them to central themes or a few key ideas. Synthesis is about organizing the different pieces to create a mosaic, a meaning greater than the sum of each shiny piece. It is a complex process but one that children, even the youngest, perform very naturally every day.

When children sit down at the dinner table at night and share the events of the day, they are synthesizing, culling out the unimportant, creating their interpretations of the day for their families. When we curl up in bed at night to ruminate about the day in our minds or in a journal, we synthesize. When we read, we have the opportunity to construct and manipulate a road map of our meaning. Synthesis is a way of saying, "I have been there, this is what I remember, and this is what I believe about what I know."

~ ~ ~

When Susan read about the Battle of Cajamarca, she synthesized during and after she read. She forced herself to slow down and think about the conclusions she drew as she read—the evolving meaning. She knew from the opening ("The most dramatic moment . . .") how important this day must have been, but needed to integrate her existing knowledge and beliefs, to figure it out *for herself* so that she would be more likely to remember it.

Susan kept an ongoing record in her mind and revised her ideas as she read, but she knew she would have to read it several times to truly understand. The first time she read, she was befuddled and intrigued by how such an extraordinary series of events could have occurred. As she reread the account and thought more about it, she came to see that the Spaniards' and the Incas' divergent religious beliefs were pivotal in explaining their behavior and motivation. Her synthesis changed and deepened.

Difference Between Summary and Synthesis

We all recall experiences from our schooling where teachers asked us to summarize a book, usually in writing. They didn't want much, just a succinct report that touched upon what they believed (but wouldn't reveal) to be the critical elements and themes in the book, roughly in the order they were presented in the text. The summary had to be less than a page long with no editorializing or accounts of personal experiences mixed in. "Oh, geez," we'd groan. It was not a process we relished.

Though our memories of being asked to summarize might not be fond, research has long indicated that teaching children to summarize is a helpful tool in teaching reading comprehension (Pearson, Roehler, Dole, and Duffy 1992). The research confirms what we know through experience and common sense: Proficient readers are able to summarize as a way of helping them recall what they read and then communicate it to others. We also know that as they reach the upper grades, students are expected to summarize more frequently; and upper-grade teachers express frustration about their students' underdeveloped summaries, particularly for nonfiction.

When we ask students to summarize, we are asking for a succinct retelling of the key points in a text in the order they were presented. Students do benefit from learning to summarize, but we know they are capable of much more than a traditional summary. They should be encouraged to incorporate schema from beyond the immediate text as well as beliefs, opinions, emotions, and values that they—rather than just the teacher—believe are important to the overall meaning. In other words, children can, and should, be taught to do both—summarize and synthesize.

To teach summary, we can think aloud about how we would retell something we had read—how we would choose the order and elements to include, how we can consider what the audience already knows, how we can capture engaging aspects without retelling the entire text. We can emphasize that a summary can help someone who has never read a book understand what it is about.

To make clear the distinction between synthesis and summary, we have only to think about what our youngest readers' summaries naturally include. When young children begin to summarize, they include what they believe to be the highlights of the text, but they often go much further. Their summaries are spirited accounts of what they read, infused with details and emotions from their own lives. They very naturally add details from other texts, opinions, and bits of prior knowledge that extend the meaning of the story for them. Through their retellings, they actually create new narratives—verbal or written syntheses that fix the meaning of the piece firmly in their memories.

Seven-year-old Alicia's retelling of Cynthia Rylant's *Dog Heaven* drove the distinction between synthesis and summary home for Ellin. One day she pulled up next to Alicia for a conference.

"Alicia, you've been talking about summary in your classroom for a while now. You've just finished reading *Dog Heaven*. Can you tell me about it?"

"Well, it's about dogs who go to heaven, not just one dog, what happens when any dog goes to heaven. Here's how it works. A dog dies and you bury him in the backyard and part of him, like the exact shape of him, but not really his body, goes to heaven and God is waiting with lots of biscuits, only they're not just the kind that we have here, they're better and in shapes like ham sandwiches and stuff. But it's supposed to make you feel better if your dog, or just any pet, has died because heaven is almost better for the dog than Earth and they can come back any time and they can be invisible!"

Her description was more than a summary, more than a simple retelling, and yet it was true to the themes in the book. Alicia elaborated her retelling, possibly to make it more memorable. She actually added concrete details about a dog's burial, not found in the book, and then extrapolated the story to all pets without compromising the key themes in Cynthia Rylant's text. She used details from the text (ham sandwiches, invisible visits to Earth) to help her arrive at a key theme—it may be better for dogs in heaven. She went beyond summary. She synthesized.

~ ~ ~

We know that students who struggle often make up their minds about the major themes and ideas in a text early in their reading. Despite abundant evidence that the plot is evolving and the meaning changing, they fail to adjust their interpretations as they read further (Allington 2006; Beers 2003).

Ellin encountered a classic example of how students struggle to synthesize during reading when observing a group of Title 1 middle school students reading a short chapter on the solar system. The piece began by comparing the planet sizes with different sports balls: Jupiter was like a basketball, Earth like a baseball. At the end of the passage, many struggling readers said the passage was mostly about balls. They latched onto a shred of meaning early on and held to it regardless of changes in the text. Showing students how they can synthesize during reading helps address this problem.

Ripples of Meaning

Years ago, Ellin introduced synthesis to Debbie Miller's first graders. She gathered the students around her for a think-aloud, using Mary Hoffman's *Amazing Grace*.

She stopped two or three times to share her thinking. "When I read a little further in this book, I change my mind. I used to think it was just going to be a book about a girl, Grace, who wants the starring role in the class play of *Peter Pan*. Now I'm thinking Grace is going to have a harder time than most kids. She has to try out for the play like everyone else, but she also has to fight people's beliefs that she can't be Peter Pan because she's a girl and she's black. These kids think because she's a girl and Peter Pan was a boy, and because she's black and Peter Pan was white in the book, Grace can't be Peter Pan. I think this book is going to be about the kinds of obstacles Grace has to face if she's going to be Peter Pan in the class play."

After several similar think-alouds, Riley raised his hand. "Mrs. Keene, can I help you out with a metaphor?"

After a moment in which Ellin had to remind herself she was teaching first graders, she thought, of course Riley and his classmates know what a metaphor is because Debbie has *taught* them what a metaphor is.

"Sure, Riley, help me out, would ya?"

"Okay, but I'm going to have to come up to the whiteboard." He rose from the floor, grabbed a marker, and turned to his peers. "Okay, here's what they're trying to say. Synthesis is like changing your mind. Here's my metaphor. You know how when you go to the mountains and you stand next to a lakeorpond?" He said "lake or pond" as if they were a single word—*lakeorpond*. He drew a rough circle on the whiteboard and a stick figure standing next to it. "Okay, if you throw a rock into the lakeorpond, it makes a big splash, you know?"

Heads nodded.

"Well, that's what they're trying to say happens at the beginning of reading a book. It's like the first few pages just make this big splash in your mind! Then you know how you get those bubbles that spread out across it?"

"Do you mean ripples, Riley?" Debbie asked.

He looked back at her and said firmly, "No. Bubbles."

"Okay, okay," Debbie quickly replied.

"You know how those bubbles go across the lakeorpond?"

Riley paused to draw a series of ripples (bubbles!) extending out from where the rock splashed into the water.

The kids nodded. "Yeah."

"Well, that's what happens when you keep reading and turning the pages of the book. The stuff the book is about keeps getting bigger and bigger the more you read. It's like bubbles. You kinda change your mind, but it's kinda still the same."

Then Riley paused. "But you know the rock's still there. You just can't see it; so that thing that you thought at the beginning of the book? It's still there, it's just under the water!" Riley had it right: Meaning expands in ripples, changing and enlarging as we read.

~ ~ ~

Through studying synthesis in primary, intermediate, and middle-grade classrooms, we discovered that children's syntheses are updated continually as they read, changing to accommodate new information. Also, their midcourse synthesis may differ significantly from their reflections about the piece after reading it in its entirety.

Synthesis goes to the heart of what text means. It is critical to encourage children to ask: "What does this really mean to me?" Teaching synthesis may require more think-alouds and more conferences than any other comprehension strategy. It is well worth the effort. When children pay attention to the evolving meaning as they read, and create new ways to think about and share the information later, there is a significant improvement in their ability to remember books and transfer the information they've synthesized to new learning situations. Something even more important happens with synthesis: Children create original interpretations of text. They "own" the evolution of their thinking and their conclusions because they are uniquely theirs.

Into the Classroom—Intermediate

It was one of those midyear mornings. Ellin was with Chryse Hutchins, a PEBC staff developer, visiting Jody Cohn's fifth-grade classroom in Denver's Samuels Elementary.

"Your touch is so evident, Chryse," Ellin said. "You and Jody have created a classroom that is just brimming with kids who really read and write with depth. It's wonderful to see. Your hard work is paying off."

Chyrse had worked with Jody for two years. "We've created a real sense of community. I really think that's where this started. Look at how these children work together now and then think back to what it was like at the beginning of last year." Chryse looked over at Jody, who nodded in agreement.

Chryse, Jody, and Ellin stood with clipboards in hand, ready to jot observations.

"Ellin," Chryse said, "Jody and I decided to try something different this year. We're having the kids study the Revolutionary War, Civil War, and World War II simultaneously. There's way too much content to teach well in fifth-grade social studies. We thought if we could ask three different groups of kids to delve deeply into this country's major war periods, eventually they could combine their knowledge and we could draw conclusions about the events that lead to war and wars' lasting effects. It's like a synthesis—a pulling together of information from different times in history. We're hoping they'll arrive at some important conclusions about universals related to wars. They've never done anything this comprehensive before, but we thought it would be a great challenge and they'd develop terrific research skills."

Ellin's mouth dropped at the magnitude of the undertaking. Right away, she noticed twenty-four fifth graders digging in. Some took notes. Some sketched. Some mapped key ideas. Some marked key themes in their books, using sticky notes. One child recorded his thoughts into a Dictaphone. Another pair compiled a list on a large butcher-paper chart.

"What great energy, Jody! And what a great way to view all the fifth-grade social studies content. You're teaching synthesis while asking them to understand—and synthesize—three different periods in American history. Talk about killing two birds with one stone!" Ellin said.

"More like four or five birds!" Jody quipped.

"This starts the moment the school year begins, and builds on everything the other teachers in this building have done," Jody said. "I'm lucky to work in a setting where my colleagues and I share the same teaching philosophy."

Ellin, Jody, and Chryse spread out to confer and observe. Ellin stopped by Marissa's desk. Marissa had developed a system using sticky notes in six colors to mark changes in her thinking as she read *My Brother Sam Is Dead*, a work of historical fiction set in the Revolutionary War. She had jotted notes, some decipherable only to her, on the sticky tags. She was busily recording key ideas and themes as well as telling details about the characters, settings, events, and resolutions in the book as she read. Each time she detected a major change in her knowledge or thinking, she recorded it on a sticky note. Ellin was flabbergasted. As Ellin watched, Marissa carefully tucked the end of each protruding note around the page where she placed it, creating a blizzard of sticky notes marking the shifts in her thinking along the pages of the closed book.

When Ellin asked Marissa why she felt it was important to mark the changes in her thinking as she read, Marissa replied confidently, "Well, it's because you really don't want to forget the big turns in the plot because that's where the author usually puts in stuff that is more than just interesting—it adds to what you know about the Revolutionary

War. When you're reading historical fiction like this, you have to read it with a real reason in mind. My reason is to figure out factual stuff about the Revolutionary War. You could read nonfiction and get facts that way or you can read fiction and get information this way, but you have to pay closer attention to what the big events are if you're going to get facts from historical fiction."

"I see. Thanks for telling me," Ellin said, thinking that if someone had explained it that clearly to her in elementary school, she might just have remembered a thing or two from American history.

That morning, Jaquil was working on a time line of the Civil War. He read at a long table in the back of the room, rotating among *Across Five Aprils*, two nonfiction books on the Civil War, and notes he had taken from a PBS documentary, *The Civil War*. His time line was taped to the long table with warnings to his classmates not to touch posted above it. His intricate drawings and captions above and below each date on the time line formed a complex synthesis of material he was learning about the Civil War.

Jody stopped behind him. "Jaquil, would you be willing to share your time line with some of the kids who are studying the Revolutionary War? They've struggled to find a way to synthesize all of their reading. You might be able to help."

Jaquil was too engaged to do more than nod.

Jaquil had, in effect, created a visible synthesis in the form of his time line. He had pulled together facts from a number of sources, culled the pieces he found most significant, and was preparing to present them in a cogent way designed to help others focus on the most salient facts related to the Civil War. His drawings emphasized what he found most interesting and significant.

The group reading books from World War II had called an impromptu meeting. They gathered around a table in the corner. Chryse, Ellin, and Jody stopped nearby to listen to their conversation— a conversation that sounded more like an argument.

"Don't go over yet," Chryse whispered. "Let's see what happens."

"It belongs!" Maria's eyes grew intense; her hands grasped her knees as she leaned across the table, speaking directly to Khoa. Chryse explained that they were creating a top ten list of issues from World War II. Their plan was to list the issues, present information to define and describe each, and draw conclusions about whether the top ten issues correlated to issues from the Revolutionary or Civil wars.

"That's good. I've never seen Maria so engaged about anything having to do with school," Jody said.

"Progress!" Chryse retorted.

"Definitely progress. But I wonder about Kaylie. She's had a hard time really getting into this and I'm not sure why. I'll go talk to her," Jody said, heading in her direction.

Kaylie sat across the room, staring out the window. Jody and Ellin knelt beside her desk.

"Hey, Kaylie, what's up?"

"I'm supposed to be meeting with them," she gestured toward the Revolutionary War group. "But I haven't read the books and so I don't have anything to say." She paused and looked out the window again. "My grandpa died in a war and there are pictures of him all over our house and I hear about him all the time and we even went to Washington to find his name on that memorial wall and we did and he wasn't in any of these wars. I could do a top ten list for Vietnam and I have about two thousand books about it at home and I could even bring in some of his stuff and Mrs. Wall in the library has some other books and she told me there is tons of stuff on the Internet about the Vietnam War."

"You don't have much time." Jody glanced at her watch. "About ten minutes till lunch, but why don't you go to the library and see what you can find on Vietnam. I have a feeling you're going to add some very important information to the discussion."

"Do you mean I can do another war?" Kaylie asked.

"If you can find the information and make the connections to the others we're studying."

"Thanks, Mrs. Cohn. I didn't want to do those wars."

"I bet she'll get more done in ten minutes than she's done in the last three days," Jody said. "I guess we've got to be flexible. Right?"

"And kids like Kaylie are the reason," Ellin said, thinking how important it is to watch children carefully.

Jody glanced at the clock. "There's time for one more conference before lunch. Julia-Claire transferred from another school a couple of months ago and the transition hasn't been easy. Let's see how she's doing."

A pile of computer printouts from Internet sources surrounded Julia-Claire.

Ellin began, "Julia-Claire, you've been so focused this morning, I can't wait to see what you're pulling out of all this information." She scanned piles of paper on Julia-Claire's desk and saw she had used a highlighting marker liberally, maybe excessively. As Ellin rifled through the piles, the yellow lines started to thin out. "What happened when you got here?" Ellin asked, pointing to the printout with only a few highlights. "Didn't you find very much that was important?"

"No, I read that stuff the day we had a crafting lesson on text structure. Remember Chryse told us there is, like, cause and effect, chronological, problem-solution, comparison-contrast, and all those ways of organizing in nonfiction."

"Whoa!" Jody exclaimed. "I'm so proud of you for remembering all of that." Jody whispered to Ellin, "Where's the principal at the great moments? Who would believe it?"

"Well," Julia-Claire continued, oblivious to their mumbles, "I started to look for words that show it is that kind of pattern, what did you call it?"

"Signal words?" Jody asked.

"Yeah, I started to look for signal words so I could get how the text was organized, and it really helped me to pay attention to the parts that I need to figure out. Now I'm working on my synthesis of all the stuff I read."

"What's your plan now?" Jody asked.

"I was thinking I would do a diary of a kid my age who lived through the Revolutionary War and tell all these facts I've found out by letting her talk. Is that okay?"

"Sounds great to me!" Jody responded. Do you know what that's called, Julia-Claire? Do you know what it's called when authors use people's talk to introduce facts or push the plot forward?"

"Nope, but I have a feeling you're going to tell me!" Julia-Claire's eyes twinkled.

"You're right about that one. I didn't learn this until college, but I wish I had known about it because I think I would have used it more consciously—on purpose. It's actually one of a set of options writers have for introducing facts or pushing the plot forward." Jody took a large sticky note and wrote:

Character Setting Conflict Theme Events Resolution Facts

at the top and below it three additional words:

Exposition   Action   Dialogue

"Basically, Julia-Claire, you can use any one of these techniques— exposition, action, and/or dialogue—to describe any one of these elements: character, setting, theme, and so forth."

"You mean, you could use dialogue—"

"Like you're doing in your diary of a child in the Revolutionary War," Jody interrupted, to bring Julia-Claire back to the current challenge.

"Okay, you could use any one of these," she pointed at the bottom of the page, "to explain any one of these in the writing."

"Exactly!" Jody said.

"But there's one I don't get—exposition—what's that?"

"Well, you just mentioned a synonym a second ago. Explain. Exposition means that you just provide a straight explanation of things in order to tell about the character or conflict or any one of the elements. As a matter of fact, that's what a lot of kids do—they just *tell* what's happening. Do you remember how, in fourth grade, you guys talked about how important it is to *show* through your writing rather than tell? Well, there are several ways to *show*. You can do it through action—letting the characters' actions show what you want to communicate. Or you can let the dialogue reveal facts or push the plot forward. Cool, huh?"

"Yeah, so I can also use action in my diary even though it's mostly in the form of dialogue to tell facts."

"Actually, a diary is more like a monologue, but I think we've covered enough territory today! We'll take that up next time I confer with you, okay? But in the meantime, yes, use actions and talk to make the facts shine through in your diary."

During Ellin's visit, she observed Jody's students sifting through information on three (then four) major wars, finding common themes and patterns in each, and developing ways to present their research. They managed the information well—discussing, thinking about, organizing—before trying to arrange it in a formal presentation. They were more than active; they were hyperaware as they read, tuning into the important issues, themes, and ideas, asking questions, creating images, relating what they read to prior knowledge, drawing conclusions, making judgments, predicting, and keeping track of what it all means. They were using a variety of means—visual, written, artistic, dramatic, and oral—to make their knowledge and opinions from a variety of sources flow together into something that would be cogent for others in the classroom (see Figure 7.2). They were, in a wide variety of ways, *synthesizing*.

Jody's classroom was not transformed overnight. She is a superb teacher and Chryse Hutchins, a highly skilled staff developer, had worked with her in her classroom for two years. Samuels School had been involved with the PEBC's professional development projects for six years, so it was a receptive environment for change and innovation. Many of Samuels' teachers had dramatically changed their teaching, and the results showed in the children. Nonetheless, this was not a privileged group of students. Eighty-five percent of the children were bused in from one of Denver's poorest neighborhoods.

As Ellin left Jody's room that day, her eyes were drawn to the mess of learning materials: papers, charts, double-entry diary forms, markers, staplers, and piles and piles of books. She was reminded of her dorm room when she was preparing for a major presentation in college and remembered the feelings of efficiency, industry, and ultimately accomplishment. Those were some of her first real feelings of excitement about learning. She left Samuels heartened to see—and a bit envious of—these children who were experiencing those feelings of intellectual rigor and excitement while still in elementary school.

~ ~ ~

When Susan read about Pizarro and Atahuallpa, she glimpsed a very different time and place. Our world has changed dramatically and she, of course, will never experience anything like that day in Cajamarca. But, through the process of synthesis, she had a series of "aha" moments about the power of belief systems and mindsets to shape diametrically different responses to the same set of circumstances, a concept that is as alive and well in this day and age (witness the situation in Iraq) as it was in 1532. Her thinking evolved as she read and even after she was finished.

Synthesis is absolutely essential—in the air and water category—for both literacy learning and life learning. The magnitude and complexity of the information we and our students must manage every day is staggering. To construct any kind of meaning in learning and in life, we must find ways to cull and prune the details with which we are confronted. We must find the essence. We must reorganize and create our own explanations for what we are learning, our own definitions of our lives at any particular juncture.

As with our reading, we cannot wait until the end to figure out what our lives have meant. The work in progress that is our lives must be synthesized along the way. When we pause long enough to reflect— to consider the synthesis of our lives—we are also bestowed with the gift of better knowing and understanding ourselves, those around us, and what we care about. No small undertaking. No small gift for our children.

Key Ideas for Comprehension Strategy Study

Synthesis

The process of synthesizing occurs during reading

- Proficient readers are aware of changes in their ideas and conclusions about a text as they read further into the text. They can articulate orally or in writing how their thinking about a given text evolves.

- Proficient readers maintain a cognitive synthesis as they read. They monitor the overall meaning and themes (there is often more than one theme in the text). Proficient readers actively revise their cognitive synthesis as they read. New information is assimilated into the reader's evolving ideas about the text, rendering some earlier decisions obsolete.

- Proficient readers are aware of the ways text elements (in fiction, character, setting, conflict, sequence of events, and resolution) "fit together" to create that overall meaning. They focus purposely on and use their knowledge of these elements to predict and synthesize as they build a sense of the overall meaning.

- Proficient readers are aware of text structures in nonfiction (cause and effect, compare/contrast, problem/solution, description, enumeration, and chronological paragraph structures). They focus purposefully on and use those structures to predict and synthesize as they build a sense of the overall meaning.

The process of synthesizing occurs after reading

- Proficient readers are able to express, through a variety of means (written, oral, artistic, or dramatic), a cogent, succinct synthesis of what they have read that includes ideas and themes relevant to the overall meaning of the text.

- A synthesis is the sum of information from the text, other relevant texts, and the reader's background knowledge, ideas, and opinions, and may be produced or shared in an original way.

- Proficient readers use syntheses to share, recommend, and critically review books they have read.

- Proficient readers can articulate how using synthesis helps them better understand what they have read.

Mosaic of Meaning

Dark human shapes could be made out in the distance, flitting indistinctly against the gloomy border of a forest, and near the river two bronze figures, leaning on tall spears, stood in the sunlight under fantastic head-dresses of spotted skins, warlike and still in statuesque repose. And from right to left along the lighted shore moved a wild and gorgeous apparition of a woman.

She walked with measured steps, draped in striped and fringed cloths, treading the earth proudly, with a slight jingle and flash of barbarous ornaments. She carried her head high; her hair was done in the shape of a helmet; she had brass leggings to the knee, brass wire gauntlets to the elbow, a crimson spot on her tawny cheek, innumerable necklaces of glass beads on her neck; bizarre things, charms, gifts of witch-men, that hung about her, glittered and trembled at every step. She must have had the value of several elephant tusks upon her. She was savage and superb, wild-eyed and magnificent; there was something ominous and stately in her deliberate progress. And in the hush that had fallen suddenly upon the whole sorrowful land, the immense wilderness, the colossal body of the fecund and mysterious life seemed to look at her, pensive, as though it had been looking at the image of its own tenebrous and passionate soul.

She came abreast of the steamer, stood still, and faced us. Her long shadow fell to the water's edge. Her face had a tragic and fierce aspect of wild sorrow and of dumb pain mingled with the fear of some struggling, half-shaped resolve. She stood looking at us without a stir, and like the wilderness itself, with an air of brooding over an inscrutable purpose. A whole minute passed, and then she made a step forward. There was a low jingle, a glint of yellow metal, a sway of fringed draperies, and she stopped as if her heart had failed her. The young fellow by my side growled. The pilgrims murmured at my back. She looked at us all as if her life had depended upon the unswerving steadiness of her glance. Suddenly she opened her bared arms and threw them up rigid above her head, as though in an uncontrollable desire to touch the sky, and at the same time the swift shadows darted out on the earth, swept around on the river, gathering the steamer into a shadowy embrace. A formidable silence hung over the scene.

She turned away slowly, walked on, following the bank, and passed into the bushes to the left. Once only her eyes gleamed back at us in the dusk of the thickets before she disappeared.

"If she had offered to come aboard, I really think I would have tried to shoot her," said the man of patches nervously. . .

— Joseph Conrad, *Heart of Darkness*

Susan's Reflections

It was this page that caught my eye as I flipped through *A Conrad Argosy*, a Joseph Conrad collection illustrated with woodcuts by Hans Mueller. It is a large, heavy book that has been carefully mended with adhesive tape to keep the cover from loosening further. In black ink on the first page is the inscription "Mrs. Paul D. Phillips, October 1942." I picture Rita, my husband Paul's mother, carefully writing her name there sixty-five years ago. It was, I believe, a difficult autograph for her. At that time she was a young woman of twenty-two, recently married, receiving the book perhaps as a birthday gift from her parents, with whom she then lived in Baltimore. Just months before, her husband Paul Sr. had been captured by the Japanese in the Philippines. For over three years—during the period that Paul Sr. was a prisoner of war, experiencing his own heart of darkness—she would not hear from him.

It is fitting that this is the book I pull out, searching for a final piece. Rita is now dead; yet I feel her careful hands where, long ago, she repaired this book with tape. I am grateful the book is now in our library. It has been much loved and cared for, and somehow, I want to capture here a sense of the love, care, and thoughtful consideration that must go into the work teachers do.

This passage leaps out at me from the page. It is the woman who captures my imagination. The first time I read it, my heart beats faster and my palms sweat. The questions begin: Why do I feel such fear for this amazing woman? Why do I sense her coming demise and with that the loss of something incalculably precious? Why, as I read, am I overwhelmed with foreboding and fascinated with this being Conrad has described?

"Dark human shapes could be made out in the distance, flitting indistinctly against the gloomy border of the forest . . ." I am taken into a dream, into a dark, murky place, a jungle completely foreign to me, a place of nightmares. My eyes and ears open and are full of images. I hear the rustling of branches and see vague shapes moving ominously on the bank, as the principal character in this scene appears: "From right to left along the lighted shore moved a wild and gorgeous apparition of a woman." She is, I suppose, a tribal leader or priestess of some sort. A vivid picture of her adorned body forms in my mind: "brass leggings to the knee," "innumerable necklaces of glass beads on her neck," "the value of several elephant tusks upon her." She is statuesque, strong, and silent. Nowhere in the passage does she make a sound. Something about Conrad's description makes me think of a leopard, an elegant, ferocious cat that cannot be tamed.

As I read on, the woman grows in my mind. I begin making inferences. She is more than a human; she is a force—that wildness in woman that has been repressed over the centuries. She becomes for me a character of mythic proportion, harking back to the goddesses of pre-Christian times.

Joseph Conrad wrote *Heart of Darkness* over a century ago, yet this passage remains eternal. The woman embodies a female power and beauty before which men stand speechless, utterly unable to respond, "the hush that had fallen suddenly upon the whole sorrowful land."

In turn the woman seems puzzled by and frightened of the steamer, the men on it, and all it represents. "Her face had a tragic and fierce aspect of wild sorrow and of dumb pain mingled with the fear of some struggling, half-shaped resolve." Is the woman the symbol of Africa? Is she the darkness in each of us, that wild part of our unconscious that we fear to confront, let alone acknowledge? Is she, in Jungian terms, a female archetype, representing a power that has been passed down through the ages?

What is her half-shaped resolve? As the dying Kurtz—one of literature's truly evil characters—is taken away on the steamer, does she know that the destruction he has caused can never be repaired? Is the wild sorrow and dumb pain a realization of all that has been lost? The questions continue, a critical part of my effort to make sense of this passage—my synthesis.

"And she stopped as if her heart had failed her ... She looked at us all as if her life had depended upon the unswerving steadiness of her glance. Suddenly she opened her bared arms and threw them up rigid above her head, as though in an uncontrollable desire to touch the sky, and at the same time the swift shadows darted out on the earth, swept around on the river, gathering the steamer into a shadowy embrace." What is she doing here? It is as if she knows her fate and yet there is something in her that goes beyond fate. Is this shadowy embrace a gesture of forgiveness, or is it her way of showing the men on the steamer that she has them in her embrace and will never let them go, though they may think they've escaped?

I read again and see that the woman's gesture is also one of futility and hopelessness. No one can really touch the sky, though we all may want to at times. Is she throwing up her arms in despair? Does she know she has lost and all she can do is make one last powerful, but futile, gesture?

What is it about the woman that the men on the steamer cannot abide? Is it her wildness, her strength, her willingness to forgive, or her inability to let go that brings out their guilt and evil? "If she had offered to come aboard, I really think I would have tried to shoot her." I infer that there is something here about the repression of those things we fear and don't understand. In this brief passage, Conrad creates a creature imbued with mystery and strength and with a few strokes shows how quickly man is prepared to destroy that which threatens or puzzles him.

I find myself reading the passage again and again, each time seeing more. Here are white men coming up the mighty river in a steamer that clangs and whistles, imposing itself on a land where it doesn't belong. The men carry rifles. They act with total disregard for the natives on the shore. They invade and plunder, believing they have every right to do so. I see the tragic clash between native peoples and Western civilization's greed. I see that the price of colonization was the destruction of cultures.

I wonder if the modern era will be remembered as that time in our history when thousands of diverse cultures were obliterated forever. I connect my experience to this writing and remember arriving at the Istanbul airport several years ago and being greeted by a huge picture of the Marlboro man. I think of Tina Turner's "What's love got to do, got to do with it" blasting from the loudspeaker at a sacred hot springs turned swimming pool in Pammukkale, a remote Turkish town with an ancient Greek theater and white travertine cliffs. And I think little has changed since Conrad's time. Our means of conquering are just different today.

I go back and reread the whole story. I first read it in college and remember skimming it years later before going to see *Apocalypse Now*, a modern-day rendition in which Vietnam was the heart of darkness and Marlon Brando the tyrant Kurtz. I get up early and read voraciously, mesmerized by the shadowy evil Conrad portrays. And as I read, I wonder if each of us has within us the potential to become a Kurtz—to be eaten up and embraced by darkness so deep and penetrating that no light can get through.

I go back to the passage of the woman, now able to put it in context and I am, more than ever, struck by the power and poetry of Conrad's language and by the dichotomies that flow through his writing, creating a mood as complex as life itself: "savage and superb," "wild-eyed and magnificent," "ominous and stately," "tragic and fierce," "wild sorrow and dumb pain," "half-shaped resolve," and "inscrutable purpose."

My prediction that the woman would be destroyed comes true—perhaps. Conrad wraps even that in ambiguity: "I pulled the string [of the steamboat whistle] time after time . . . Only the barbarous and superb woman did not so much as flinch, and stretched tragically her bare arms after us over the somber and glittering river . . . And then that imbecile crowd [the men with rifles] down on the deck started their little fun, and I could see nothing more for the smoke."

As I read, I consciously and subconsciously use the strategies we've discussed in this book. I synthesize. I question. I infer. I create vivid sensory images. I relate the piece to my own experience. I tease out what I think is most important. I draw conclusions about what I think the key points of the passage are. Sometimes I use the strategies purposefully; other times they surface randomly. They are the tools I use, sometimes effortlessly, sometimes purposefully, to construct a meaning. They intertwine and merge and I switch quickly among them, frequently using them simultaneously. They are the instruments that, as I became more familiar with them, give me the ability to read more critically. They are a means to an end. For proficient readers, they are second nature.

Teachers as Sculptors

Years ago, Ellin gave Susan *Where the Bluebird Sings to the Lemonade Springs*, a series of essays by Wallace Stegner. She gave it to Susan when she left the Public Education and Business Coalition to embark on a writer's life and inscribed it, "to call forth that all-important sense of place; to surround you with peace and wonder on your journey."

Many essays in that book have guided Susan, but the last one she returns to year after year. In it Stegner says, "The writers I admired, and still admire, were not carpenters but sculptors. Their art was and is a real probe of troubling human confusions. They spurned replicas, they despised commercialized entertainment. They were after the mystery implicit in the stone."

Repeatedly, we find ourselves substituting the word *teacher* for *writer* in this passage. The teachers we admire—the teachers whose classrooms we have visited in this book as well as many others—are not carpenters but sculptors. They are after the mystery implicit in the stone. They guide their students on a search for the mystery and ponder with them as "troubling human confusions" are revealed.

These teachers create the environment and provide the tools students need to read deeply and thoughtfully, so they can contemplate ideas alone and with others, and write persuasively about what they read. They are teachers who embrace the wide range of responses their students give to the same text, and challenge the students to read books they believe they cannot. They relish every day with children and recall why they went into teaching in the first place. They are teachers who know that what matters most is the joy of learning.

We have all had those teachers, inside and outside the classroom: people who believed in us, who trusted our uniqueness, who unleashed our dormant talents, and who gave us the skills and confidence to carve away at the stone ourselves. We remember them for their gifts to us.

Perhaps their greatest gift was the standard they set as curious and passionate learners.

Unless we use them ourselves, we cannot expect to be able to teach these techniques for increasing the scope and depth of a child's comprehension. It is through our own experience in reading—using these strategies very consciously at times—that we internalize and are able to teach them. By teaching the strategies, we give children the tools they need to exercise their critical thinking faculties, to struggle with human confusions, and to embark on their own explorations of the mystery and beauty of life.

John Cheever once said that he wrote "to try to make sense of my life." We read for the same reason: to make sense of our lives and to connect to those who have come before us as well as those who now share the planet with us. We read to do our jobs, to learn, to explore, to adventure, to bring order to chaos, to open new vistas, to better understand the world around us, and to develop compassion for the human condition.

Great writing leaves us with more questions than answers. Each of us must look deep within to determine what a great novel, poem, or essay means to us. The comprehension strategies discussed in this book are the tools to chisel meaning deep into a reader's long-term memory as he or she discusses with others, writes about the piece, or explores it further through research or additional reading.

Each time we encounter a great piece of writing, we set out on a personal journey of self-discovery with a destination as unknown as that of Columbus. By the mysterious alchemy of the written word, we range over time and space, expanding our experiences, enriching our souls, and ultimately becoming more fully, more consciously human.

Thinking Strategies Used by Proficient Learners

Monitoring Meaning and Comprehension

READERS

- Readers monitor their comprehension during reading. They know when the text they are reading or listening to makes sense, when it does not, what does not make sense, and whether the unclear portions are critical to overall understanding of the piece.

- Readers can identify ways in which a text gradually becomes more understandable by reading past an unclear portion and/or by rereading parts or the whole text.

- Readers are aware of the processes they can use to make meaning clear. They check, evaluate, and make revisions to their evolving interpretation of the text while reading.

- Readers can identify confusing ideas, themes, and/or surface elements (words, sentence or text structures, graphs, tables, etc.) and can suggest a variety of different means to solve the problems they have.

- Readers are aware of what they need to comprehend in relation to their purpose for reading.

- Readers must learn how to pause, consider the meanings in text, reflect on their understandings, and use different strategies to enhance their understanding. This process is best learned by watching proficient models "think aloud" and gradually taking responsibility for monitoring their own comprehension as they read independently.

WRITERS

- Writers monitor during their composition process to ensure that their text makes sense for their intended audience at the word, sentence, and text levels.

- Writers read their work aloud to find and hear their voice.

- Writers share their work so others can help them monitor the clarity and impact of the work.

- Writers pay attention to their style and purpose. They purposefully write with clarity and honesty. They strive to write boldly, simply, and concisely by keeping those standards alive in their minds during the writing process.

- Writers pause to consider the impact of their work and make conscious decisions about when to turn a small piece into a larger project, when revisions are complete, or when to abandon a piece.

MATHEMATICIANS

- Mathematicians check to make sure answers are reasonable.

- Mathematicians use manipulatives/charts/diagrams to help themselves make sense of the problem.

- Mathematicians understand that others will build meaning in different ways and solve problems with different problem-solving strategies.

- Mathematicians write in order to better understand.

- Mathematicians check their work in many ways: working backwards, redoing problems, and so on.

- Mathematicians agree/disagree with solutions and ideas.

- Mathematicians express in think-alouds what's going on in their head as they work through a problem. They are metacognitive.

- Mathematicians continually ask themselves if each step makes sense.

- Mathematicians discuss problems with others and write about their problem-solving process to clarify their thinking and make problems clearer.

- Mathematicians use accurate math vocabulary and show their work in clear, concise forms so others can follow their thinking without asking questions.

(Note: Readers will be enlightened, informed, and engaged by *Comprehending Math,* Arthur Hyde's [2006] new book on translating the strategies for use in math classrooms.)

RESEARCHERS

- Researchers are aware of what they need to find out and learn about.
- Researchers can identify when they comprehend and take steps to repair comprehension when they don't.
- Researchers pause to reflect and evaluate information.
- Researchers choose effective ways of organizing information—taking notes, webbing, outlining, and so forth.
- Researchers use several sources to validate information and check for accuracy.
- Researchers revise and edit for clarity, accuracy, and interest.
- Researchers check sources for appropriate references and copyrights.

Using Prior Knowledge—Schema

READERS

- Readers spontaneously activate relevant, prior knowledge before, during, and after reading text.
- Readers assimilate information from text into their schema and make changes in that schema to accommodate the new information.
- Readers use schema to relate text to their world knowledge, text knowledge, and personal experience.
- Readers use their schema to enhance their understanding of text and to store text information in long-term memory.
- Readers use their schema for specific authors and their styles to better understand text.

- Readers recognize when they have inadequate background information and know how to create it—to build schema—to get the information they need.

WRITERS

- Writers frequently choose their own topics and write about subjects they care about.
- A writer's content comes from and builds on his or her experiences.
- Writers think about and use what they know about genre, text structure, and conventions as they write.
- Writers seek to better recognize and capitalize on their own voice for specific effects in their compositions.
- Writers know when their schema for a topic or text format is inadequate and they create the necessary background knowledge.
- Writers use knowledge of their audience to make decisions about content inclusions/exclusions.

MATHEMATICIANS

- Mathematicians use current understandings as first steps in the problem-solving process.
- Mathematicians use their number sense to understand a problem.
- Mathematicians add to schema by trying more challenging problems and hearing from others about different problem-solving methods.
- Mathematicians build understanding based on prior knowledge of math concepts.
- Mathematicians develop purpose based on prior knowledge.
- Mathematicians use their prior knowledge to generalize about similar problems and to choose problem-solving strategies.
- Mathematicians develop their own problems.

RESEARCHERS

- Researchers frequently choose topics they know and care about.
- Researchers use their prior knowledge and experience to launch investigations and ask questions.

- Researchers consider what they already know to decide what they need to find out; they self-evaluate according to background knowledge of what constitutes high-quality products/presentations.

Asking Questions

READERS

- Readers spontaneously generate questions before, during, and after reading.
- Readers ask questions for different purposes, including to clarify meaning, make predictions, determine an author's style, content, or format, locate a specific answer in text, or consider rhetorical questions inspired by the text.
- Readers use questions to focus their attention on important components of the text.
- Readers are aware that other readers' questions may inspire new questions for them.

WRITERS

- Writers compose in a way that causes the reader to form question as they read.
- Writers monitor their progress by asking questions about their choices as they write.
- Writers ask questions of other writers in order to confirm their choices and make revisions.
- Writers' questions lead to revision in their own work and in the pieces to which they respond for other writers.

MATHEMATICIANS

- Mathematicians ask questions before, during, and after doing a math problem.
  - Could it be this?
  - What happens if?
  - How else could I do this?
  - Have I seen this problem before?
  - What does this mean?

- Mathematicians test theories/answers/a hypothesis by using different approaches to a problem.
- Mathematicians question others to understand their own process and to clarify problems.
- Mathematicians extend their thinking by asking themselves questions they don't have an answer to.

RESEARCHERS

- Researchers ask questions to narrow a search and find a topic.
- Researchers ask questions to clarify meaning and purpose.
- Researchers ask themselves:
  - What are the most effective resources and how will I access them?
  - Do I have enough information?
  - Have I used a variety of sources?
  - What more do I need?
  - Does the concept make sense?
  - Have I told enough?
  - Is my thinking interesting and original and does my writing have voice?

Drawing Inferences

READERS

- Readers use their schema and textual information to draw conclusions and form unique interpretations from text.
- Readers make predictions about text, confirm their predictions, and test their developing meaning as they read on.
- Readers know when and how to use text in combination with their own background knowledge to seek answers to questions.
- Readers create interpretations to enrich and deepen their experience in a text.

WRITERS

- Writers make decisions about content inclusions/exclusions and genre/text structure that permit or encourage inference on the part of the reader.

- Writers carefully consider their audience in making decisions about what to describe explicitly and what to leave to the reader's interpretation.

- Writers, particularly fiction and poetry writers, are aware of far more detail than they reveal in the texts they compose. This encourages inferences such as drawing conclusions, making critical judgments, predictions, and connections to other texts and experiences possible for their readers.

MATHEMATICIANS

- Mathematicians predict, generalize, and estimate.

- As mathematicians read a problem, they make problem-solving decisions based on their conceptual understanding of math concepts (e.g., operations, fractions).

- Mathematicians compose (like a writer) by drawing pictures, using charts, and creating equations.

- Mathematicians solve problems in different ways and support their methods through proof, number sentences, pictures, charts, and graphs.

- Mathematicians use reasoning and make connections throughout the problem-solving process.

- Mathematicians conjecture (infer based on evidence).

- Mathematicians use patterns (consistencies) and relationships to generalize and infer what comes next in the problem-solving process.

RESEARCHERS

- Researchers think about the value and reliability of their sources.

- Researchers consider what is important to a reader or audience.

Using Sensory and Emotional Images

READERS

- Readers create sensory images during and after reading. These may include visual, auditory, and other sensory images as well as emotional connections to the text and are rooted in prior knowledge.

- Readers use images to draw conclusions and to create unique interpretations of the text. Images from reading frequently become part of the reader's writing. Images from personal experience frequently become part of the reader's comprehension.

- Readers use their images to clarify and enhance comprehension.

- Readers use images to immerse themselves in rich detail as they read. The detail gives depth and dimension to the reading, engaging the reader more deeply and making the text more memorable.

- Readers adapt their images in response to the shared images of other readers.

- Readers adapt their images as they read to incorporate new information revealed through the text and new interpretations they develop.

WRITERS

- Writers consciously attempt to create strong images in their compositions using strategically placed detail.

- Writers create impact through the use of strong nouns and verbs whenever possible.

- Writers use images to explore their own ideas. They consciously study their mental images for direction in their pieces.

- Writers learn from the images created in their minds as they read. They study other authors' use of images as a way to improve their own.

MATHEMATICIANS

- Mathematicians use mental pictures and models of shapes, numbers, and processes to build understanding of concepts and problems and to experiment with ideas.

- Mathematicians use concrete models and manipulatives to build understanding and visualize problems.
- Mathematicians visually represent thinking through drawings, pictures, graphs, and charts.
- Mathematicians picture story problems like a movie in the mind to help understand the problem.
- Mathematicians visualize concepts (parallel lines, fractions, etc.).

RESEARCHERS

- Researchers create rich mental pictures to better understand text.
- Researchers interweave written images with multisensory (auditory, visual, kinesthetic) components to enhance comprehension.
- Researchers use words, visual images, sounds, and other sensory experiences to communicate understanding of a topic (which can lead to further questions for research).

Determining What Is Important in Text

READERS

- Readers identify key ideas or themes as they read.
- Readers distinguish important from unimportant information in relation to key ideas or themes in text. They can distinguish important information at the word, sentence, and text levels.
- Readers utilize text structures and text features (such as bold or italicized print, figures and photographs) to help them distinguish important from unimportant information.
- Readers use their knowledge of important and relevant parts of text to prioritize in long-term memory and synthesize text for others.

WRITERS

- Writers observe their world and record what they believe is significant.
- Writers make decisions about the most important ideas to include in the pieces they write. They make decisions about the best genre and structure to communicate their ideas.

- Writers reveal their biases by emphasizing some elements over others.
- Writers provide only essential details to reveal the meaning and produce the effect desired.
- Writers delete information irrelevant to their larger purpose.

MATHEMATICIANS

- Mathematicians look for patterns and relationships.
- Mathematicians identify and use key words to build an understanding of the problem.
- Mathematicians gather text information from graphs, charts, and tables.
- Mathematicians decide what information is relevant to a problem and what is irrelevant.

RESEARCHERS

- Researchers evaluate and think critically about information.
- Researchers sort and analyze information to better understand it.
- Researchers make decisions about the quality and usefulness of information.
- Researchers decide what's important to remember and what isn't.
- Researchers choose the most effective reporting platform.

Synthesizing Information

READERS

- Readers maintain a cognitive synthesis as they read. They monitor the overall meaning, important concepts, and themes in the text and are aware of ways text elements "fit together" to create the overarching ideas. They use their knowledge of the text elements to make decisions about the overall meaning of a passage, chapter, or book.
- Readers retell or synthesize in order to better understand what they have read. They attend to the most important information and to the clarity of the synthesis itself.

- Readers capitalize on opportunities to share, recommend, and critique books they have read.

- Readers may respond to text in a variety of ways, independently or in groups of other readers. These include written, oral, dramatic, and artistic responses and interpretations of text.

- A proficient reader's synthesis is likely to extend the literal meaning of a text to the inferential level.

WRITERS

- Writers make global and focal plans for their writing before and during the drafting process. They use their knowledge of text elements such as character, setting, conflict, sequence of events, and resolution to create a structure for their writing.

- Writers study other writers and draw conclusions about what makes good writing. They work to replicate the style of authors they find compelling.

- Writers reveal themes in a way that suggests their importance to readers. Readers can create a cogent synthesis from well-written material.

MATHEMATICIANS

- Mathematicians generalize from patterns they observe.

- Mathematicians generalize in words, equations, charts, and graphs to retell or synthesize.

- Mathematicians synthesize math concepts when they use them in real-life applications.

- Mathematicians use deductive reasoning (e.g., reach conclusions based on knowns).

RESEARCHERS

- Researchers develop insight about a topic to create new knowledge or understanding.

- Researchers utilize information from a variety of resources.

- Researchers enhance their understanding of a topic by considering different perspectives, opinions, and sources.

Thinking Rubric

Name _____

Teacher _____

Date _____

Directions

Use this rubric to rate the quality of your thinking on a comprehension strategy. The rubric can be used to review written, oral, artistic, or dramatic expressions of your thinking about a book.

When you can go beyond describing your use of a strategy to tell how using that strategy helps you comprehend better, your work should be scored at least a 4.

Thinks Aloud

(Used for a general think-aloud on a text—any strategy can be used, and many can be used together)

1. I can't think of any response; I can't contribute to the discussion about this text or strategy.

2. My thinking is related more to the pictures than text and I'm generally pretty confused about what is going on in the book.

3. I understand some of the events and content, but I feel like I have some of it wrong—some of it doesn't really seem to fit together. I may be thinking more about things that have happened to me than this book. I think I could probably retell generally what's happening in the book.

4. I find myself asking questions and making some inferences in this book. I know what's happening with the main characters and the conflict. I can make some connections between text events and my own experience; it's possible to make predictions about the book's overall meaning. I could probably retell this book in some detail.

5. My thinking is very clear about this book. I have a strong idea about the central ideas or themes. When I think about my thinking, I understand this text much more clearly; I can even tell you how thinking about my own thinking helps me in other books I read.

Monitors Comprehension

1. I can't think of any response; I can't contribute to the discussion about this text or strategy.

2. I can tell you where I have problems in this book; the problems are usually on hard words. I'm not sure that I read this book well enough to really understand it and I'm not quite sure what to do to fix the problems.

3. I have some problems when reading this book. Some are on words and some relate to the ideas in the book, but I usually know what to do to solve the problems.

4. I understand much of this book and when I do have problems I can solve them quickly. If that doesn't work I have a lot of other ways I can fix the problem—most of the problems I do have relate to ideas, not words.

5. I can identify whenever I have a problem, whether it's at the word or idea level, and I have a lot of word and comprehension strategies I can experiment with until I fix the problem. I use different strategies depending on the problem and the purpose I have for reading and can tell you how using those strategies helps me understand any book I read.

Uses Schema

1. I can't think of any response; I can't contribute to the discussion about this text or strategy.

2. I can tell you what this text reminds me of but it would be really hard to explain how those connections fit with the book.

3. I have a very clear idea of how my own experiences, beliefs, and feelings relate to the characters and events or topics in this text.

4. I can describe my background knowledge that relates to this book and even develop new thinking and interpretations for it using my schema. I can discuss my schema for this author, and maybe even for the way the text is laid out—the text structure. I may have some questions because my schema for some of the content doesn't seem to fit with the way things happen in this text.

5. I can explain how my schema helps me understand this or any other text much more clearly; I'm even more aware of how my schema helps me understand other texts. The connections I make go beyond my own life experience and this book. I am able to think about connections to other issues and other people's experiences.

Questions

1. I can't think of any response; I can't contribute to the discussion about this text or strategy.

2. I can think of a couple of questions that can probably be answered by reading further or rereading the text.

3. The questions I think of mostly help me figure out exactly what is happening in this book or what the main topics are.

4. The questions I pose make me understand more about the book itself but I'm not sure I can explain exactly how posing these questions deepens my comprehension.

5. I can use questions to challenge an author's message or point of view; I can question whether he or she is right or shares my beliefs, feelings, and opinions. I can tell you exactly how my questions help me understand this text or any text I read better; most of my questions are the kind that can't be answered directly in the text and would probably lead to interesting discussion.

Infers

1. I can't think of any response; I can't contribute to the discussion about this text or strategy.

2. Sometimes I have predictions or decide things about this book, but

I'm not sure how they relate to the book or if the author wanted me to draw these conclusions.

3. The predictions and conclusions I draw from this text are probably aligned with what the author would think and with my background knowledge.

4. I can draw conclusions, interpret, and/or predict and can explain how I came up with my conclusions, interpretations, or predictions for this book.

5. I can develop my own predictions, interpretations, and/or conclusions about the text that include connections between the text and my background knowledge or my ideas and beliefs. When I create these inferences I can describe how I understand more about the book or any book I read and why those books are likely to be more memorable to me.

Uses Sensory and Emotional Images

1. I can't think of any response; I can't contribute to the discussion about this text or strategy.

2. I have a few pictures in my head, but I'm not sure how they relate to the book.

3. I can tell you about my images. Most of them are visual. My images include more than just what is in the book or pictures. Sometimes I have some emotional images that make me want to read this book more or reread it.

4. I have images that come from emotions as well as sight, sound, smell, touch, and even taste. I can use them to help me understand this text better.

5. I can tell you a lot about how my images help me better understand this book or any book I read.

Determines What Is Important in Text

1. I can't think of any response; I can't contribute to the discussion about this text or strategy.

2. I can point out some parts of the text, mostly pictures, that must be pretty important for understanding this text's meaning, but I'm not quite sure how or why these parts are important.

3. I can point out certain words, characters, and/or events as more important to the meaning and I can explain why I think something is important. If I'm reading expository text I can use text features such as bold print and captions to help me decide what is important. I can usually explain why the concepts are important.

4. I am sure I can point out and explain at least one key concept, idea, or theme as important to understanding the overall text meaning.

5. I can explain several ideas or themes that are very important for understanding this text; I can tell you why they're important and why the author might have emphasized them given his/her purpose. I can tell you how thinking about these important ideas helps me to better understand this text or any other book I read.

Synthesizes

1. I can't think of any response; I can't contribute to the discussion about this text or strategy.

2. I can tell you some parts of text for fiction and nonfiction. I can tell you generally how things are happening in this book, but I'm not really sure what the author is trying to tell me.

3. I have a pretty good idea about the order for this text and how the ideas are organized, like the beginning, middle, end. I understand that the order helps me understand better. I can tell you a little about how my thinking changed as I read this book.

4. When I think about how my thinking is changing, how I'm synthesizing, I understand this text much better. Sometimes I use my schema or my knowledge of what characters usually do, the problem, the setting, and the conclusion or resolution; I can tell you about the key themes and I can describe how my thinking changed from the beginning to the end of the passage.

5. I can synthesize using everything I know about story structures, text formats, and genres. I can identify the key themes and tell you how

synthesizing helps me understand more in this or any book I read. I can represent my understandings and opinions in a way you'll clearly understand after my reading.

Epigraphs from the First Edition

On the following pages are the opening short pieces from the first edition of *Mosaic of Thought*. Over the years we have gotten excellent feedback about how useful these are to introduce and practice using the strategies in study groups. Therefore, we wanted to make them available to you in this new edition.

Salvador, Late or Early

Salvador with eyes the color of caterpillar, Salvador of the crooked hair and crooked teeth, Salvador whose name the teacher cannot remember, is a boy who is no one's friend, runs along somewhere in that vague direction where homes are the color of bad weather, lives behind a raw wood doorway, shakes the sleepy brothers awake, ties their shoes, combs their hair with water, feeds them milk and corn flakes from a tin cup in the dim dark of the morning.

Salvador, late or early, sooner or later arrives with the string of younger brothers ready. Helps his mama, who is busy with the business of the baby. Tugs the arms of Cecilio, Arturito, makes them hurry, because today, like yesterday, Arturito has dropped the cigar box of crayons, has let go the hundred little fingers of red, green, yellow, blue, and nub of black sticks that tumble and spill over and beyond the asphalt puddles until the crossing-guard lady holds back the blur of traffic for Salvador to collect them again.

Salvador inside that wrinkled shirt, inside the throat that must clear itself and apologize each time it speaks, inside that forty-pound body of boy with its geography of scars, its history of hurt, limbs stuffed with feathers and rags, in what part of the eyes, in what part of the heart, in that cage of the chest where something throbs with both fists and knows only what Salvador knows, inside that body too small to contain the hundred balloons of happiness, the single guitar of grief, is a boy like any other disappearing out the door, beside the schoolyard gate, where he has told his brothers they must wait. Collects the hands of Cecilio and Arturito, scuttles off dodging the many schoolyard colors, the elbows and wrists criss-crossing, the several shoes running. Grows small and smaller to the eye, dissolves into the bright horizon, flutters in the air before disappearing like a memory of kites.

Sandra Cisneros, *Woman Hollering Creek and Other Stories*

I cried then for a while because I wasn't absolutely certain I wanted to spend my life with the boy who lay sleeping next to me. I cried for my bed at home and for my parents. . . . After that, I gave up trying to sleep and decided to sneak into the bathroom to read. Bobbe spotted me when I crept past her door.

"Faygele," she called. "Are you all right? What are you doing up so late?". . .

"I can't sleep either," she said. "Come, keep me company."

She lifted the heavy quilt and patted the bed beside her. I can remember so clearly how gingerly I crawled into the tiny bed, struggling to keep myself at the edge so I would not have to touch the misshapen little bone-bag that was her body. She pulled the blanket up over us both and said, "When you are old, you never want to sleep because there are so many years to sleep soon, anyway."

"I had a dream last night," she told me. "I saw your father-in-law (who had recently died) and I asked, Frank, are you happy where you are? I think he couldn't speak, but he handed me a piece of bread and honey and he motioned for me to eat. You will have a boy," she said firmly, putting her hand on my stomach. A fat little boy and he will have Frank's name. That's what the dream meant."

Still keeping a death grip on the edge of the mattress, I started to tell her how the five-year plan made no provision for fat little boys, but I changed my mind. Instead, I let go, rolling to the hollow where our bodies touched, feeling my firm, moist arms, embarrassing in their ripeness, against her powdery, translucent flesh, fearing my chunky body would crush her brittle, twiglike limbs.

Bobbe threw off the covers and took down boxes in her closet. She showed me her wig, a saucy unexpected auburn, part of her dowry when, as a sixteen-year-old, she had married her first husband. From another box, she drew out a thick brown braid glistening with naphthalene. I had the strangest feeling touching the crumbling hair that if I stretched my fingers far enough I could touch, too, the tender young bride who must have cried so bitterly when the women came to shear her heavy hair.

Faye Moskowitz, *A Leak in the Heart: Tales from a Woman's Life*

I am not free of the condition I describe here. I cannot be certain how far back in human history the habit of denial can be traced. But it is at least as old as I am. In our common history, I have found it in the legends surrounding the battle of Troy, and in my own family I have traced it three generations back, to that recent time past when there had been no world wars and my grandparents were young. All that I was taught at home or in school was colored by denial, and thus it became so familiar to me that I did not see it. Only now have I begun to recognize that there were many closely guarded family secrets that I kept, and many that were kept from me.

When my father was still a small boy, his mother did something unforgivable. It was a source of shame as many secrets are, and hence kept hidden from my father and, eventually, from me. My great-aunt would have told me this secret before she died, but by that time she could not remember it. I have always sensed that my grandmother's transgression was sexual. Whatever she did was taken as cause by my grandfather and his mother to abandon her. They left her in Canada and moved to California, taking her two sons, my father and his brother, with them.

My father was not allowed to cry over his lost mother. Not to speak her name. He could not give in to his grief but instead was taught to practice the military virtue of forbearance and to set an example in his manhood for his younger brother, Roland. In this way I suppose my grandfather hoped to erase the memory of my grandmother from all of our minds. But her loss has haunted us.

How old is the habit of denial? We keep secrets from ourselves that all along we know. The public was told that old Dresden was bombed to destroy strategic railway lines. There were no railway lines in that part of the city. But it would be years before that story came to the surface.

I do not see my life as separate from history. In my mind my family secrets mingle with the secrets of statesmen and bombers. Nor is my life divided from the lives of others. I, who am a woman, have my father's face. And he, I suspect, had his mother's face.

There is a characteristic way my father's eyelids fold, and you can see this in my face and in a photograph I have of him as a little boy. In the same photograph there is a silent sorrow mapped on his face, and this sorrow is mine too.

I place this photograph next to two others which are on my desk. Tracing the genesis of the bombing of civilians, I have come across a photograph of Dresden taken in 1945. A few dark figures hunch over a sea of corpses. There are ruined buildings in the background and smoke from a fire. The other photograph was sent to me by my cousin, after I asked her if she knew the name of my paternal grandmother, or if she might have a picture of her.

The photograph my cousin did send me has a haunted quality though it was taken in Canada before the erasure of my grandmother. It is not a picture of my grandmother. It is a picture of my grandfather with my father. It was taken a few years before masses of soldiers died on the battlefields of World War I, and over three decades before the bombing of Dresden, the concentration camps, Hiroshima. And yet, my grandfather's face bears an expression of grief just as if he were looking over a scene of senseless destruction, a field of bodies. What was his sorrow? . . .

If I tell here all the secrets that I know, public and private, perhaps I will begin to see the way the old sometimes see, Monet, recording light and spirit in his paintings, or the way those see who have been trapped by circumstances—a death, a loss, a cataclysm of history—grasping the essential.

Susan Griffin, *A Chorus of Stones: A Private Life of War*

An Unspoken Hunger

It is an unspoken hunger we deflect with knives—one avocado between us, cut neatly in half, twisted then separated from the large wooden pit. With the green fleshy boats in hand, we slice vertical strips from one end to the other. Vegetable planks. We smother the avocado with salsa, hot chiles at noon in the desert. We look at each other and smile, eating avocados with sharp silver blades, risking the blood of our tongues repeatedly.

Terry Tempest Williams, *An Unspoken Hunger: Stories from the Field*

Three Small Oranges

My old flannel nightgown, the elbows out,
one shoulder torn . . . Instead of putting it
away with the clean wash, I cut it up
for rags, removing the arms and opening
their seams, scissoring across the breast
and upper back, then tearing the thin
cloth of the body into long rectangles.
Suddenly an immense sadness . . .
Making supper, I listen to news
from the war, of torture where the air
is black at noon with burning oil,
and of a market in Baghdad, bombed
by accident, where yesterday an old man
carried in his basket a piece of fish
wrapped in paper and tied with string,
and three small hard green oranges.

Jane Kenyon, *Constance: Poems*

We who lived in concentration camps can remember the men who walked through the huts comforting others, giving away their last piece of bread. They may have been few in number, but they offer sufficient proof that everything can be taken from a man but one thing: the last of the human freedoms—to choose one's attitude in any given set of circumstances, to choose one's own way.

A thought transfixed me: for the first time in my life I saw the truth as it is set into song by so many poets, proclaimed as the final wisdom by so many thinkers. The truth—that love is the ultimate and the highest goal to which man can aspire. Then I grasped the meaning of the greatest secret that human poetry and human thought and belief have to impart: The salvation of man is through love and in love. I understood how a man who has nothing left in this world still may know bliss, be it only for a brief moment, in the contemplation of his beloved. In a position of utter desolation, when man cannot express himself in positive action, when his only achievement may consist in enduring his sufferings in the right way—an honorable way—in such a position man can, through loving contemplation of the image he carries of his beloved, achieve fulfillment.

Viktor E. Frankl, *Man's Search for Meaning*

Comrade Past & Mister Present

Can the misfortune of a dog owned by vegetarians
be felt by a woolen creature exuding class privilege?
Looking through windows to glimpse tits I saw this
instead. It wasn't in the manual. But
applying private cures to collective diseases
occupied every page, it was The Book of
the Transparent Tombstone. You could see
all the heroes inside, and downtown Chicago,
men like Mr. Wrigley and buildings like the Tribune
Tower, and what they felt being there like that,
men and buildings squashed inside the look
of a drunk poet chased by wind
like a Sunday supplement on Monday morn.
You could read their desires but not their thoughts,
because you can read those like cigarettes in Lebanon
or Madagascar, and they said,
The thing to be is dead. Complete
thought evacuation. The cold wind
said that. The buildings themselves said
other things, having to do with stubbornness,
heart, commerce, stability, the will
of large men who know the world well
enough to sell it, and when.
You cannot throw up a building in Chicago,
my friend Debra says, and what, say I,
do I look big enough to throw up buildings?
Maybe my steak, but not a whole edifice, no.
You cannot, she says, do that unless it says
something, and the buildings in Chicago say
some pretty strange things these days. I look.
They do. . . .

     Andrei Codrescu, *Comrade Past & Mister Present*

References

Children's Literature

Aliki. 1979. *The Two of Them*. New York: Greenwillow Books.

Bagnold, Enid, 1935. *National Velvet*. New York: William Morrow.

Baylor, Byrd. 1977. *The Way to Start a Day*. New York: Simon & Schuster.

———. 1988. *I'm in Charge of Celebrations*. New York: Simon & Schuster.

_____. 1974. *Everybody Needs a Rock*. New York: Simon & Schuster.

Bridges, Ruby. 1999. *Through My Eyes*. New York: Scholastic.

Burnett, Frances Hodgson. 1911. *The Secret Garden*. New York: HarperCollins.

Cleary, Beverly. 1983. *Dear Mr. Henshaw*. New York: William Morrow.

Coles, Robert. 1995. *The Story of Ruby Bridges*. New York: Scholastic.

Collier, James, and Lincoln Collier. 1974. *My Brother Sam Is Dead*. New York: Four Winds Press.

de Paola, Tomie. 1973. *Nana Upstairs, Nana Downstairs*. New York: Penguin

———. 1975. *The Cloud Book*. New York: Holiday Books.

Fox, Mem. 1988. *Koala Lou*. New York: Harcourt, Inc.

Goble, Paul. 1975. *The Friendly Wolf*. New York: Simon & Schuster.

———. 1978. *The Girl Who Loved Wild Horses*. New York: Simon & Schuster.

Grant, James P., and Maurice Sendak. 2001. *I Dream of Peace*. New York: HarperCollins.

Gray, Libba More. 1993. *Dear Willie Rudd*. New York: Simon & Schuster.

Heard, Georgia. 1997. "Elephant Warning." In *Creatures of the Earth, Sea, and Sky*. Honesdale, PA: Boyds Mills Press.

Hoffman, Mary. 1995. *Amazing Grace*. New York: Dial Books.

Hunt, Irene. 1964. *Across Five Aprils*. Chicago, IL: Follet.

Innocenti, Roberto. 1985. *Rose Blanche*. New York: Harcourt Brace.

Johnston, Tony. 1994. *Amber on the Mountain*. New York: Penguin.

Locker, Thomas. 1994. *Where the River Begins*. New York: Penguin.

Martin, Bill, Jr. 1987. *Knots on a Counting Rope*. New York: Henry Holt.

Martin, Rafe. 1992. *The Rough-Face Girl*. New York: G. P. Putnam's Sons.

Mayer, Mercer. 1998. *Just Me and My Babysitter*. New York: Golden Books.

Morrison, Toni. 2004. *Remember*. New York: Houghton Mifflin.

Muth, Jon. 2002. *The Three Questions*. New York: Scholastic.

Naylor, Phyllis Reynolds, and Barry Moser. 2000. *Shiloh*. New York: Simon & Schuster.

Polacco, Patricia. 1988. *The Keeping Quilt*. New York: Simon & Schuster.

———. 1990. *Just Plain Fancy*. New York: Random House.

———. 1992. *Mrs. Katz and Tush*. New York: Bantam/Doubleday.

Rylant, Cynthia. 1982. *When I Was Young in the Mountains*. New York: Penguin.

———. 1985. *The Relatives Came*. New York: Simon & Schuster.

———. 1991. *Appalachia*. New York: Harcourt, Brace & Company.

———. 1995. *Dog Heaven*. New York: Scholastic.

Sewell, Anna. 1877, 1998. *Black Beauty*. New York: Random House.

Stroud, Virginia. 1994. *Doesn't Fall Off His Horse: A Cherokee Tale*. New York: Dial Books.

Van Allsburg, Chris. 1991. *The Wretched Stone*. New York: Houghton Mifflin.

White, E. B. 1970. *The Trumpet of the Swan*. New York: HarperCollins.

Wick, Walter. 1997. *A Drop of Water*. New York: Scholastic.

Woodson, Jacqueline. 2002. *The Other Side*. New York: G. P. Putnam's Sons.

Zimmer, Paul. 1989. "Yellow Sonnet." In *The Great Bird of Love*. Champaign/Urbana, IL: The University of Illinois Press.

Zolotow, Charlotte. 1972. *William's Doll*. New York: HarperTrophy.

Adult Literature

Gordimer, Nadine. 1990. *My Son's Story*. New York: Farrar, Straus & Giroux.

Kingsolver, Barbara. 1988. *The Bean Trees*. New York: Harper & Row.

Marquez, Gabriel Garcia. 1988. *Love in the Time of Cholera*. New York: Penguin.

Miller, Arthur. 1949. *The Death of a Salesman*. New York: Penguin.

Morrison, Toni. 1987. *Beloved*. New York: Alfred Knopf.

Pasternak, Boris. 1958. *Dr. Zhivago*. London: Wm. Collins & Sons, Ltd.

Porter, Katherine Anne. 1945. *Ship of Fools*. New York: Little, Brown.

Stegner, Wallace. 1987. *Crossing to Safety*. New York: Random House.

Stegner, Wallace. 1992. *Where the Bluebird Sings to the Lemonade Springs*. New York: Random House.

Thornton, Lawrence. 1987 *Imagining Argentina*. New York: Doubleday.

Zimmermann, Susan. 2005. *Keeping Katherine*. New York: Three Rivers Press.

Chapter Opening Selections

Angelou, Maya. 1969. *I Know Why the Caged Bird Sings.* New York: Random House.

Collins, Billy. 1988. "Books." In *The Apple That Astonished Paris.* Fayetteville, AR: The University of Arkansas Press.

———. 1991. "First Reader." In *Questions About Angels.* Pittsburgh, PA: The University of Pittsburgh Press.

Conrad, Joseph. 1899/1942. *Heart of Darkness.* In *A Conrad Argosy.* New York: Doubleday, Doran & Co.

Diamond, Jared. 1997. *Guns, Germs, Steel.* New York: W. W. Norton.

Kincaid, Jamaica. 1978. "Girl." *The New Yorker,* June 26.

Galleano, Eduardo. 1992. "Celebration of the Human Voice." In *The Book of Embraces.* New York: W. W. Norton.

Humes, Harry. 1996. "The Cough." In Jerome Stern, ed., *Micro Fiction: An Anthology of Really Short Stories.* New York: W. W. Norton.

Levin, Gail. 1995. "Inventing My Parents." In *The Poetry of Solitude.* New York: Universe.

O'Brien, Tim. 1990. "Stockings." In *The Things They Carried.* New York: Houghton Mifflin.

Professional Resources

Allington, Richard. 2006. *What Really Matters for Struggling Readers: Designing Research-Based Programs.* 2nd ed. Boston: Pearson/Allyn & Bacon.

Beers, Kylene. 2003. *When Kids Can't Read, What Teachers Can Do.* Portsmouth, NH: Heinemann.

Beers, Kylene, Linda Rief, and Robert Probst, eds. 2007. *Adolescent Literacy: Turning Promise into Practice.* Portsmouth, NH: Heinemann.

Bernstein, Jeremy. 1981. "Profiles: Marvin Minsky." *The New Yorker,* December 14: 50–128.

Block, Cathy, Linda Gambrell, and Michael Pressley. 2002. *Improving Comprehension Instruction: Rethinking Research, Theory, and Classroom Practice.* San Francisco: Jossey-Bass, 2002.

Block, Cathy, and Michael Pressley. 2002. *Comprehension Instruction: Research-Based Best Practices.* New York: The Guilford Press.

Cipielewski, J., and K. Stanovich. 1992. "Predicting growth in reading ability from children's exposure to print." *Journal of Experimental Child Psychology 54*: 74–89.

Gambrell, Linda, Lesley Mandel Morrow, Susan Neuman, and Michael Pressley, eds. 1999. *Best Practices in Literacy Instruction.* New York: The Guilford Press.

Grimes, Sharon, 2006. *Reading Is Our Business: How Libraries Can Foster Reading Comprehension.* Chicago: American Library Association.

Harvey, Stephanie, 1998. *Nonfiction Matters: Reading, Writing, and Research in Grades 3–8.* Portland, ME: Stenhouse.

Harvey, Stephanie, and Anne Goudvis. 2000. *Strategies That Work.* Portland, ME: Stenhouse.

Hoyt, Linda, ed. 2005. *Spotlight on Comprehension.* Portsmouth, NH: Heinemann.

Hyde, Arthur. 2006. *Comprehending Math: Adapting Reading Strategies to Teach Mathematics, K–6.* Portsmouth, NH: Heinemann.

Johnston, Peter. 2004. *Choice Words.* Portland, ME: Stenhouse.

Keene, Ellin Oliver. 2006. *Assessing Comprehension Thinking Strategies.* Huntington Beach, CA: Shell Educational Publishing.

Keene, Ellin Oliver. Forthcoming. *To Understand.* Portsmouth, NH: Heinemann.

Keene, Ellin Oliver, and Susan Zimmermann. 1997. *Mosaic of Thought.* Portsmouth, NH: Heinemann.

Langer, Judith. January 2002. On AERA science blog: http://www.scienceblog.com/community/older/archives.

Larner, Marjorie. 2004. *Pathways.* Portsmouth, NH: Heinemann.

Maria, K. 1990. *Reading Comprehension Instruction: Issues and Strategies.* Timonium, MD: York Press.

Mason, Pamela, and Jeanne Shay Schumm, eds. 2004. *Promising Practices for Urban Reading Instruction.* Newark, DE: International Reading Association.

Miller, Debbie. 2002. *Reading with Meaning.* Portland, ME: Stenhouse.

Morgan, Bruce. 2005. *Writing Through the Tween Years.* Portland, ME: Stenhouse.

National Assessment of Educational Progress. 1999. *1998 NAEP Reading Report Card for the Nation and States.* Washington, DC: U.S. Department of Education.

National Endowment for the Arts. 2004. *Reading at Risk: A Survey of Literary Reading in America.* Washington, DC National Endowment for the Arts.

Pearson, P. David, and M. C. Gallagher. 1983. "The Instruction of Reading Comprehension. *Contemporary Educational Psychology 8*: 317–344.

Pearson, P. D., Roehler, J. A. Dole, and G. G. Duffy, 1992. "Developing Expertise in Reading Comprehension." In J. Samuels and A. Farstrup, eds., *What Research Has to Say About Reading Instruction.* Newark, DE: International Reading Association.

Pressley, Michael. 2002. *Reading Instruction That Works.* 2nd ed. New York: The Guilford Press.

RAND Reading Study Group, RAND Education. 2001. *Reading for Understanding: Towards an R&D Program in Reading Comprehension.* Washington, DC: RAND Education.

Smith, Frank. 1983. "Twelve Ways to Make Learning to Read Difficult." *Essays Into Literacy.* Portsmouth, NH: Heinemann.

Stanovich, Keith E. 2000. *Progress in Understanding Reading.* New York: The Guilford Press.

Sweeney, Diane. 2003. *Learning Along the Way: Professional Development by and for Teachers.* Portland, ME: Stenhouse.

Tovani, Cris. 2000. *I Read It, But I Don't Get It.* Portland, ME: Stenhouse.

———. 2004. *Do I Really Have to Teach Reading?* Portland, ME: Stenhouse.

Zimmermann, Susan, and Chryse Hutchins. 2003. *7 Keys to Comprehension.* New York: Three Rivers Press.

Index

Accountability, 28–29

Across Five Aprils, 237

Aliki, 82

Allen, Patrick, 19, 20

Amazing Grace, 233

Angelou, Maya, 66, 67, 68, 69, 99

Apocalypse Now, 251

Appalachia, 191

The Apple That Astonished Paris, 2

Assessing Comprehension Thinking Strategies, 98, 124

Assessment
in comprehension instruction, 27
high-stakes testing, 28–29, 30

Background knowledge
using, 67–71
See also Schema

Baylor, Byrd, 96, 125

The Bean Trees, 51

Beloved, 15

Best Practices in Literacy Instruction, 26

Blauman, Leslie, 13, 17, 18, 19, 20

The Book of Embraces, 138

Book selection, guidelines for, 160

"Books," 2, 4, 6, 23

At the Bottom of the River, 45

Brando, Marlon, 251

Bridges, Ruby, 89

Buddy, Colleen, 19, 20, 36–37

Calkins, Lucy, 22

Call, Jan, 5

Carlstrom, Nancy White, 92

"Celebration of the Human Voice," 138, 139–142, 144

Cheever, John, 253

Choice Words, 40

A Chorus of Stones: A Private Life of War, 276–277

Cisneros, Sandra, 274

The Civil War (PBS), 237

Classrooms

reflection in, 152
thoughtful, 29–30

Cleary, Beverly, 213

The Cloud Book, 96

Coan, Sabrina, classroom of, 180–183

Codrescu, Andrei, 280

Cohn, Jody, classroom of, 235–242

Coles, Robert, 85

Collins, Billy, 2, 3, 4, 22

Composing sessions
effectiveness of, 185
purpose of, 184–185

Comprehending Math, 37, 257

Comprehension Instruction, 26

Comprehension strategies, 13
example of integration of, 247–252
experimenting with, 18–23
integration of, 35–36
metacognitive, 14
research on, 26–28
in thoughtful classrooms, 29–30
universality of use of, 20
use by proficient students, 42–43

Comprehension strategy instruction, 18–20
across curriculum, 36–37
based on student reading level, 34–35
demonstrating in, 147
format of, 35–36
importance of, 32–33
modeling in, 147
order of, 34, 37
think-alouds in, 147

Comrade Past & Mister Present, 280

Conferences
importance of, 154–155
student role in, 165
teacher role in, 164–165
use in primary classroom, 157–159, 161–163

Conrad, Joseph, 247, 249

A Conrad Argosy, 247

Considerate text, 212

Constance: Poems, 278

Contentive words, 210

1170 44